Women
and Public
Service

Women and Public Service

Barriers, Challenges, and Opportunities

Mohamad G. Alkadry **and** Leslie E. Tower

Routledge
Taylor & Francis Group

LONDON AND NEW YORK

First published 2014 by M.E. Sharpe

Published 2015 by Routledge
2 Park Square, Milton Park, Abingdon, Oxon OX14 4RN
711 Third Avenue, New York, NY 10017, USA

Routledge is an imprint of the Taylor & Francis Group, an informa business

Notices
No responsibility is assumed by the publisher for any injury and/or damage to
persons or property as a matter of products liability, negligence or otherwise,
or from any use of operation of any methods, products, instructions or ideas
contained in the material herein.

Practitioners and researchers must always rely on their own experience and
knowledge in evaluating and using any information, methods, compounds, or
experiments described herein. In using such information or methods they should
be mindful of their own safety and the safety of others, including parties for
whom they have a professional responsibility.

Product or corporate names may be trademarks or registered trademarks, and
are used only for identification and explanation without intent to infringe.

Library of Congress Cataloging-in-Publication Data

Alkadry, Mohamad G., 1970–
  Women and public service : barriers, challenges, and opportunities / by Mohamad G.
Alkadry and Leslie E. Tower.
     pages cm.
  Includes bibliographical references.
  ISBN 978-0-7656-3102-2 (hardcover : alk. paper)—ISBN 978-0-7656-3103-9 (pbk. : alk. paper)
  1. Women in the civil service—United States. 2. Discrimination in employment—
United States. 3. Women—Employment—United States. 4. Diversity in the workplace—
United States. I. Tower, Leslie E., 1971– II. Title.

JK721.A67 2013
352.6'30820973--dc23   2013004786

                              ISBN 13: 9780765631039 (pbk)
                              ISBN 13: 9780765631022 (hbk)

Contents

Foreword

The issue of gender in the public service, once almost totally ignored, has made its way over the past two decades into the light of day. For such a central influence on virtually everything we do (What is the first question we ask about a new baby?), it has been quite a slog to get it noticed. As the publication of this book attests, the difference that gender makes is now a question no one who cares about organizational effectiveness can afford to neglect.

Gender has been the elephant in the room, hiding behind a screen of bureaucratic neutrality. Max Weber told us long ago that bureaucracies are typified by strict adherence to objectivity. He offered them to us as a replacement for patriarchy, though he knew the price modernity would pay for its quintessential instrument. (Not for nothing did he speak in terms of iron cages.) Little did Weber recognize, however, that patriarchy would continue to lurk within the modern organization, hidden by the match between bureaucratic norms and those of masculinity: objectivity, reason, linearity, and dispassionate action. A fine neutrality, indeed.

Since they first entered government work in the mid-nineteenth century, women's work life in public agencies has been fundamentally different from men's. Women have been paid less, done a lopsided share of the routine work, struggled with how to adapt themselves to practices shaped by men, brooded over how to turn aside men's advances without losing their jobs, and fought to balance work demands with what was expected of them—what they expected of themselves—on the domestic front. Women have fought to win not just acceptance but respect and a fair shot at the top of the modern organization—the same as men. Their experience taught them, however, that they did not (or were not permitted to) fit. Calling attention to this fact only made them fit even less.

Women and Public Service is a practical, sane, clear-sighted, and altogether helpful book. The authors recognize the difference between what managers can (and should) do and the external forces that continue to make gender equality a slog. It is a topic forever at risk of lapsing again into invisibility. The 2012 national elections are a case in point: no mention of women, except obliquely in bizarre discussions of "legitimate rape" and "binders full of qualified females." Have we decided to settle for 2056 as the target date for equal pay? Have we given up on shattering glass ceilings and walls? Would it not be pretty to think that gender equality will come about "naturally!"

I am not at all sure that rates of progress in the future can be projected based on previous experience. The entire world of work is on a downward slide. Things employers once took for granted that they owed their employees are disappearing—that is, if the company itself has not disappeared to Mexico or Southeast Asia. Benefits? Full-time work? A regular schedule? Surely you are joking. And we are assured that employees "like the flexibility." Salaries and wages have stagnated since the 1970s, and the proportion of women in the labor force has soared because families were not getting by on just one paycheck. In recent years, many people's savings have been wiped out, and guaranteed pensions are fast becoming a thing of the past. In this world, gender equality has a way of seeming frivolous. "If only we had the luxury to be able to worry about *that*!"

Yet I do believe that progress will continue to be made, albeit slowly. Much of that progress will come about because people in positions of responsibility, like many of those who will read this book, use the discretionary power they have, at crucial everyday moments, in the name of justice. The revolution may not be tweeted, as one wag had it. It may, however be accomplished in agency discussions and work assignments, in managerial alertness to stereotypes and willingness to work against them, in perceptive performance evaluations, and in the determination to hire people not because "they think like we do," as one manager pressed on the issue of diversity said, but for their new perspectives and ideas, differing life experiences, and fresh approaches, along with the desire to commit themselves to the organization and its goals.

Let us refuse to emulate the Norwegian pioneers in tenth-century Greenland, who starved to death amid herds of reindeer because they had a taboo against eating meat. Let us not be ruled by mores and prejudices of which, half the time, we are only half aware. In what is given to us as necessary and inevitable, let us look for what is contingent and subject to change. And in this work of freedom, let women and men become equal partners.

Camilla Stivers

Acknowledgments

Eight years before this book was published, we started working together on gender issues in public administration. Our coauthored works included pay equity, authority and women, representation issues, spirituality, institutional climates, and finally this book, which is our way to conclude eight years of collaborative research on the subject. It is also our way of providing an important resource to our current and future public servants and public service human resources managers.

In writing this work, we owe a great deal of gratitude to our graduate students and academic homes. Our graduate students at West Virginia University, Old Dominion University, and Florida International University have seen different versions of this book used in our lectures and discussions. They helped inspire this project on many levels. They listened to us discuss the barriers and challenges, and sometimes the opportunities, facing women in public organizations. Both female and male students always appeared thrilled to learn about women's issues. In a sense they were our audience for testing the relevance of our materials to what students would want to learn. Whether they were in an introductory, specialized class or capstone class, they often claimed to be hearing about these issues for the first time. The thought that some students could have graduated without learning about issues that face half of the workforce is the true inspiration behind this work. This book addresses, in accessible form, the needs of women and the challenges to their fair integration in public service organizations. As such, we believe that public administration students at all levels and public sector employees at all levels should have an understanding about the issues that we raise. And, based on the small sample that includes our own students, we believe that the next generation of public servants, men and women, white and people of color, Hispanic and non-Hispanic, conservative and liberal, and pre-service and in-service, all understand the importance of learning about women's and related work–life balance and work–family balance issues.

Many colleagues, graduate students, friends, and family members have contributed to this project. We wish to first acknowledge Babatunde Epoyun, Gleema Nambiar, and Gretha Burchard from Florida International University for their patience and thoroughness in reading earlier versions of this manuscript. We are forever grateful to them, although we continue to claim credit for any mistakes that may have been made.

We are honored that Professor Camilla Stivers, a public administration scholar whom we both deeply admire, agreed to write the foreword. Her pioneering works on gender images and on settlement women continue to inspire generations of public servants and public service scholars. We would also like to express our appreciation to Harry Briggs and Elizabeth Parker from M.E. Sharpe for their support during this project.

We want to thank West Virginia University's Eberly College of Arts and Sciences for the sabbatical that they awarded to Leslie Tower to dedicate to this book project. We want to also thank Florida International University for the administrative and logistical support provided to Mohamad Alkadry while he was working on this publication.

We both owe plenty of gratitude to our mentors, colleagues, and friends who have encouraged us along the way. Finally, thanks to the countless others that have assisted us broadly, in our professional development, and more specifically, with this book.

We want to thank our parents, Ghazi Alkadry and Nahla Khoayer (Mohamad's) and Arthur and Kay Gomberg (Leslie's) for a lifetime of support that has truly allowed us to pursue our passions and goals. We are forever grateful for and in awe of their continued influence in our lives.

We want to also thank our life-partners, Robert Tower and Rania Salem, for their support, encouragement, sense of humor, and patience as we completed the different stages of this work. The time we spent writing this book is ultimately time that we spent away from our awesome children, Benjamin and Toria Tower and Kenda and Jad Alkadry. The joy they bring to our lives, their laughter, imagination, and enthusiastic insights have all created the ultimate positive energy and motivation to complete this project.

Introduction

Frank Carollo, a city commissioner for the city of Miami had recently become a father. While he was in city hall one day in 2011, Mr. Carollo took his one-year-old daughter to the men's bathroom for a diaper change. But a changing table was not available. He looked around in other men's rooms in city hall, and later in city offices elsewhere. He discovered that the entire city of Miami had only 35 diaper stations in the 200 men's bathrooms within its facilities.

Upon further investigation and some research on pricing, the commissioner proposed to the full city commission, the installation of 165 changing stations in men's bathrooms in the remaining city buildings. The total estimated cost was $45,000. What seemed to be an easy decision to bring the city into conformity with its own building standards turned into political theatrics. It took four commission meetings to finally vote in favor of adding the diaper-changing stations. The president of the Fraternal Order of Police had a problem with the city's spending frivolously on something that it did not "need to have" while the police department needed funding for essentials such as guns, equipment, and apparently for repairing a leaky roof. In an article titled, "Daddy Diaper Duty OK'd by Miami Commission," the *Miami Herald* quoted the police order president as saying, "We must differentiate between 'need to have,' and 'good to have.'"

The above story ended with Mr. Carollo promising to find private sources for funding the "extravagant" venture of adding diaper-changing stations to men's bathrooms in city hall and other city buildings. That promise reassured the hesitant commissioners who voted in favor of the diaper-changing stations. While the story might be mildly entertaining, the resistance to the commissioner's bill is quite symptomatic of the need for this book project, and it reflects a thorny path in dealing with issues of gender equity.

In a public organization, it should have been instantly clear to elected and nonelected commissioners that men too should have the facilities to care for children in their company. It might be uncomfortable, and in some cases even convenient, for a man to say, "Honey, you have to change the baby because the men's room does not have a changing room." But, is that not forcing women into the gender role of the "only caregiver" that has haunted women for ages? Moreover, what is a male caregiver to do when he is not with a woman? Or, if his partner is not a woman? This story is about a lot more than the convenience of changing stations in men's rooms. This is about regimented gender roles that assign the caring function, in this case the diaper-changing function, exclusively to women. The discrepancy in treatment of men and women here enforces existing gender roles. The underlying assumption is a question: "Why do men need changing stations in their restrooms if women are supposed to change the diapers?" It is this assumption that makes diaper-changing tables in women's rooms "need to have" items, but those in men's rooms "nice to have" items.

In order to treat everyone equally, public officials cannot assume that only women would be walking into city hall with diapered children. By making such an assumption, public organizations are perpetuating these uneven gender roles. Therefore, installing diaper-changing stations in men's bathrooms is unquestionably a gender equity issue. Moreover, these diaper-changing tables offer men the opportunity to change a child's diaper and relieve women from the expectation that they are the only diaper-changing parent, at least when they are in public.

The idea behind this book stems from the authors' realization of the compelling need to deal with the many issues that affect women in the workplace. We delve into these issues—everything from representation, to pay equity, to social costs of careers, to mentoring and negotiating, and to bullying and sexual harassment. The book looks at past policies and court cases, and looks forward to future policy actions that would enhance the role of women in public service organizations. At each stop, or chapter, the authors discuss barriers, challenges, and opportunities for women.

Why Write a Book on Women in Public Service Organizations?

Research on women in public service organizations has been limited and inconsistent. Researchers who conduct studies on women in the field of public organizations are few and far between. In 1988, Kathy Ferguson wrote a landmark book, *The Feminist Case Against Bureaucracy*. She critiqued bureaucracy through a radical feminist's lens. She argued that bureaucracy is not "A-OK" for women. It is rather a system that counts on domination and the socialization into domination roles not only of women but also of men. Women are left with the choice between staying out of the bureaucracy or entering it at their own risk. The risks are simple: get co-opted into the existing culture and swim with the tide, or swim against the tide and suffer the consequences. Ferguson (1985) was hardly optimistic about the ability of women to succeed in bureaucratic organizations.

Almost six years later, Camilla Stivers (1993) introduced another landmark book titled *Gender Images in Public Administration*. Like Ferguson, Stivers argued that resolving the problems that face women in organizations requires a comprehensive look at society and the gender roles it assigns to women. Stivers did not follow Ferguson (1985) in pointing at domination as the source of the problem—rather she argued that women are kept away from leadership positions primarily because leadership is associated with societal masculine images that contradict the societal feminine images of caring that are associated with women.

In a second book—*Bureau Men, Settlement Women: Constructing Public Administration in the Progressive Era* (2000), Stivers strengthens this discussion of gender roles with a historic discussion of roles and management styles of women and men. This book not only challenges the roles assigned to men and women but also looks deeper into women's approaches to problem solving. Advancing Stivers's discussion, particularly of settlement women's management styles, we argue in this book that management strategies that have dominated administrative and management reforms in the 1990s and beyond have adopted many of the management styles that have historically been associated with settlement women and their approaches to problem solving. Listening skills, consultation, and participative management were often associated with the management styles of settlement women. In many ways, one can argue that the historic stereotypes of women managers have become the mainstream of management today.

These three books to a large extent influence the approach of this current work. Primarily, we acknowledge that it is difficult to separate what happens within the organization from what goes on outside it—particularly in the area of gender images and societal gender roles.

Women pay a higher social cost for their careers than men largely because of society's gender roles, which assign the caring function to women. Therefore, it is harder to deal with the issue of costs without reverting to the very source of the problem—gender roles. For a field that deals with 22 million employees in the public sector and at least as many in the nonprofit sector in the United States alone, we are not paying due attention to women's issues.

Principles Guiding the Book

This book is not intended as a manifesto of principles—but rather as an examination of the status of women in public service organizations, their history, and the issues and policies affecting them. It is based on theory and research studies that have been well documented and referenced. As authors, we do not make the cliché claim of objectivity in our writing. However, we are not driven by an intentional bias other than the agenda of informing employees and managers of the challenges that face women in organizations. Our agenda is a better workplace for men and women, and our biases are unintentional biases driven by our own experiences as employees, scholars, and individuals. We understand that one's own life experiences and principles guide what one deliberately sees and what one unintentionally ignores. That is why it is important to disclose the principles and authors' values as they relate to this book project.

First, we believe that men and women are equal. We are not biological determinists and do not start with the assumption that men are built physically, mentally, or emotionally to take on certain male jobs or roles. We believe that any differences between men and women (other than body parts) are socially constructed. Women grow up to be nurses, teachers, and social workers not because of some natural inclination but rather because of their socialization into these roles. In her 2009 book, *Pink Brain, Blue Brain*, Lisa Eliot, a neuroscientist, concludes that there are few meaningful differences between boys and girls brains. Children's brains are very malleable, and they develop and respond to their environment, not to any inherent biological traits. Therefore, we argue that gender differences are generally caused by society, including parents and teachers (inadvertently or not) who reinforce gender stereotypes in the way they treat children, in the directions in which they point children, in experiences they offer to children, and so on.

We follow Young's (1990b) "Throwing Like a Girl: A Phenomenology of Feminine Body Comportment, Motility, and Spatiality." Young, according to Alkadry (1997):

> demonstrates the existence of a set of body habits which constrain and restrict women in their own bodies. She uses the analogy of her own tennis game, which was only made difficult by her inability to perform certain moves and maneuvers. [Playing tennis with her daughter,] Young (19[9]0) realized that her body was able to perform more functions than she was willing to let it perform. She was not constrained by her body's "natural" inflexibility. She was rather constrained by her unwillingness to use her body to its utmost limits. She felt confined to her space on the tennis court. She simply did not have the full ownership of her court. That ownership and comfort with the space are essential for tennis players to perfect their game. Young was in every sense confined in her own body and space. The confinement of women to spaces defined by society and their inhibitions in their movements are but limitations on women's assertion of their presence in society and in organizations. (Alkadry, 1997, p. 107)

So, there is no legitimate reason to explain why women cannot be competent firefighters, construction workers, engineers, army combat soldiers, elite navy seals, army generals, and commanders in chief. The old arguments based on biological determinism seem invalid from Eliot's (2009) and Young's (1990b) perspectives, and from the perspective of the authors of this book. Troubling as it may seem, socialization into specific gender roles can have implications for physical behavior. What appears to be physiological is deeply rooted in social construction and essentially nonphysiological social roots.

Second, the authors of this book assume that gender parity means that 50 percent of workers, commissioners, or elected officials are men and 50 percent are women. In our popular culture, many organizations tout a single female leader as evidence that women are represented in management. We recently saw evidence of this behavior in the 2012 national conventions of the Republican and Democratic parties in the United States. Both conventions rushed to identify several women in leadership positions as evidence that women are represented. In reality, neither Democrat nor Republican national administrations have achieved parity in the representation of women in cabinets, in congressional nominations, or in state gubernatorial elections. Women continue to be underrepresented in senior administrative organizations run by both parties.

We contend that a proper representation of women in the workplace is not only 50 percent (+/−) but also has to ensure that 50 percent (+/−) of the decision-making power is held by women. This is not radical—just a literal interpretation of the word "parity."

Third, the authors of this book believe that time is capable of resolving some things, but not everything. Therefore, the discussion leaves matters for time only if time is what it takes to correct the issue at hand. For example, if an organization has only 20 percent women and 80 percent men, and the organization is losing 30 percent of its workforce every ten years, it is fair to say that time will fix the problem if 50 percent of the newly hired employees are women. If parity exists among new hires, then it should not take more than thirty years—a typical organizational career span—to remedy any gender imbalance issues within any organization. Therefore, only parity in hiring, and not reverse discrimination, will solve that organization's problems. The authors of this book wish for parity, not affirmative action. However, as later chapters will clearly show, we are far from parity among new hires, and the claim that time will cure all problems is highly questionable. And time might be acceptable to resolve things such as representation (if parity in hiring exists), but it is not acceptable to rely on time to resolve issues of pay equity. Some studies, for instance, estimate that pay parity will be in place by 2056—nearly a century after civil rights reforms and the removal of most discriminatory provisions from the law in the United States. There is no justification for allowing generations of female employees to suffer pay inequity. Equal pay can be achieved in a few years through resolute deliberate policies and actions taken by policymakers and public service leadership. It should take weeks not decades, or almost a century, to eradicate discrimination in pay.

Fourth, images of how leaders are supposed to behave are changing from historically masculine (by society's definition) to what we have historically looked at as feminine traits. In other words, mainstream management consultants are finally embracing settlement house women's strategies, such as listening and participative leadership/management. Assertiveness as a leadership trait has largely given way to participative management ideas. Employee empowerment is far more important in today's organizations than control of employees. Therefore, the stereotypic discussion of a male/female assertive/caring dichotomy has little value, as most organizations have adopted principles of participative management that essentially favor caring and listening over assertive characteristics.

Fifth, we do not believe in a strict separation between the private sphere and the public sphere. We argue in later chapters that fairness for women in the workplace and their ability to excel in their careers is largely dependent on how well women negotiate their roles at home. Dismantling the conventional ideology of working men and family women (Johnson and Duerst-Lahti, 1992)—which is one of the most compelling structural problems facing women in organizations—requires changes in women's role in the family as well as at work. Therefore, we go beyond the traditional liberal feminists' separation between public and private spheres. This separation is a luxury that most women and men with families simply do not have.

Finally, we believe that progress over the years in the status of women in organizations has occurred after decades of struggle by progressive men and women. When we discuss progress over the years, we do not focus much on the efforts of activists and politicians in driving these changes. The mechanical approach of this book and its near silence on linking activism and social movements to the progress of women should not be interpreted as undervaluing the contributions of these movements. Many things have driven positive changes to the status of women over the past five decades. Attempting to allocate causes for these positive changes would be a major distraction for this discussion. The book intends to make a statement about where we are today, and the barriers, challenges, and opportunities for the future.

Barriers, Challenges, and Opportunities

Chapter conclusions are presented in the form of barriers, challenges, and opportunities. It is important in this introduction to explain what these three terms mean in the context of a book dealing with women working in public service organizations. *Barriers* are forces or obstacles beyond the reach of organizations. Organizations cannot change barriers, as they often occur outside the workplace. A common barrier cited in the book is the effect of social images and gender roles on women in society in general, and in organizations in particular. In an attempt to be positive, the book cites as *challenges* situations or patterns that organizations have the influence to change. If mentoring and other policies within the organization can help women move into upper ranks, then the segregation of women in lower echelon positions is presented as a *challenge*. Finally, *opportunities* are circumstances that organizations can look forward to in order to change the status of women in the near future.

Outline of the Book

In chapter 1, we make a case that diversity is important, not just because of issues of fairness but also for more practical reasons of effectiveness. The chapter argues that administrative reforms and equitable representation of minorities and women have to go hand in hand if the goal of reforms is a more responsive, and therefore, effective management. The chapter introduces the concept of representative bureaucracy and the idea that representation is important in unelected institutions, as much as it is important in elected institutions. Diversity theories and concepts such as active and passive representation are also introduced in this chapter—which acts as the theoretical backbone of the book.

Chapter 2 discusses key pieces of legislation that affect women. When discussing workplace legislative protections, we can think about laws that either (a) protect against discrimination (e.g., Title VII of the Civil Rights Act of 1964), or (b) guarantee benefits (e.g., the Family and Medical Leave Act). We also need to look beyond our borders for a more thorough understanding of policy options, namely, to the European Union (EU). The EU offers us a framework to challenge the dominant norm of worker–workplace relations in the United States, that of the "organization man."

Chapter 3 covers executive orders and court decisions that affect women at work. This chapter also looks at the experience of other nations in implementing policies that improve the status of women in organizations. While the U.S. Supreme Court has had the tendency to limit policy aimed at increasing diversity, the European Court of Justice has been expanding its reach to improve representation of women in the workplace. It is fair to point out, however, that women in the United States have made laudable strides in terms of representation over the past few decades, despite the tendencies of the U.S. Supreme Court to discount inequalities.

Chapter 4 presents progress that women have made over the past few decades. It also discusses problems of representation that women continue to face, particularly issues of segregation of women in certain agencies, occupations, and organizational hierarchy levels (lower ones). The chapter includes data on administrations at the state and local levels as well as at the federal level. The chapter's main thesis is that while progress is clear, the pace and inconsistency of progress are causes for concern. The analogy of the lawn that grows unevenly is most relevant here. Women continue to be underrepresented, even among new hires, in traditionally male-dominated fields, occupations, and agencies.

Chapter 5 addresses issues of equal pay that have affected women in the past and continue to affect them today. Reasonable estimates suggest that pay inequity will continue to affect women, at least until 2056. The chapter explores the reasons behind pay inequity, and the link between pay inequity and segregation of women to lower paying female-dominated fields, occupations, and agencies. The chapter also compares pay disparities in the United States with those in other countries.

Chapter 6 addresses the issue of social costs incurred by women disproportionately as a result of having careers. Alternatively, women may forgo their career for family, which also comes with associated costs. Throughout this chapter we offer tips to minimize the costs associated with choices related to favoring career, family, or both. Work–life satisfaction policies that have been implemented in organizations are also discussed.

Chapter 7 covers issues that affect the climate of organizations. Institutional climate, also referred to as "working conditions" or "organizational environment," is increasingly being associated with better productivity and enhanced loyalty to organizations. Working conditions obviously affect men and women in organizations. Women workers face more challenges in the workplace than their male counterparts. Women face sexual harassment at higher rates than men. They experience workplace bullying at higher rates than men. This chapter focuses on the issues that women face in their everyday organizational lives. Each chapter concludes with a discussion of barriers, challenges, and opportunities in matters that are addressed in the chapter.

Women
and Public
Service

1

From Representation to Diversity: The Road Ahead

Women should be properly represented in public service organizations because that is the right thing to do, and because their presence in these organizations is critical for the success of policy implementation. This is not only a statement of principle. This chapter argues that it is rather a statement of fact. Representation in general, and representation of women and minorities in particular, has been linked to the success of policymaking and policy implementation by many scholars in the fields of public policy and public administration. It is fair for women to have equal representation because (a) women are entitled to the same political rights as men, including in competing for public service jobs, and (b) women constitute more than half of the recipients of public services.

In this chapter, we address the fundamental questions of equality, representation, and diversity. Although the answers might seem obvious to many, it is very important to articulate why the representation of women in public service organizations is critical to the ability of organizations to perform their day-to-day tasks. It is also important to tackle the issue of representation of women and the move from "passive representation" to "active representation," to "issue representation" in the context of representative bureaucracy. In this chapter, we make a case for an effective role for women in the running of public service organizations. We also present a discussion of work–life issues, particularly as they affect women and women's organizational life. Finally, this chapter discusses diversity and implicit bias theories.

From Diversity to Representation

What does diversity mean? Generally, *diversity* is respect for individuals of different characteristics such as color, race, ethnicity, gender, age, religion, sexual orientation, or way of thinking. A diverse organization mirrors the diversity in the population and provides a workplace that is friendly to different lifestyles and ideas. A diverse organization is not only a demographically diverse place in terms of sex, race/ethnicity, sexual orientation, age, national origin, or other characteristics. It is also a place where all ideas are respected and represented. And, it is an organization where the capability to see the world can be seen from multiple perspectives.

For many decades, popular culture has supported the idea that organizations are populated and run by the "good old boys." The good old boys are usually people who think alike, have similar values, and often are alike in terms of race, gender, class, and ethnicity. Such an organization is homogeneous, not diverse. Conflict is minimal, but creativity in problem solving is impeded by pressure to conform.

A homogeneous workplace is associated with two fundamental problems based on arguments related to equity and consumerism: An *equity-based argument* charges that there is injustice in excluding segments of society because they are different. A *consumerist-based argument* holds that individuals of a single sex or race have a limited ability to understand and solve the complex problems of a diverse citizenry. Therefore, from a normative principled equity perspective and from a more practical consumerist perspective, organizations serve their diverse customers better if they mirror the diversity of their citizens.

The following two sections explore the equity-based argument and the consumerist-based argument for diversity. The goal of these two sections is to make the case that diversity is important not only for political reasons but also for the effective provision of services. Following these two sections, we discuss the issue of *representative bureaucracy*—passive and active—and how demographic representation may or may not lead to the desired diversity outcomes.

Equity-Based Arguments for Diversity

Beginning with the founding fathers of the American republic, legitimacy of the administrative state has been linked to the concept of popular sovereignty. *Popular sovereignty* is the idea that citizens are the fundamental source of political power. Because political power is derived from "the will of the people," or what is popular, citizens play a central role in decisions that affect them. Under this premise, the legitimacy of the political system is uncompromised as long as elected officials are making decisions on behalf of the electorate.

Under the *politics–administration dichotomy* advanced by Woodrow Wilson in 1887, the people exercise their rights by electing officials who in turn play a central role in making policies mandated by the citizens. Administrators focus on the efficient delivery of services, while politicians make political policy decisions. Politicians make the policy, while politicians execute and implement these policies. Over time, questions have arisen about whether the political will of the people is being adequately achieved through the election of representatives. In addition, questions have surfaced about the feasibility of separating politics from administration. Starting in the 1970s, and largely in response to the civil rights movement, administrative scholars have also looked at representation in nonelected institutions as a way to augment representation through politically elected offices.

Influence of Public Administrators

Wilson's (1887) politics–administration dichotomy notwithstanding, administrative organizations today play a fundamental policy role through input in legislation, rule making, and policy implementation. For years, public affairs research focused only on the administrative role in policy implementation. However, and increasingly in the past few decades, administrative scholars have been exploring the role of administrators in the legislative and rule-making scenes.

Input in Legislation. Administrators often participate in and influence legislative policy through their participation in hearings and sometimes directly in writing legislation for elected bodies. As an example, immediately following the terrorist attacks of September 11, 2001, Congress passed the Uniting and Strengthening America by Providing Appropriate Tools Required to Intercept and Obstruct Terrorism (USA PATRIOT Act) Act of 2001. The USA PATRIOT Act was drafted almost entirely by officials of the U.S. Department of Justice. Within forty-eight hours of its introduction in committees, both houses of Congress passed the legislation without any amendments. Administrators held the expertise in the area of counterterrorism and they effectively made the policy. The administrative action might have been understandable given the circumstances surrounding the attacks of September 11, 2001. While administrators do not usually influence most legislation to this extent, they tend to influence most legislation to some degree. The famous iron triangle of policymaking includes unelected public officials, interest groups/lobbyists, and elected congressional committee members. If the three groups are in agreement, legislation will likely have a smooth ride to passage.

Rule Making. Administrators play a central policy role in public policy through the process of rule making. At the federal level, rules help administrators to implement public laws passed by Congress and signed by the president. At the state and local levels, some form of *rule making* also takes place. These rules are very important in creating policy because administrators participate in interpreting legislative will and laws into actionable rules. After the 2010 midterm election in which Democrats lost their majority in the federal House of Representatives, many analysts and media pundits suggested that the executive branch would turn to making policy through rule making, particularly in relation to the newly passed health-care law (Patient Protections and Affordable Care Act of 2010). Soon thereafter, we witnessed a national debate about requiring insurance companies and employees to cover contraception. The administrative actions are part of the rule-making stage of policymaking. This is a testament to the importance of this rule-making stage in the process of making and implementing policy.

Policy Implementation. Administrators implement policies. Policy does not interact with citizens, but administrators do, as they implement laws and regulations. Over the years many have written about the roles of street-level bureaucrats in influencing policy through implementation. Many scholars have argued that policy is indeed made during implementation. This dates back to the famous Friedrich-Finer debate, which took place in the 1930s, about the role of discretion in policy implementation. The debate was carried forward by such scholars as Lipsky (1980) in his prominent book *Street-Level Bureaucracy*, in which he argues that administrative action is more responsive to the situations that administrators face in day-to-day policy implementation than it is to the policy itself.

Table 1.1

Definitions of Representative Democracy and Representative Bureaucracy

Concept	Definition
Representative democracy	Founded in the concept of popular sovereignty and an important foundation in the American republic form of government, representative democracy refers to the electoral process of selecting representatives by citizens. These representatives, according to this concept, will represent the citizens in the process of making policy.
Representative bureaucracy	Founded in the realization that nonelected administrators play a major role in policymaking and implementation, representative bureaucracy refers to the representation of diverse societal groups in the administrative organizations of government. Representative bureaucracy is rooted in the post–civil rights movement era, and is also often associated with the intellectual heritage of the New Public Administration—often referred to as the Minnowbrook Conference.

Administrators, sometimes, though not always, choose responsiveness at the expense of compliance with policy.

In summary, administrative organizations play a central policy role as advisers in the legislative process, as rule makers and as implementers of policy. To remain truthful to the principles of popular sovereignty, these organizations need to be equally representative of their citizens. Thus, the concept of *representative bureaucracy* was born, with the explicit assumption that when administrators reflect the demographic characteristics of the people, they are more likely to serve them better. Representative bureaucracy is not a substitute for *representative democracy*. Rather, it is a supplement to representative democracy institutions. Table 1.1 compares representative democracy and representative bureaucracy.

The Road from Representative Democracy to Representative Bureaucracy

There are two important sociopolitical arguments for the representation of women and other historically disadvantaged groups in the labor force: diversity and equality. Founded in the concept of popular sovereignty, and an important foundation in the American republic form of government, representative democracy refers to the electoral process of selecting representatives by citizens. These representatives, according to this concept, will represent the citizens in the process of making policy. Whereas, founded in the realization that nonelected administrators play a major role in policymaking and implementation, representative bureaucracy refers to the representation of diverse societal groups in the administrative organizations of government. Representative bureaucracy is rooted in the post–civil rights movement era and is also associated with a generation of administration scholars who were influenced by the civil rights movement and the resulting social movements of the 1960s.

The road from representative democracy to representative bureaucracy is important and of interest to public service scholars and practitioners. Prior to the emergence of representative bureaucracy, the field of public administration relied on the Wilson–Weber orthodoxy, which assumes neutrality, objectivity, and the irrelevance of personal and demographic attributes of administrators.

Under representative democracy, and given the lingering bureaucratic thinking of the Wilson–Weber orthodoxy, political institutions such as legislative bodies and city/county councils/commissions are representative, while implementation institutions and agencies that deliver services are supposed to be neutral, apolitical, and essentially nonrelated to any representation function. Representative bureaucracy, on the other hand, seems to relegate representation to public administration organizations, which are essentially implementation institutions. On the other hand, the function of representing the public is essentially a political function and is relegated to elected institutions not appointed ones.

Representative democracy rests on the assumption that administrators take administrative actions while politicians make policy. If administrators stay out of the policy process, and if implementation does not affect the outcomes of policy delivery, then one could reasonably assume that representative institutions will deliver popular sovereignty. On the other hand, representative bureaucracy rests on the idea that "the social composition of the bureaucracy should reflect that of the population as a whole; and that larger numbers from certain underrepresented groups should be brought [into] the public service" (Kernaghan and Siegel, 1991, p. 470). Riggs (1970) has linked this ability to mirror the population to the ability of governments to command the loyalty of their own citizens.

The idea of representative bureaucracy is closely associated with the public administration scholarly movement known as the "New Public

Administration" and the social sciences critical theories of the 1960s and 1970s, which mostly dismiss the concept that public administration and social science are value free. A product of the scholarly work presented at the Minnowbrook Conference in 1969, New Public Administration scholars argue that the main value driving governance is the equalization of economic and political power (Thompson, 1975; Marini, 1971). This value-oriented approach defines the success or failure of a certain organization according to how well it serves its values. Attendees at the Minnowbrook Conference pushed the boundaries of representation beyond racial, gender, or ability-determined classifications to include equitable representation at all demographic levels including socioeconomic status and age.

The New Public Administration undermines judging organizations by their responsiveness "to an unconcerned majority or [their] efficiency in achieving [their] assigned goals" (Riggs, 1970, p. 570). Fred Riggs relates representation in "all organizations of government" to the stability of that government. He cites examples from various countries of how the failure to have an equitable representation in government and its administration could result in public rebellion. Riggs also argues that a government draws its authority or legitimacy from its own diverse composition. He argues for the "need for diverse elements in a population to be adequately represented in order for a government to command their loyalty as a legitimate expression of common welfare" (ibid.).

One could argue that injustice inflicted by nonrepresentative institutions suffers from a poor ability to justify the fairness of their actions. If this argument holds true then an all-male jury would appear biased in rendering a guilty verdict on a woman who harms her abusive partner, while a jury that includes as many women as men could appear more fair or legitimate when it renders the same verdict using the same evidence. At issue here is not only the appearance of diversity and therefore legitimacy but also an assumption that evidence was examined from multiple perspectives. In the context of public administration, one could use the same logic when discussing policing actions, zoning, code enforcement, or any other situation where administrators make decisions affecting the public they serve. An all-white police force will face many more questions of improper behavior in conducting racial and ethnic profiling than a diverse police force. An all-white bureaucracy faces many more questions in code enforcement that specifically targets an African American neighborhood. Questions of improper actions are still asked of diverse workforces, but the issue of bias frequently becomes less central to these questions.

Riggs (1970) argues that economic growth and the emergence of efficiency-oriented governments have given rise to the idea of government capabilities as opposed to the "need for representativeness." This new orientation would stress a monolithic type of government structure if it is to lead to efficiency and economic growth (Weber, 1967). Riggs criticizes such a form of government because it will promote neither political representation nor effective administration:

> The effectiveness of any government depends not only on how well its machinery for implementing decisions operates, but also on its ability to command the continuing support and loyalty of its population. (Riggs, 1970, p. 573)

In the United States in the 1980s, administrative reforms should have gone hand in hand with the introduction of diversity programs. Administrative reforms seeking more capable, efficient, and effective government administration might also benefit from advocating for a more equitable representation of minorities or disadvantaged majorities such as women and the poor in some countries. Riggs further argues that

> if we concentrate on the effort to improve capacity by administrative reform without simultaneously making sure that the need for more political equality is met, then revolutionary turbulence will undermine and destroy whatever gains might have been made in the struggle for greater efficiency.
> . . . [S]ometimes the best way to improve administration may be to work for a more representative political system and, conversely, of course, that the most promising road to political reform will sometimes be to strive for greater administrative capabilities. (Riggs 1970, pp. 573–574)

Riggs's association between administrative and political reform was dominant in the discussion of representation by the Treasury Board of Canada (equivalent to the Office of Personnel Management in the United States): "If the Public Service is, or should be, a mirror of our highest ideals, then there are distortions within the mirror that cause us, as members of Canada's visible minority community, great concern" (Visible Minority Consultation Group, Canada, 1993, p. iv). In this argument we differ with Riggs, who does not necessarily view representativeness of institutions as a form of administrative reform, but rather, appears to see administrative reform and representativeness as exclusive terms. Conversely, we see representativeness of institutions as a fundamental component of administrative reform. The following discussion of consumerist reasons behind the representativeness of institutions alleges that without representative administrative institutions, it is difficult to deliver public services effectively. In other words, we argue that the more representative an institution is, the more responsive and effective it will be. In Western nations, since the 1980s, responsiveness and effectiveness have been the holy grail of administrative reforms.

The Consumerist Argument for Representative Bureaucracy

One can take issue with the continued relevance of Riggs's classification of reform advocates as being either political or administrative. Reforms to improve representation are both political and administrative. Inclusion of historically disadvantaged groups serves a political goal. However, it also fundamentally serves an administrative goal because representative organizations can deliver better services to a diverse population. Given that most private sector organizations are more interested in the administrative rather than the political reforms, some private sector organizations have voluntarily adopted programs to improve the diversity of their workforces with the underlying rationale that diversity is a necessary business strategy.

Private organizations have historically opposed government-imposed equal-opportunity regulation because it may interfere with day-to-day operations. Today, most companies accept the idea that diversity is good for business. Why? Diversity benefits private organizations because a diverse citizenry is best served by a diverse workforce. A diverse workplace also welcomes with open arms the best talent, regardless of sex, race, ethnicity, or other characteristics that have rendered individuals less welcome in prediversity workplaces.

Jain and Hackett (1989) sent questionnaires in 1985 to 648 public and private organizations. A follow-up questionnaire was sent in 1987 to 60 organizations selected from the first sample. Survey results showed that organizations that had applied diversity programs were very satisfied with the potential of these programs on the excellent human resource management system due to fewer discrimination complaints. Aside from the good marketing and service edge that result from workforce diversity, one executive argues that employment equality results in "more motivated employees, improved productivity, better retention, and improved recruitment" (Government of Canada, 1994, p. 5).

Identity Diversity and Functional Diversity

There are two types of diversity: identity diversity and functional diversity. *Identity diversity* refers to differences based on demographics, ethnic, and cultural backgrounds as well as training and experience. *Functional diversity* refers to differences in how individuals solve problems (Hong and Page, 2004). Identity diversity is linked to functional diversity.

Hong and Page (2004) contend that "diversity trumps ability" (p. 16386). Their research demonstrates that diverse groups of individuals tend to outperform groups composed of the "best" individuals. How? Diverse preferences, experiences, and interpretations lead to more potential solutions and superior problem-solving capacity (Page, 2007, p. 296). Why? When approaching a problem, individuals have:

1. *Perspective*—the way an individual represents the problem in his/her mind; the internal language used to understand the problem.
2. *Heuristics*—mental shortcuts that allows people to solve problems and make judgments quickly and efficiently. The rules of thumb for how an individual searches for a solution to a problem; an algorithm, system, or process to find solutions.

(Hong and Page, 2001, 2004)

Having individuals with diverse problem-solving approaches, rooted in their perspective/heuristic pair, may be more important than any one individual's ability to solve the problem. It is important here to contrast this idea with Kathy Ferguson's (1985) *Feminist Case Against Bureaucracy* where diversity within a bureaucratic organization (not all organizations are bureaucratic by definition) is replaced with conformity to organization culture. Organization culture forces this one way of doing things that limits the ability of individuals (women in this case) to influence that culture or decision outcomes in an effective way.

Another limitation of functional diversity theory is that it does not account for communication and learning differences or incentives that may impede optimal solutions. This means that we may unconsciously discrimi-

Figure 1.1   **Minority Representation in the Workforce, 2011 and 2050**

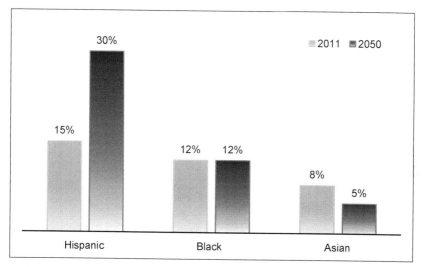

Source: M. Toossi, 2002. *A Century of Change: the US Labor Force 1950–2050.* Washington, DC: Bureau of Labor Statistics. http://www.bls.gov/opub/mlr/2002/05/art2full.pdf.

nate against diverse individuals, consciously believing and knowing that diversity is desired for optimal organizational outcomes (and fairness). In summary, it is very important to note that public service organizations deal with distressing problems involving diverse citizenry and requiring a diversity of problem-solving approaches that functional diversity promises.

Given American demographic realities and the importance of functional forms of diversity for organizations, there is a justifiable argument that a diverse workforce is essential for the future survival of any private as well as public organization. This fundamentally challenges the prevalent antiaffirmative-action argument that diversity programs shift the focus from "corporate image or demographic changes and better utilization of human resources" to "meeting Legislative/regulatory requirements" (Benimadu and Paulsen, 1992, p. 23). On the contrary, the country's demographics are changing in such a way that the workforce and the markets are becoming increasingly more diverse. Diversity programs have become an unavoidable human resources concern because the pool of target applicants is likely to be diverse. Therefore, employment equity programs extend a hand to a "broader pool of talent," and at the same time a broader market of customers.

Figure 1.2   **Percentage of 25–29-Year-Olds Who Attained University Degrees, 1971–2009**

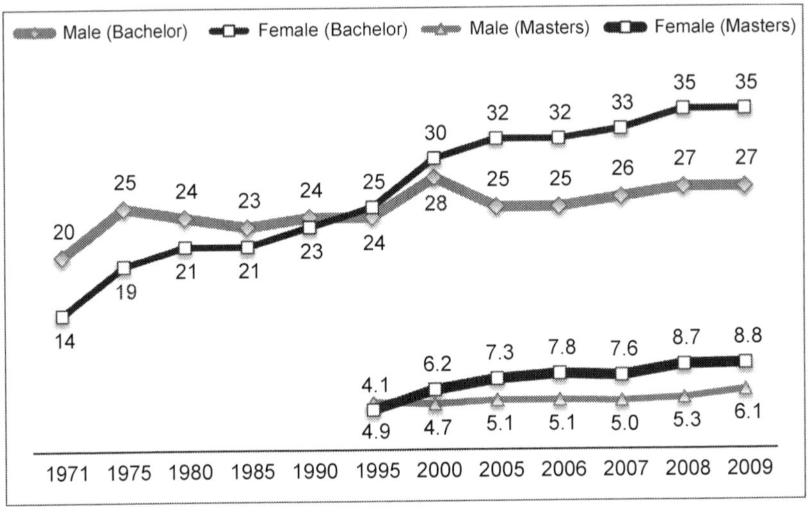

Source: National Center for Education Statistics, 2011.

Women are increasingly representing a larger segment of the workforce in terms of talent and qualifications. By larger, we do not mean that there are more women than before. We mean that more women than men are receiving higher education degrees (see Figure 1.2). Not to extend a hand to that segment of the workforce would deprive organizations, public and private, of access to that talent pool. This is the case not only for representation of women in organizations but also in terms of ensuring that workplaces are friendly to women.

Therefore, given that the population is becoming more diverse—which directly translates into a diverse citizenry and a diverse pool of applicants and employees—diversity of organizations and diversity competencies of public employees become critical to serving the needs of a diverse citizenry and to recruiting the most qualified employees in the workforce. However, the drive to create diverse organizations is not without risks and challenges. One of the foremost challenges to the concept of representative bureaucracy is its heavy reliance on the representation of societal groups in organizations. For instance, to mirror the representation of American society, an organization's workforce would have to be 12 percent African American, 8 percent Asian, 15 percent Hispanic, and 51 percent female. The complex question that will likely remain unanswered after the following discussion is whether this is adequate to achieve a representative bureaucracy that would better represent a diverse citizenry, that would better serve them, and that would welcome a diverse pool of talented and skilled employees regardless of sex, race, ethnicity, or other diversity categories.

Diversity and the Challenge of Representing Groups

In a narrow sense, diversity in organizations is interpreted as representation, management, retention, and hierarchical progression of women and minorities in an organization. Most organizations, public and private, aim to improve the representation of individuals belonging to different groups based on sex, ethnicity, race, and other societal groups. The representation of groups raises two interesting challenges. First, relegating to individuals the function of representing underrepresented groups creates pressure that disfavors individuality, but favors behavior that conforms to group norms and to an extent stereotypes—it forces them to "speak as" members of groups (Spivak and Gunew, 1993). Second, there is a concern that group-based representation has the tendency to yield *passive representation*. In other words, a picture-perfect mirror may be formed that creates the illusion of representation, but does little to empower underrepresented members of organizations to influence change.

Achieving diversity in recruitment, retention, and advancement is important to reverse the trends of excluding women and minorities from leadership positions. An example is the election of an African American president or a female president. After such an election, it is difficult for people to think that a woman or an African American cannot be president. However, such an election does not change the everyday lives of women or African Americans. In organizations, hiring a woman because she is a "good fit" for an organizational culture often results in hiring women who will follow the existing organizational culture without challenging it. Her perspective is muted by an expectation that she will follow the company line. There is not any functional diversity at that point. This form of identity diversity rarely serves the interests of minorities and women in organizations.

Passive and Active Representation

Representation comes in different shades. Organizations can aspire to have a "picture-perfect collection" of minorities and women in their workforce, or they go farther to ensure that minorities and women have some power and can liberally express their ideas and contribute to the delivery of the organizational objectives. While having a representative workforce is essential for them to be heard, some organizations treat that representation as an end by itself. There is a distinction between passive and *active representation*. Passive representation involves the mirroring of society's diversity in organizations. Active representation involves ensuring that the representation is meaningful in terms of influencing decision making within the organization.

Active representation is more sensitive to the representation of interests rather than the physical representation of cultural/ethnic/gender/sexual orientation groups (Hindera and Young, 1998; Young, 1990a). With active representation, the diverse workforce is empowered in the decision-making and implementation stages. Active representation involves the direct influence of women and minorities in setting organizational priorities and making decisions. Passive representation is achieved when the bureaucracy mirrors society in terms of group representation (Hindera and Young, 1998; Thompson, 1975). Alkadry (2007) argues:

> The main flaw of passive representation rests in its inability to provide meaningful results-oriented representation. The most that such a form of representation could hope for is a bureaucracy that reflects the visible diversity in society. Such a form of representative bureaucracy would not necessarily serve the functions of participatory democracy. (p. 159)

Passive representation might yield a change in organizational behavior toward different groups, and it might result in better responsiveness (Meier, 1993). Hindera and Young (1998, p. 656) suggest that "the relationship between passive and active representations changes at three critical points: when the critical mass is reached; when the group constitutes a plurality (i.e., social prominence) of agency personnel; and when the group constitutes a majority (i.e., social dominance)." Passive representation is therefore very important to achieving responsive organizations, but effectively turns representative bureaucracy into a form of tokenism.

There is a general agreement in social sciences and public administration in particular that a true form of representation would engage women and minorities in all types of organizations, in all fields and occupations, and at all levels of the hierarchy. That would ensure true representation and would set the foundation for associating this representation with decision-making power. However, and for many reasons, women continue to be segregated in certain agencies, certain occupations, and certain fields. In chapter 4, we focus on the issue of segregation of women in lower echelon positions, in lower paying female-dominated positions, and in specific occupations.

We all have families. Our familial roles may change throughout our lives, as do the associated time and energy demands they require: child bearing, sibling role-modeling, cousin, aunt/uncle, and niece/nephew welfare, partner supporting, parent caring, grandparent well-being, as well as other additional relationships we cherish. This book's authors believe that the most compelling challenge facing public, private, and nonprofit organizations is to reverse what is known as the conventional ideology of working men and family women (Johnson and Duerst-Lahti, 1992). In sociological circles, this is largely associated with the concept of patriarchy. Patriarchy, or the conventional ideology of working men and family women, is fundamentally entrenched in organizational culture that rests on assumptions of full commitment and dedication by employees to the organization—the production of "organization men" (Whyte, 1956) and later "organization women." This ideology will be referenced throughout the book as a challenge for organizations. The foremost problem with this ideology is its assumption that family responsibilities, and we all have them to some extent, are the sole domain of a support person, customarily a wife. This ideology and its assumptions fundamentally act to disadvantage women, who are often expected to function as caregivers at the expense of career success. Work–life balance and satisfaction with both work and life conditions is fundamental in combating this ideology.

Work–Life Balance, Fit, or Satisfaction

Most male and female adults participate in the workforce. These workers want to spend time with their families. There is also an increased expectation for parenthood to be time-, energy-, and money-intensive. These factors and more (e.g., caring for a child with special needs) lead to work–life conflict. Work–life balance is an issue that affects men as well as women. Work–life conflict, however, tends to hit women harder because of societal norms and expectations that women bear the larger burden of family responsibilities.

Table 1.2

Work–Life Conflict Differences by Employment Class

Upper/middle-class employees	Working-class employees
Have some control over schedule.	Have little or no control over schedule (e.g., when to take breaks).
Flexibility to make/receive telephone calls; arrive late/leave early.	Personal business frequently forbidden, unless during breaks or lunch.
May be able to arrange workday to attend school event or take a child to a doctor's appointment.	Rigid schedules that may need to be accounted for by "punching in." Discipline or dismissal for not adhering.
Travel may be required.	Scheduled work shift may change without notice.
Extension of workplace into the home through technology (see "third" and "fourth" shifts in chapter 4.	Nonstandard working hours (e.g., evening or night shift). Mandatory overtime.

Source: Williams (2010).

Work–life conflict/work–family conflict may be defined as concerns about insufficient time to take care of family responsibilities because of work responsibilities or vice versa (Blair-Loy and Wharton, 2004). This conflict is not only an issue that affects women more than men but also an issue of social class. Work–life conflict affects people in the upper-middle class differently than it affects working-class employees. Table 1.2 lists differences in workplace norms that affect work–life conflict experienced by upper/middle-class workers compared to working-class workers.

How to manage work–life conflict is frequently negotiated within the family. In a traditional marriage, for example, couples frequently make decisions related to work and family that tend to enhance the husband's earning capacity (Chang, 2010). How does this happen? Some women may exit the workforce to dedicate more time to family, allowing their partners to be more dedicated to work, while other women may turn down promotions or switch to jobs (full-time or part-time) that do not require long hours, long commutes, extensive travel, or even relocation. When women turn down promotions or switch jobs to support their husbands' careers, it is termed *downshifting*. While downshifting their careers may reduce work–life conflict of the family unit, it decreases women's lifelong earning trajectory and enhances men's. This can be devastating financially and otherwise, especially when couples separate.

Families should not find themselves stuck between a rock and hard place when it comes to making a choice between commitment to work and commitment to personal and family issues. Work–life conflict may be minimized by changes in policies (mandated by the government or voluntarily implemented by organizations) and changes in women's behaviors. *Family-friendly* or *work–life policies* may be defined as workplace policies with the goal of helping employees balance their work and family responsibilities. Williams (2010, pp. 64–71) makes the case that organizations should adapt to the changing realities of the workforce in order to optimize organizational effectiveness. Offering some control and flexibility to workers can:

1. Improve employee and consumer safety—reducing employees' exposure to distraction that may lead to injury to the employee, coworkers, or consumer.
2. Reduce employee stress—leading to less turnover, absenteeism, and insurance costs.
3. Increase employee loyalty—leading to higher quality products/ services because employees care about what they are doing.
4. Increase employee productivity.
5. Reduce turnover and improve recruitment.

Critics may argue that it is not possible to structure flexibility into working-class jobs. But, flexibility and reliable staffing are not incompatible. Williams (2010) offers multiple examples of approaches to achieve both flexibility and reliable staffing. For example, cross-training workers, computerized bidding systems for shifts, and backup systems for workers who call off work.

Women may also implement behaviors to minimize work–life conflict. Some refer to this as work–life fit (Yost, 2004) or work–life satisfaction (AWIS, 2001). The idea is that the solution to working outside of the home and having a family is individually based and may change throughout the life cycle. For example, you may need more time with your family when your children are toddlers and less time when your children have left home (empty nest). The Association of Women in Science (AWIS) conceptualized a model to achieve work–life satisfaction (Figure 1.3).

Work–life conflict may be minimized by work–life balance policies

Figure 1.3   **Achieving Work–Life Balance**

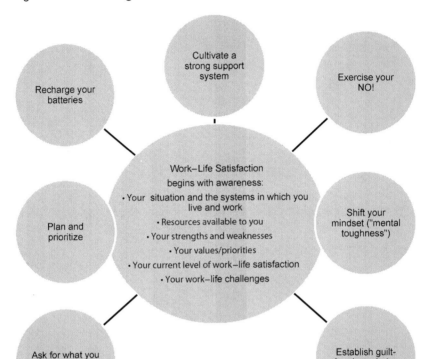

as well as changes in one's own behaviors. While each of us can control our own behaviors, it is important for organizations to be responsive to the demographic realities of today's workers: both working class and upper/middle class.

Diversity Theories

Before describing policy that protects individuals from discrimination in the workplace, it is important to understand two theories related to diversity. One is about *gender roles,* and the other is about the concept of implicit bias. Gender roles are more about society and societal expecta-

Table 1.3

Gender Roles Prevalent in the United States

Masculine roles	Feminine roles
Breadwinner	Dependent
Ambitious	Supportive
Competitive	Nurturing
Stoic	Communicative
Strong	Gentle
Assertive	Deferential
Confident	Compassionate

tions. However, it is very difficult to separate these gender roles from organizational life—especially as they relate to family commitments and organizational leadership expectations. Implicit bias theories are about our unconscious biases. We all have unconscious bias that may lead us, at times, to unintentionally discriminate against individuals.

Gender and Roles

What are gender roles/norms? *Gender norms* are attitudes or behaviors that are socially acceptable for one's gender. Gender norms vary by culture and historical time period. Table 1.3 displays dominant assumptions about gender roles in the United States. These gender roles continue to exist despite their dwindling effects. Men have historically been assigned the role of breadwinner. As such, they are expected to behave ambitiously, competitively, stoically, assertively, and confidently. On the other hand, women have been assigned the role of support person, with the associated behavioral traits: dependent, supportive, nurturing, communicative, gentle, deferential, and compassionate.

Individual men and women, however, may embody any of these roles, given the situation. Rigidly adhering to these gender roles may hurt men (and women). We limit our discussion here to men, as the application to women will be discussed in subsequent chapters. For men who rigidly adhere to masculine gender norms, they and their female partners tend to be less satisfied with their intimate relationship (Burn and Ward, 2005). Men who put in long hours at the office, with the aspiration and stress associated with the status of the sole breadwinner, may lose the ability to fully participate in their family life. But, men who do not live up to

Table 1.4

Strategies to Overcome Barriers of Gender Inequity

Barrier	Strategies
Apathy	Show men how they may benefit from gender equity: • Share financial responsibilities with partner • Improve relationship with partner • Increase parental involvement, leading to better relationship with children • Freedom to define self • Better physical and psychological health Show men how they may be hurt by gender inequity
Fear of losing status, being seen as sexist, other men's disapproval	Discourage fixed-pie thinking—that there are limited rewards. If women are given more, there is less for men Include men Introduce men to male role models
Ignorance of gender bias	Organize men-only groups to discuss the costs of gender inequity to them personally Include men in developing solutions to gender bias Expose men to women mentors

Source: Prime, Moss-Racusin, and Foust-Cummings (2009).

the perfect image of masculinity may also be penalized. These men may experience gender discrimination in the workplace.

Because gender roles are stereotypes that translate into expectations of appropriate behavior that penalize men, men have a stake in redefining gender roles and gender equity. But there are obstacles that prevent more men from becoming change agents. Prime, Moss-Racusin, and Foust-Cummings (2009) identified the following barriers to men becoming champions of gender equity; likewise, they offer strategies to overcome these barriers (see Table 1.4).

Gender norms heavily influence how work is organized and individuals' behaviors are interpreted. Both men and women experience problems as a result of gender role expectations. Therefore, it makes sense for men to be part of the conversation to change gender norms.

Implicit Bias

Let us take a closer look at our assumptions about gender roles. Whether you intend to discriminate against a minority (based on race, sex, etc.)

or not, you have probably done it. While this may be difficult to accept, we will show you how this works, as well as ways to minimize implicit biases—biases that you may not even be aware that you have (implicit attitudes or biases). Individuals who may be disadvantaged themselves by these biases often hold these unintentional biases (Shields, Zawadzki, and Johnson, 2011). Even others who consciously "try not to" discriminate also hold these unintentional biases. In other words, both women and men hold and apply similar implicit assumptions. Implicit bias is related neither to explicit bias nor to behavior (Karpinski and Hilton, 2001). So, even if one abhors sexism, that individual might still be susceptible to bias against women and people of color. You should not take our word for it. Try it:

1. Harvard Implicit Bias Test (IAT): https://implicit.harvard.edu/implicit/demo/
2. University of Chicago Shooter Test: http://home.uchicago.edu/~jcorrell/TPOD.html

How does unintentional, implicit, or unconscious bias work? In order to process the volumes of information that individuals encounter, we tend to take shortcuts, or rely on schemas or stereotypes. These heuristics cause us to overlook traits and behaviors that are inconsistent with our expectations as well as to notice traits and behaviors that are consistent with our expectations. Schemas may also cause us to negatively attribute the same behavior differently depending on whether a man or woman engages in it. For example, if a woman takes on the role of being a leader, she is likely to be perceived more negatively than a man taking on the leadership role. Why? Eagly and Karau (2002) explain that women's gender roles are incongruent with leadership roles. Therefore, not only do women have a more difficult time attaining a leadership role, but when women are leaders, they are perceived less effectively.

These disadvantages that result from our schemas compound over time, resulting in important disparities in career advancement, compensation, and opportunities (Valian, 1998). Men's performance, for example, tends to be overrated while women's performance tends to be underrated. There is much empirical support for implicit bias in the workplace, for example, in evaluating job applicants (Bertrand and Mullainathan, 2004), writing and interpreting letters of recommendation (Trix and Psenka, 2003), and reviewing employees' job performance (Lyness and Heilman, 2006).

Table 1.5

Reducing Implicit Bias

Adequate time	Devoting adequate time to evaluations
Full attention	Devoting one's full attention to the evaluation
Accountability	Knowing that a higher authority will review the evaluators' evaluations
Adequate number of women in the candidate pool	Having sufficient numbers of women in the hiring pool to be able to compare them to other women (vs. just men); strive for greater than 25 percent of the pool
Avoid other reasoning errors	Cognitive psychologists have identified numerous human reasoning errors. Three related to evaluations include: failure to appreciate covariation, blocking of relevant hypotheses, and illusory correlation
Visual priming	Display pictures of professional women and people of color in the room where candidates/candidates' materials are evaluated
Audio priming	Prior to evaluating candidates, simply stating/hearing the group leader remind the group to avoid prejudice results in more objective evaluations

Sources: Blair, Ma, and Lenton (2001); Dasgupta and Greenwald (2001); Lowery, Harkin, and Sinclair (2001); Valian (1998).

Men are able to accumulate advantages at a faster rate than women. These small advantages accumulate, leading to substantial differences across a career trajectory. Likewise, small setbacks/disadvantages for women and other minorities accumulate to cause disproportioned disadvantages across a career. Table 1.5 displays strategies for reducing implicit bias.

Institutional Discrimination

Institutional discrimination is often unconscious and unintentional. Institutional discrimination tends to be built into the normal operations of the organization. It comes from everyday practices, policies, and procedures: how work is organized, and how work gets done. For example, an agency that has mandatory weekly staff meetings at 3:00 p.m. will cause women to have a more difficult time attending that meeting. Not being present may affect her performance as well as management's view of her commitment to the organization. But women are largely responsible for the transportation of their school-age children to and from school. In this example, gender roles (women as homemakers and men as breadwinners), implicit bias (women are more committed to their family than their work), and institutional discrimination (meetings at a time that is difficult for women to attend) tend to support and reinforce each other. Bobbitt-Zeher (2011) found that discrimination is often the result of gender stereotyping, the sex composition of the organization, and policy rules as well as managers' discretion related to employees using the policy.

Barriers, Challenges, and Opportunities

Political culture is a very important barrier. In the United States, there is hardly a national consensus that representative bureaucracy is essential to achieving better representation or delivering better services. In fact, there are frequently efforts to curtail government actions to improve the representation of women and minorities not only in the workplace but also in colleges and universities. Historic discrimination resulted in the status quo. Efforts to correct the past would boost or accelerate the achievement of representative bureaucracy. Associating efforts to correct the past injustices or imbalance in representation with efforts to improve the representation of women and other underrepresented groups is one of the major barriers to achieving representative bureaucracy. These two issues—actions to correct the imbalance in the status quo and representative bureaucracy—are related but not the same.

Other major barriers are societal expectations and gender roles. These expectations are changing, but not as rapidly as women's education and employment potential in the labor force. As women become the better-educated sex, they need to be relieved of archaic expectations that women are responsible for the larger share of family care. Reversing the conventional ideology of working men and family women (Johnson and Duerst-Lahti, 1992) requires reversal of both the idea of "working men" and the idea of "family women." Such reversal should not result in family men and working women. It should rather be based on the concept of work–life balance for all working men and women.

Ridding organizations of the working-men assumption is within reach of the organization itself. The trend of increasing work–life initiatives, while reducing the expectation that employees give complete dedica-

Figure 1.4   **Age Distribution of Employees by Sector**

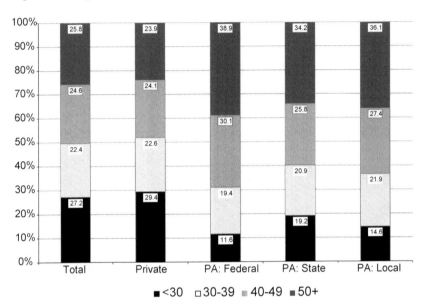

tion to work, organizations, or overtime may do away with the idea of
organization men or organization women. Reversing the idea of family
women, however, is far more complex and is not within the reach of
organizations. Rather, deconstructing the role of family women rests
with society at large.

Perhaps the biggest challenge to achieving representative bureaucracy
is time. Time is important. If the public sector were a ship, it would have
22 million passengers. Turning this mega-ship is a process that takes time.
There is also the challenge of convincing public service organizations to
follow in the footsteps of major private corporations, which have already
realized that family women (and family men) are too critical to forgo as
talented employees. Work–life programs are seen as an important human
resource strategy to recruit, retain, and promote talented individuals who
are looking for a better fit between their work and personal lives. At times
of financial constraint and negative attitudes toward the public sector, it is
challenging for public organizations to promote human resource policies
that would appear to make a public servant's life more enjoyable.

As more employees retire from the public sector, there will be a golden
opportunity for administrators and political leaders to attain better representation in institutions. Figure 1.4 displays the aging of the federal, state,

and local government workforce. Within fifteen years, 36 percent of the local government workforce, 34 percent of state government workforce, and 39 percent of federal government workforce will retire. With high rates of retirees exiting the government workforce, coupled with the demographic shift of women being the majority of college graduates and holders of graduate degrees, the public service faces the unprecedented and enormous opportunity to create more representative organizations that will meet the current and future demands of a diverse citizenry.

Key Terms

Active representation
Consumerist-based argument
Downshifting
Equity-based argument
Family-friendly or work–life
   policies
Functional diversity
Gender norms
Gender roles
Heuristics
Identity diversity
Implicit bias

Institutional discrimination
Passive representation
Perspective
Politics–administration
   dichotomy
Popular sovereignty
Representative bureaucracy
Representative democracy
Rule making
Work–life conflict/work–
   family conflict

2

Legislation Affecting Women

Legislation and public policies since the 1960s have progressively provided legal protections for women in the workplace. Legislation has also improved the workplace for individuals, both men and women, with family. However, the legislative bag is still full of tricks that prevent women and members of minority groups from balancing work and family, while obtaining wages comparable to men in jobs requiring similar skills and education. In this chapter, we outline key U.S. laws, make comparisons to international laws, and discuss legislation that would likely help provide an equitable workplace for women in terms of pay and promotion while allowing them to achieve a good work–life fit.

When discussing workplace legislative protections, we can think about laws that either (a) protect against discrimination, or (b) guarantee benefits. In the beginning of this chapter we discuss legislation that protects against workplace discrimination. First, there are laws that prohibit sex-based discrimination, such as Title VII of the Civil Rights Act, and the Pregnancy Discrimination Act. Second, there are laws that prohibit unequal pay, such as the Equal Pay Act and the Lilly Ledbetter Fair Pay Act. Third, there are laws that protect against other forms of discrimination, including the Americans with Disabilities Act and the Genetic Information Nondiscrimination Act.

The chapter then goes on to discuss laws that guarantee benefits relate to one's ability to work or take leave including laws regulating family medical leave, support for women to continue breastfeeding when returning to work, and child-care support.

By comparison, the European Union (EU) has a history of, and continues to strive for, both broad nondiscriminatory (based on "arbitrary ascriptive or acquired criteria") practices as well as equality between men and women in and beyond the workplace, through progressive policies (Eurofound, 2011b). Because the United States is so broad and diverse, politicians look to other U.S. states for policy ideas, but it is necessary that we look beyond our borders for a more thorough understanding of policy options. It is also helpful to look to the EU for a framework to challenge the ideal norm of a worker in the United States, that of the "organization man" (Whyte, 1956). The EU tends to have stronger antidiscrimination policies. For example, "The Treaty of Lisbon of 1 December 2009, includes in Article 21(1) a general prohibition of any discrimination based on any ground, such as sex, race, colour, ethnic or social origin, genetic features, language, religion or belief, political or any other opinion, membership of a national minority, property, birth, disability, age or sexual orientation" (Eurofound, 2011a). As will be discussed later, the protections as well as workplace benefits offered by the EU typically go well beyond what is offered in the United States.

At this point, it is important to warn that legislation can achieve only so much. Even though the EU has stronger antidiscrimination laws and better employment benefits, sex equity in the EU has yet to be achieved. Nevertheless, better policies at the federal, state, and local levels in the United States are very important for the dual purpose of protecting women's rights in the workplace and ensuring that the workplace is female-friendly. It is also important for current and future managers to educate co-workers, subordinates, and superiors on the benefits that organizations reap from implementing workplace protections that go beyond the minimums required by law. A female-friendly workplace is important not only for women, but for the organization's ability to recruit, reward, promote, and retain the best employees, regardless of sex.

Employment Discrimination Legislation

The Civil Rights Act of 1964 represented a foundational moment in U.S. history. This piece of federal legislation outlawed common overt acts of sex discrimination within organizations. Title VII of the act bars certain employers from discriminating against employees on the basis of race, color, religion, sex, or national origin. While women and other oppressed groups benefited from their inclusion in the Civil Rights Act, it should be noted that the impetus to passing the act was actually the Civil Rights Movement (mid-1950s to late 1960s), which drew attention to racial injustices.

While this landmark legislation may be criticized today for not taking the important step of adding protections against discrimination on the basis of sexual orientation, it is unrealistic to impose today's standards on historical events. With this said, the U.S. federal government has failed to pass the *Employment Non-Discrimination Act (ENDA)* that would offer employment discrimination protections to gay, lesbian, and transgender individuals, despite its introduction in nearly every Congress since 1994. In contrast to the United States, the European Union passed employment-based protections, in 2000, on the grounds of sexual orientation as well as beliefs related to morality and philosophy (Bell, Chopin, and Palmer, 2007; Ellis, 2005).

Since the enactment of the Civil Rights Act, particularly Title VII, significant policy changes have improved the workplace for women and others. Several workplace-related antidiscrimination laws followed the Civil Rights Act, including the Pregnancy Discrimination Act, and Section 4207 of the Patient Protection and Affordable Care Act of 2010.

Sex-Based Employment Discrimination

Title VII of the Civil Rights Act

A formative piece of U.S. legislation is *Title VII of the Civil Rights Act of 1964* (U.S. EEOC, 1964). Title VII prohibits private employers with fifteen or more employees and state and local governments from discriminating on the basis of race, color, religion, sex, or national origin. Age (forty and older) was added to the list of protected attributes in 1967. Title VII established the Equal Opportunity Employment Commission (EEOC) to enforce it. The EEOC will be described more fully in this chapter when we cover federal agencies.

Title VII prohibits discrimination based on three theories: (a) *disparate treatment*; (b) *disparate impact*; and (c) *pattern of practice. Disparate treatment* is defined as treating a member of a protected group differently. Disparate treatment is explicit discrimination. It only requires one incident or one person to prove discrimination.

To prove disparate treatment it is no longer necessary to prove *intent* to discriminate or prove there was a *motive* to discriminate (*EEOC v. Joe's Stone Crab* [11th Cir. 2000]). This 2000 decision focuses on differential treatment of the employee from a protected class (e.g., a woman). Therefore, it is important to find a comparator—an employee who is not from the protected class (e.g., a man)—to establish that he was treated more favorably or less adversely.

The U.S. Supreme Court broadened the reach of Title VII in *Griggs v. Duke Power Co.*, 404 U.S. 424 (1971) from the prohibition of disparate treatment, to the prohibition of disparate impact. The theory of *disparate impact* holds that a seemingly neutral practice that has an adverse effect on members of a protected group is illegal. Disparate impact was codified in law under the Civil Rights Act of 1991. The legal principle of disparate impact makes institutional discrimination, discussed in chapter 1, illegal. To prove disparate impact, a statistical pattern must be shown. An employer's intent to discriminate, or not, is not relevant. Historically, disparate impact theory was used by women to challenge height and weight requirements for jobs (U.S. EEOC, 2010). Disparate impact may remain a problem when employers use tests to screen and select employees. For example, does a cognitive test, physical ability test, or personality test disproportionately exclude women?

Discrimination based on a *pattern of practice* was determined to be illegal under Title VII in *Teamsters v. U.S.*, 431 U.S. 324 (1977). The company was found to have hired minorities for less desirable and lower paying positions (e.g., local city drivers or servicemen vs. long-distance drivers). Transferring to a desirable position meant forfeiting one's seniority, as per the union's seniority system. The discriminatory pattern in hiring as well as the seniority system rule that perpetuated the discrimination was in violation of Title VII. Pattern or practice discrimination is often used in class action lawsuits asserting a pattern of widespread discrimination (*Teamsters v. United States*, 431 U.S. 324 [1977]).

Title VII includes several exceptions. One important exception to disparate treatment of an individual may occur when an employer requires a certain attribute in the individual for the normal operation of the business, termed *bona fide occupational qualification* (BFOQ). For example, a public or private hospital may seek to hire a male nurse to perform catheterizations at the increasing request of male patients. A hospital may also seek a female gynecologist at the request of female patients. Race and color may never be a BFOQ, while religion, national origin, and sex may be permissible in some instances.

The U.S. EEOC (2010) offers a list of employer best practices, including use of validated tests. If a test overly excludes a protected group, the EEOC recommends finding an alternative test and updating the test, as job requirements change.

Pregnancy Discrimination Act

While Title VII offered equal protection in the workplace with regard to hiring, promotion, retention, and overtime pay, it failed to protect women from real biological differences between men and women. This gap in protection led to the passage of the Pregnancy Discrimination Act (O'Leary, 2007). The *Pregnancy Discrimination Act of 1978* amended Title VII, making it illegal to discriminate on the basis of "pregnancy, childbirth, or related medical conditions" (U.S. EEOC, 1978). The law requires pregnant women to be treated similarly to other employees.

The Pregnancy Discrimination Act does *not*, however, compel employers to provide pregnancy-related leave, which is the norm internationally. While the Pregnancy Discrimination Act of 1978 requires employers to allow pregnant women to use their sick leave for "pregnancy, childbirth, or related medical conditions" the law does not mandate that employers offer sick or pregnancy leave (U.S. EEOC, 1978).

In summary, Title VII of the Civil Rights Act prohibits private employers with fifteen or more employees and state and local governments from discriminating on the basis of race, color, religion, sex, or national origin. Because Title VII did not protect against biological differences in sex (i.e., pregnancy), the Pregnancy Discrimination Act amended Title VII to fill that gap by legislating equal protection in the workplace with regard to hiring, promotion, retention, and overtime pay.

Equal Pay Legislation

As will be discussed in detail in chapter 5, equal pay legislation offers another area of federal antidiscrimination protection. Remarkably, equal pay became an important election issue during the 2008 presidential elections. Then Senator Obama promised to sign a new equal pay bill to reverse the current trend that results in women getting paid less for the same work in some cases. Is current legislation effective at eliminating pay inequity between women and men? It is well documented that women and men have not achieved equal pay in the United States (Table 2.1). As shown in Table 2.1, on average, white women earn about 63 percent of what white men earn (or $0.63 compared to a white man's $1). Not only does being female negatively affect pay, but race does too. As shown in Table 2.1, when looking at people of a single race, on average, white employees earn more than Asians, followed by blacks, and then Hispanic/Latinos.

Table 2.1

Median Earnings, for Population Sixteen Years and Older by Gender
(in 2005 inflation-adjusted dollars)

Race	Men (%)	Women (%)
White alone	100	63
Black alone	70	56
Hispanic/Latino alone	60	43
Asian alone	99	70
American Indian/Alaska Native alone	65	47
Native Hawaiian/Pacific Islander alone	72	57
Other race alone	60	43
Two or more races	70	49

Source: U.S. Census Bureau.

This section will discuss legislation aimed at guaranteeing equal pay based on sex. There are some serious doubts about the ability of existing legislation to protect women from pay discrimination and to deliver equality in pay in the workplace. Therefore, this section also discusses other previously proposed legislation that would deliver this equality, even though such legislation has not passed into law.

Equal Pay Act of 1963 and Lilly Ledbetter Fair Pay Act of 2009

The *Equal Pay Act of 1963* (U.S. EEOC, 1963) requires an employer to pay the same wage to employees holding the same job. One of the major strengths of the law is that jobs need not be identical to qualify for protection under this law—they must only be "substantially equal." It is the content of the job, rather than the job title that is important. But U.S. courts have frequently narrowed the interpretation of this already limited law to render it somewhat ineffective.

The Equal Pay Act allows four affirmative defenses—justifications for disparate pay—against liability: merit, seniority, quality/quantity of production, and a difference based on "any factor other than sex." This last defense is quite broad. The Equal Pay Act has numerous other weaknesses. The Fair Paycheck Act attempts to remove these weaknesses as well as clarify parts of the Equal Pay Act that have been limited by U.S. courts.

In 2007, the U.S. Supreme Court ruled that a person must bring a lawsuit within 180 days of the company's original discrimination under the Equal Pay Act of 1963. This ruling will be discussed in more detail in a later section of this chapter. *The Lilly Ledbetter Fair Pay Act of 2009* nullified the 2007 Supreme Court decision, which narrowed the interpretation of the Equal Pay Act. The Ledbetter Act amended Title VII of the Civil Rights Act. The new law extends the statute of limitations 180 days after *each* paycheck (the way it was interpreted for twenty-five years prior to the 2007 decision).

Fair Paycheck Legislation

The Lilly Ledbetter Fair Pay Act fixed a specific recent interpretation of the Equal Pay Act, its companion legislation; the Fair Paycheck Act is a comprehensive fix to the Equal Pay Act. Although the legislation was supported by then Senator Obama during the 2008 presidential campaign, the bill has yet to become law. The Fair Paycheck Act, if passed, promises to:

1. Increase damages allowed—allowing compensatory and punitive damages that are available for discrimination based on ethnicity or race.
2. Make class action lawsuits easier to file—allowing class action lawsuits for equal pay claims to conform with the Federal Rules of Civil Procedure (FRCP), which allows plaintiffs to opt *out* if they choose. At present, plaintiffs need to opt *in* to a lawsuit, making it more difficult to bring a class action lawsuit.
3. Prohibit retaliation from employers—if employees discuss salary information, which is necessary to discover, if one is to discover pay disparities.
4. Close loopholes from court interpretations and roll back harmful Department of Labor (DOL) regulations—
   a. Loopholes—clarifies that comparisons between employees do not need to be in the same physical location; tightens an employer defense and limits the "any factor other than sex" defense to those that are actually caused by something other than sex, for example, differences in experience, education, or training.
   b. Rollbacks—requires the DOL to reinstate investigation and enforcement tools that were prohibited during the Bush era.

Exhibit 2.1

Steps to Determine Comparable Worth

1. Write a job description for each job
2. Identify common job characteristics (e.g., education, degree of skill, mental demands, working conditions, responsibility)
3. Assign a weight to each job characteristic
4. Evaluate job descriptions to determine degree of job characteristic found in each job

Source: Arnault et al. (2001, p. 809).

5. Require proactive actions to reduce pay discrimination by the federal government—increasing training for EEOC employees to recognize and respond to complaints; collecting more data; developing training for women and girls to better negotiate.
6. Increase training, education, and research.

(National Women's Law Center, 2005, 2009)

If passed, the Fair Paycheck Act would make the rules around filing lawsuits for disparate pay consistent with the rules for filing lawsuits for other forms of discrimination.

Comparable Worth Legislation

What is comparable worth? *Comparable worth* policies are those that evaluate jobs on the basis of characteristics (e.g., education or degree of skill). These characteristics are weighted ratings that are assigned to each attribute found in a job. A score is computed and a determination is made about whether a comparable worth adjustment is needed. Specific steps to engaging in comparable worth are found in Exhibit 2.1.

As the sex composition of an occupation changes, so do the wages. As the percentage of women in a job increases, the total compensation for that job decreases (e.g., Elvira and Graham, 2002). Comparable worth policies, legislation, and actions by organizations are the primary mechanisms to reduce the effect of occupational and agency segregation on women's pay, without the need to alter the composition of female/male-dominated agencies or fields. In other words, women may be concentrated in certain agencies or occupations. Such segregation should not be an excuse for these jobs to pay less than positions in male-dominated fields and agencies that require the same types of skills and education.

Comparable worth lost momentum after a ruling by the 9th Circuit Federal Court of Appeals. In *AFSCME (American Federation of State, County and Municipal Employees) v. State of Washington*, the court upheld the state's right to determine pay based on prevailing market rates. The court rejected the argument that pay disparities may be demonstrated under Title VII of the Civil Rights Act through a comparable worth study that showed male-dominated jobs paid more than female-dominated jobs. Comparable worth can be revived with the Fair Paycheck Act.

Comparable Worth vs. Market Rate

The goal of comparable worth is for all jobs within an organization to be compensated based on the value of the job rather than the market rate. The market rate can be problematic as it is often based on historical and discriminatory norms. From our perspective, for example, a social worker who has a Masters of Social Work degree, should not be paid significantly less than an engineer who has a Bachelor of Engineering degree.

Comparable worth attempts to fix the pattern that low wages are disproportionately paid to women simply because women occupy these jobs. Before the passage of the Equal Pay Act of 1963, it was legal, and common, to advertise jobs by the sex of the worker. Newspapers had separate listings for "Help wanted—Female" and "Help wanted—Male" jobs (*AFSCME v. Washington*, 1985). Women's jobs offered lower pay because women's work was not valued. In addition, it was assumed that a woman had a man in her life, father or husband, to properly support her. In other words, it was presumed that women worked for extra spending money and men worked to support a family. Sometimes jobs were listed for both sexes, but the pay scale was lower when advertised for women. The problem, according to comparable worth supporters, is that *today's pay scales continue to reflect this illegal bias.* Comparable worth seeks to correct this historical discrimination that may be reinforced by the prevailing market rate. Comparable worth could decrease pay disparities that result from occupational and agency segregation.

Critics of comparable worth argue that wages reflect market rates, determined by such factors as availability of workers, effectiveness of collective bargaining efforts, and so on. They also contend that comparable worth inflates wages in the interest of parity between male- and female-dominated occupations. Critics further argue that comparable worth stifles organizations' ability to respond to the labor market and makes organizations less globally competitive. But, comparable worth policies have been implemented internationally in Australia, New Zealand, the European Union, and Canada (Baker and Fortin, 2004; Borland, 1999, p. 268; Gunderson and Riddell, 1992)—and comparable worth practices have not been cited even once as stifling the competitive advantage of these countries. While the wage gap has not been eliminated internationally, comparable worth policy has been credited for narrowing it in the countries that have taken that issue seriously.

Effectiveness of Comparable Worth

Why have comparable worth policies failed to eliminate the wage gap? Comparable worth is difficult to implement. The lack of an agreed-upon method to determine the score assigned to each characteristic or weight assigned to each attribute in the overall job worth is a major drawback of comparable worth practices. In an experiment of three professional job evaluators, evaluating twenty-seven jobs, the evaluators were not consistent in rating the worth of the jobs (Arnault et al., 2001). Therefore, determining job worth is not easy to objectively define or to reliably measure; therefore, any outcome of a comparable worth system would be heavily influenced by the evaluator who performs it (Arnault et al., 2001, p. 814). To minimize bias, De Ruijter, Schippers, and Van Doorne-Huiskes (2004) suggest using at least six judgments per job: two job evaluators, two vocational advisers, and two social scientists. Although this process may be reliable, it is costly and may not allow adequate rewards for personal contributions and job performance.

Internationally, comparable worth has found more acceptance and largely been implemented in the public sector. In fact, comparable worth is embedded in the EU's definition of equal pay, "the principle of equal pay for women and men, states that the principle of equal pay, means, for the same work or *for work to which equal value* is attributed, the elimination of all discrimination on grounds of sex with regard to all aspects and conditions of remuneration. In particular, where a job classification system is used for determining pay, it must be based on the same criteria for both men and women and so drawn up as to exclude any discrimination on grounds of sex (Council Directive, 1975, Article 1)" [emphasis added]. In practice, however, the pay gap tends to vary by country, being as low as 2 percent in

Malta to as high as 25 percent in Austria, while the Czech Republic comes in with an average of 17 percent. While improvements are still very much needed, the EU is doing better than the United States, and the EU has had a long-term commitment to equal pay that continues today.

An exception to this rule that comparable worth is more common internationally in the public sector than in the private sector may be found in our northern neighbor, Canada. A study examining comparable worth outcomes of the private sector in Ontario, Canada, found that small employers tended not to comply with the policy (Baker and Fortin, 2004). Small firms lacked the resources to create job evaluation programs and delineate job classification systems, and also lacked adequate samples of male and female jobs to make meaningful comparisons. But comparable worth was modestly successful for larger firms, particularly among women who were not represented by a union or who occupied undervalued jobs (e.g., clerical). The authors conclude that stronger enforcement mechanisms are necessary for success in the smaller firms.

No U.S. state has achieved pay parity between the sexes, the gap ranges from as low as a 7 percent difference, to as high as a 37 percent difference in pay between men and women (National Women's Law Center, 2009). Absent national legislation and action on comparable worth, the states were left to legislate in the area of comparable worth. About half of the states (including, e.g., Washington and Minnesota) and some local governments have implemented comparable worth (O'Neill, 2011).

This section described U.S. law and other policy with the goal of equalizing pay inequity between men and women: The Equal Pay Act of 1963 and Lilly Ledbetter Fair Pay Act of 2009 require equal pay for the same job. They do not require comparable worth, a tool that has been used globally and in some U.S. states and local governments to narrow the pay gap.

Disability and Genetics Legislation

The *Americans with Disabilities Act (ADA) of 1990* prohibits discrimination based on disability. The intent of ADA is to remove barriers that prevent people with disabilities from fully participating in mainstream society. The ADA is a broad law covering employment discrimination, access to public services and businesses, and telecommunications. While access to public services and businesses is important for public service students and scholars to focus on, this book's focus will be on the implications of the ADA for employment discrimination.

The ADA defines a disability as a physical or mental impairment that substantially limits one or more major life activities. There must be a clear record of such impairment, or the employee must be regarded as having such impairment. The *ADA Amendments Act (ADAA) of 2008* expanded the definition of disability, to cover more people (Job Accomodation Network [JAN], 2011).

The Act provided many additions to the definition of who is covered under the ADA protections. First, the definition of "major life activities," such as seeing, hearing, eating, walking, was expanded to include major bodily functions (e.g., functions of the immune system). This added coverage to people living with HIV/AIDS. Second, the standard for considering whether a worker is "substantially limited" was lowered. Workers who are able to control symptoms of their disability, for example, through the use of medication, are now considered disabled. Third, workers who experience episodic conditions or remission now fall under the definition of disability (JAN, 2011, pp. 1–6).

While the ADA prohibits discrimination based on disability, the *Genetic Information Nondiscrimination Act (GINA)* of 2008 prohibits discrimination based on genetic information. GINA was largely a reaction to rapid advances in genetics and diffusion of this technology. The reaction was preemptive, as few cases documenting genetic discrimination exist (Pullman and Lemmens, 2010).

Legislation on Workplace Benefits

Workplace protections for U.S. workers tend to lag behind those of other developed countries, translating into important implications for the lives of U.S. workers and their families. Although U.S. policy has some workplace protections, we fall behind other industrialized countries on various entitlements. Out of 177 countries studied, the United States does not guarantee any of the following:

1. 169 out of 173 countries provide paid leave for childbirth
2. 145 countries provide paid sick leave
3. 134 countries have a cap on hours worked per week
4. 126 countries guarantee a 24-hour break from work each week
5. 50 countries mandate wage premiums for night/evening work; 28 have restrictions
6. 40 countries provide paid leave for major family events (e.g., marriage)

(Heymann, Earle, and Hayes, pp. 1–6)

Considering international law may help readers look beyond our own societal expectations of workplace protections that reinforced the "organization man" standard.

An explanation and critique of the Family and Medical Leave Act will ensue, including how few women qualify for it and how few women can afford to use it in cases of childbirth or caring for an aging family member. It is important to keep in mind that U.S. policy, organizational practices, and women's "choices" tend to adversely affect women throughout their lives. As will be discussed, the United States lacks a social safety net, and when this is added to the punitive eligibility requirements for government programs and stringent eligibility requirements for employer benefits, it results in much higher rates of poverty among children and families. It is instructive to note that single moms are usually the hardest hit, and that poverty continues into old age for women.

Family Medical Leave

The *Family and Medical Leave Act (FMLA) of 1993* is a seminal piece of U.S. legislation for employees. It provides some protections for workers with family issues that could affect their ability to work. The legislation, however, falls short on many other fronts. Some eligibility requirements for both the employee and employer limit the use of the FMLA, particularly among women. Because states may be laboratories for federal programs, a discussion of *paid* leave policies in states such as California and New Jersey will follow. When we compare the FMLA to policies in most other nations, it appears that most developed countries have leave that is (a) universal, (b) paid, and (c) longer than that offered by the FMLA.

Federal Legislation

Before the FMLA, sick leave/family leave was offered at the discretion of the employer. As a result, organizations dismissed employees for taking "too much" leave. This had the double effect of (a) discriminating against women as well as (b) forcing women to "choose" between having a family and a career. Women faced discrimination based on their physiology and gender roles. Women's physiological issues focused on birthing babies, an event that required time for recovery and time for bonding with the baby. On the other hand, women's gender roles tend to dictate that women are the primary caregivers of children and adult family members. Women were given the nonchoice of sacrificing having children to continue their career trajectory, or being fired for taking time off after childbirth or to care for a family member.

FMLA seeks to prevent employers from being able to fire workers for using sick leave/family leave, at least within the parameters of the law. FMLA is a federal law that normally guarantees employees job security while they are using up to twelve weeks of leave to take care of a family member for medical issues. The law does not require that family medical leave be paid. More specifically, the FMLA may be used for the birth or adoption of a child, to care for a family member (i.e., child, spouse, or parent) with a serious medical condition, or to take medical leave for a serious personal health problem. The definition of "child" goes beyond that of a legal or biological relationship to also include those who take on the role of caring for a child (U.S. DOL, 2012).

Effective in 2009, caregivers for wounded service members are permitted to take twenty-six weeks of *unpaid* leave, and family members of National Guard or Reservists may take twelve weeks of *unpaid* leave to prepare for, or cope with (for example) short-notice of deployment, set up child care, or make financial arrangements (DOL, 2008).

There are eligibility requirements of both the employee and employer that limit the use of the FMLA, particularly among women:

1. An employee must have worked for the employer for at least 1,250 hours in the past twelve months. This requirement makes it less likely that female employees will be eligible for family and medical leave because female workers are more likely to work part-time or exit the workforce to care for family members.
2. Private employers with fifty or more employees and all government agencies, regardless of size, are subject to FMLA. Women are more likely to work in small businesses and therefore to be ineligible for family and medical leave.

FMLA conditions, coupled with women's gender roles and concomitant work patterns, disqualify many female workers. It does not always address the needs of the very employees who disproportionately need the policy's protection. FMLA covers only about 40 percent of the private sector (National Partnership for Women and Families, 2009), and 62 percent of all employees. Forty-eight percent of female workers, compared to 52 percent of male workers, qualify for family and medical leave; yet 58 percent of women compared to 42 percent of men utilized it (Heymann, Earle, and Hayes, 2007). In other words, fewer women qualify for FMLA, but more women use it.

Data from the Congressional Commission on the Family and Medical Leave Act indicate that women are significantly more likely to use the FMLA than men (Armenia and Gerstel, 2005). Here are some trends in leave usage:

1. After controlling for other variables, women are almost two times as likely to take leave.
2. Regardless of race, length of leave—taken to care for a sick spouse, sick parent, or seriously ill child—are similar among women and men.
3. Regardless of race, women take longer leaves to care for newborns than men—on average, fifteen days longer.
4. Never-married individuals are significantly less likely to take leave.
5. Individuals with higher incomes, or paid a salary are more likely to take leave.

(Armenia and Gerstel, 2005)

Wage replacement is a critical component in a successful leave policy. Only one in five U.S. middle class families have sufficient assets to live without income for twelve weeks (Wheary, Shapiro, and Draut, 2007). Therefore, unpaid leave is a significant barrier for most working families.

Table 2.2 lists proposals to increase the number of individuals who are covered by and able to use the FMLA. Proposals may target employer requirements, for example, mandating partial or full pay for employees who utilize the FMLA. Proposals also include relaxing employee eligibility and usage requirements, such as reducing the number of hours an employee has to work to qualify for family and medical leave.

State Legislation

A few states have stronger family and medical leave laws than the Family and Medical Leave Act. State laws may reduce the number of employees necessary for individuals to qualify for the FMLA. For example, Vermont

Table 2.2

Proposals to Increase Individuals Covered and Usage of the FMLA

	Example
Employer requirements	
Include firms with fewer than 50 employees	25 or 10 employees
Mandate partial or full pay	55% up to $987 per week (indexed for inflation)
Employee requirements	
Widen the definition of family	Siblings, grandparents/in-laws, domestic partners, or aunt/uncle
Increase the types of reasons that one is permitted to take family and medical leave under the FMLA	Domestic violence, sexual assault, or stalking; school activities and teacher conferences
Reduce number of hours worked to qualify for FMLA leave	Part-time workers (e.g., 625 hours)
Reduce the length of time with the current employer to qualify	6 or 3 months

Source: Pyle and Pelletier (2003).

extends parental leave to organizations with ten or more employees, and family and medical leave to organizations with fifteen or more employees. States have expanded the definition of family that is covered by the FMLA to include categories such as domestic partner/civil union partner, domestic partner's child, grandparent, grandparent-in-law, parent-in-law, or sibling. State laws have also expanded the uses of the FMLA, for example, to attend a child's educational activity, for routine medical visits, or to manage the effects of domestic violence, stalking, or sexual assault (National Partnership for Women and Families, 2009).

While only five states provide paid family and medical leave to its workforce, state workers may use other types of leave to help fund leave after a baby (e.g., sick leave and vacation). An individual thus has to accrue leave or sick days and spend them on this event. Some organizations, however, do not allow birth mothers to use accrued sick leave beyond the period of recovery from childbirth; these organizations do not allow the second parent to use accrued sick leave at all. In other words, some organizations will allow sick leave to be used only for one's own illness. Organizations that limit sick leave usage this way further limit employees' options.

No U.S. state guarantees 100 percent wage replacement and job protection while on leave (Grant, Hatcher, and Patel, 2005). Only California and New Jersey offer partial paid leave (Appelbaum and Milkman, 2011). Table 2.3 compares provisions in California and New Jersey law.

The California Paid Family Leave program has proved quite successful, boasting the following outcomes:

1. Cost savings for employers (e.g., reduced turnover)
2. Gendered division of labor more equalized: men increased their use of leave
3. Breastfeeding median duration of new mothers doubled
4. Wage replacement higher for those using Paid Family Leave than those who did not

The Paid Family Leave program was possible in California and New Jersey because these states taxed employee payrolls, rather than employers. The disability pay in Washington is a flat $250 per week, for up to five weeks. However, it has not been implemented because funding has not been identified (Applebaum and Milkman, 2011).

Other Countries

When comparing other nations' policies to the Family and Medical Leave Act, distinct patterns emerge. Policies in other countries tend to be longer and more universal. They are universal in the sense that they cover all working parents. For most countries, the average leave period is ten months. Leave comes with some wage replacement or income supplementation. All new mothers are covered; while some countries also cover fathers (Waldfogel, 2001). Paid leave in Europe is largely funded by social insurance or general taxes, thereby shifting the cost to society as a whole and reducing the opposition of employers (Pyle and Pelletier, 2003).

What are the pros and cons of longer paid leave? We saw from the discussion on the FMLA in the United States that unpaid leave is not an option for many women, particularly those among the working poor and the lower levels of the middle class. But longer leaves are associated with healthier women and children (Spangler, 2000). Longer leaves have also

Table 2.3

California and New Jersey Legislation on Leave and Wage Replacement

	California 2002	New Jersey 2009
Disability Insurance	55% up to $987 per week for 6 weeks (indexed for CA average weekly wage)	2/3 salary for 6 weeks up to $561 in 2010 (indexed for NJ average weekly wage)
Employee Payroll Tax	1.2%	.09%
Employer Payroll Tax	0	0
Eligible	Employee earned at least $300 in an SDI-covered job (p. 2)	Employee worked 1 year (1,000 hours) in prior 12 months. Exceptions: 5% of highest salaried employees or 7 highest paid individuals

Source: Appelbaum and Milkman (2011); New Jersey Office of the Attorney General (2011).

been linked to better parenting. For example, Feldman, Sussman, and Zigler (2004) found that mothers who took leaves of less than twelve weeks were less knowledgeable (e.g., did not search for infant development information), perceived their baby as more difficult, and perceived the birth to have a less positive effect on their self-esteem and marriage. Longer leaves may allow women to initiate and sustain a breastfeeding relationship. As will be discussed later, breastfeeding is also associated with positive health outcomes for mother and child.

On the other hand, longer leaves may reinforce traditional gender roles and hinder gender equity in the workforce. If women take longer leaves, employers may be more likely to discriminate against women in employment matters—hiring, promoting, training, and compensation— because they anticipate that their investment in women will not be returned. However, antidiscrimination legislation could meaningfully curb discrimination if it were accessible to victims, had strong consequences for offenders, and had strong enforcement for violations.

In sum, the FMLA gives a limited number of U.S. employees job security for up to twelve weeks of *unpaid* leave to take care of themselves or a particular family member for certain reasons (e.g., medical issues). Several U.S. states offer better protections. In light of economic constraints, additional states embracing more generous family leave policies, or a successful federal effort to require universal paid family leave is unlikely for the near future. By comparison to other nations, especially industrialized ones, the FMLA leaves much to be desired in terms of its ability to provide universal, paid, and longer leaves to women.

Breastfeeding and the Law

Section 4207 of the Patient Protection and Affordable Care Act of 2010 (also known as the 2010 Health Care Reform Law) protects women who wish to continue breastfeeding after returning to work. The law states that organizations with fifty or more employees will provide a private, nonbathroom space to express breast milk. Employees are entitled to a reasonable amount of time, *each time* she has the need, to do so. These breaks may be unpaid, and this protection is limited until the child is one year old (Section 4207 of the Patient Protection and Affordable Care Act). While the law does not require the designation of a separate room for this purpose, the room must meet these requirements across all sites (e.g., a boardroom with no/or covered windows and a lock).

Publicly Supported Child Care and Education

Child care in the United States is viewed differently than it is around the world. In Europe, children are viewed through the "public good" notion: essential for population and economic growth, a societal benefit that all may enjoy whether they pay for it or not. Therefore, quality child care and education are regarded as a social investment, a way to socialize the next generation of the country's citizens, who will contribute to the nation's economy (Williams and Cooper, 2004). Parents devote money, time, and care to rearing children whom society ultimately benefits from. Therefore, the state helps pay for some costs associated with raising children. As a result, European countries tend to provide high quality child care, and poverty rates among children are relatively low.

How is child care viewed in the United States in terms of policy and resources used to support it (vs. the lip service given to the importance of "family" in political speeches)? The assumption that undergirds policy related to children and families in the United States may be understood through the *"children-as-pet" notion:* "those who want children ought to pay for them" (England and Folbre, 1999, p. 195). In the United

States, it is mothers, in particular, who absorb most of the costs related to raising children—financial costs, time devoted to care, and reduced earnings. Furthermore, child care is devalued, whether it is provided by family members (most often mom) or "strangers" (child-care facilities, overwhelmingly staffed by women). The former are given no societal compensation for providing unpaid familial care. Instead, mothers (and other caregivers) who do not engage in paid employment are penalized by government policies (e.g., they do not receive Social Security if they do not engage in paid employment). As a result of the U.S. attitude toward children and its concomitant effect on policy, child care is deemed the responsibility of the family, the quality of child care is uneven, and U.S. children have one of the highest rates of poverty in the industrialized world.

The availability of child care affects family finances, child development, and women's attitudes toward work (Donovan, Pieper, and Ponce, 2007). This section will review publicly supported child-care efforts in the United States as well as abroad.

Federal and State

In contrast to many European countries, child care in the United States is not viewed as an entitlement. It is largely subsidized through tax credits and the welfare system. A *tax credit* is the amount of money a taxpayer can deduct from the taxes owed to the government. The federal government provides the following tax credits:

1. Child Tax Credit—In 2010, parents were permitted to reduce their federal income tax up to $1,000 for each child age sixteen and younger (i.e., tax credit of $1,000 per child) (IRS, 2011a).
2. Child and Dependent Care Credit—In 2010, parents were permitted to reduce their federal income tax up to $3,000 for one child or $6,000 for two or more children (IRS 2011b).

Tax breaks offered by the federal government do not come close to offsetting real child-care costs. The tax breaks, however, are provided only to parents who are working—if both parents are living with a child, they both have to work (or study full-time). States may also offer tax credits.

The *welfare system* also provides limited child-care services to families, although it is based on income. The *Child Care and Development Block Grant (CCDBG)* is the federal financial support mechanism. It largely helps low-income families pay for child care, but 4 percent must be spent on initiatives to improve quality in child care.

Some states (e.g., Ohio) provide financial assistance to eligible parents to pay for child care in private facilities. Other states offer publicly funded child care, often in conjunction with their Head Start Program. Head Start offers grants to public, nonprofit, and for-profit agencies to provide comprehensive child development services to low-income children (Administration for Children and Families, 2011). The focus of Head Start is to prepare preschoolers to be successful in school.

A recent trend in child-care subsidization is happening at the state level: there is a movement toward universal pre-K. Some states extend pre-K to four-year-olds. Others provide pre-K for three-year-olds as well. Although the objective of this trend is to standardize and improve children's readiness for school, it shifts child-care expenses from families to taxpayers.

School-aged children also need safe and enriching opportunities after school hours. Yet, most children do not have access to affordable after-school care (Heymann, Penrose, and Earle, 2006). These authors suggest extending the school day and school year to address this gap to improve students' academic achievement and subsidize child care.

Other Countries

Broadly, three types of child-care policies are found internationally. Although in the U.S. we do not typically view parental leave as childcare, providing paid parental leave encourages a parent or parents to deliver the childcare themselves. Please see Table 2.4 to understand the outcome that is likely given the continuum from limited to generous policies offered.

   a. Parental leave policies—allow employed parent(s) to stay home to provide care themselves.
   b. Child-care policies—give parent subsidies to pay for child care or provide child care directly in publicly operated facilities.
   c. Early childhood benefits—confer cash to parents. Cash may be used to pay for child care or reimburse a parent for lost wages.

(Waldfogel, 2001, p. 101).

Although child care is expensive in the United States, quality tends to vary across sites due to weak state regulations (e.g., in regard to provider training) (Meyers and Gornick, 2005). One aspect of quality relates to

Table 2.4

Leave and Child-Care Policies Related Outcome

Parental leave	Child care	Outcome
Limited	Generous	Moms return to work earlier.
Generous	Limited	Moms provide care for their infants.
Limited	Limited	Moms completely withdraw from workforce, or return to work earlier.
Generous	Generous	Gives families real choice.

Source: Meyers and Gornick (2005); Waldfogel (2001).

the children per staff ratio. The number of children per staff ratio in the United States tends to be higher than most other nations (Heymann, Penrose, and Earle, 2006). U.S. children in higher-quality settings display better cognitive, language, and social competencies at the time of day care and in the future. Not only children benefit from high quality child care, society also reaps benefits:

- Lower taxes by reducing the need for special education and grade retention
- Larger pool of more productive employees
- Future reductions in crime
- Future reductions in welfare programs utilization.

(Vandell and Wolfe, 2000)

Despite economic justification for public intervention to improve child-care quality, state governments are not doing enough. Schulman and Blank (2011) of the National Women's Law Center conducted a survey of successful state strategies to improve quality. The most common initiatives used by states include:

1. Establishing a Quality Rating and Improvement System (QRIS) rate and offering financial incentives to improve quality;
2. Offering educational development opportunities and increased compensation to these providers;
3. Offering resources to assist child-care program in meeting social, emotional, and health needs of children;
4. Strengthening collaboration among programs providing services to children (e.g., Head Start, Early Head Start, state Pre-K); and

5. Offering guidance/mentoring to providers who care for very young children.

Because of the role of government in foreign countries, quality standards tend to be more uniform and rigorously enforced (Waldfogel, 2001, p. 107).

Reconsidering Policy: An Opportunity?

As has been described, and compared to other countries, the United States lacks a robust social safety net. Children are viewed as a choice, rather than as essential for economic and population growth—a public good in a sense. As a result, it is each family's responsibility, often the mother's rather than society's, to bear the financial burden. The United States does not offer worker protections found in Europe and elsewhere. As a result, U.S. organizations are free to impose restrictive employment benefits on U.S. workers. And poverty continues into old age for women.

When women exit the workforce to care for a family member, they do not receive credit toward Social Security. The calculation for Social Security is based on the ideal worker norm of thirty-five years of employment: The highest thirty-five years of earnings are applied to formulas. If an individual does not work thirty-five years, "0" will be included in those years. The "0" entries can substantially bring down the average, as can low-wage, part-time employment.

Should a mother exit the workforce to perform caregiving and then become divorced, she can anticipate a significant drop in her and her offsprings' standard of living, but not in her ex-husband's (Crittenden, 2001). Crittenden explains that family law fails to recognize an economic partnership, hence assigning income and property to the person who "earns" it. Chang (2010) reminds us that work–life conflict is negotiated within the family, with couples frequently deciding to enhance the husband's earning capacity at the expense of the wife's. Wives may downshift or exit their careers (i.e., those that require long hours, long commutes, extensive travel, or even relocation) so they are available for family responsibilities while their husband can commit to these time-intensive work schedules. In other words, to reduce work–life conflict for the family unit, the wife may reduce her work responsibilities to support her husband's career. In a divorce, even equal distribution of the assets does not adequately compensate her for her forgone earning capacity trajectory (and his increased earning capacity) that was based on a joint decision.

Furthermore, if she is given custody, she will be further financially disadvantaged: she will need to remain in career downshift mode, which comes with a wage penalty now and in the future. U.S. Census data, in 2009 for example, show that 30 percent (3,371 mothers) of mothers who were owed child support received nothing, and only 42 percent (4,720 mothers) of mothers received the full amount of child support owed to them (Grall, 2011).

Given what we know about work–life conflict and how families cope with it, it is important to reconceptualize what policy looks like. An important step would be decoupling full-time employment with company benefits (e.g., health insurance) and government benefits (e.g., FMLA). This would go a long way to reducing poverty among women and families (see Exhibit 2.2).

Stone and Kuperberg (2005) found that pay equity policy reduces poverty and discriminatory pay, whereas living wage reform maintains discriminatory pay, but does reduce poverty by raising the wages of the lowest wage earners.

Family Responsibility Discrimination, a New Frontier

Five of the statutes described in this chapter—Title VII, Pregnancy Discrimination Act, Equal Pay Act, FMLA, Americans with Disabilities Act—have been used successfully to sue employers for discrimination against "employees with family responsibilities." What is family responsibility discrimination (FRD)? *Family responsibility discrimination* occurs when a personnel decision is based on stereotypes about how a caregiver will or should behave (WorkLife Law, http://worklifelaw.org/frd/). For example, FRD may occur if a mother is not promoted because the employer assumes she will not travel, as required by the job.

The Center for WorkLife Law, at the University of California Hastings College of the Law, is a "nonprofit research and advocacy group" that is at the vanguard of the FRD debate. While no federal law explicitly outlaws this type of discrimination, some state and local governments expressly forbid such discrimination. The center found more than sixty-three local governments in twenty-two states that expressly prohibit the practice (Bornstein and Rathmell, 2009). It is important for more state governments and the federal government to pass protections.

Exhibit 2.2

Policies to Reduce Poverty for Women and Families

1. Limit the workweek to 35 hours per week. This would allow all workers more time with their families. Fewer women would need to drop out of the workforce or reduce their hours to part-time.
2. Curtail employers' ability to mandate overtime; allow unlimited voluntary overtime.
3. Forbid discrimination against part-time workers
   - Require proportional pay, benefits, training, and advancement
   - Unless there is a legitimate business reason not to, allow employees to decrease or increase their hours
   - Require part-time workers be eligible for
     - Government benefits (e.g., FMLA, pensions, unemployment insurance, workers compensation, disability insurance)
     - Employer-based benefits (health insurance, sick leave, and other employer benefits) (Williams and Cooper, 2004).
4. Offer the right to request workplace flexibility "modeled on legislation in the United Kingdom and introduced in the 111th Congress in the House by Rep. Carolyn Maloney (D-NY)—the Working Families Flexibility Act, H.R. 1274—to give Americans the right to request a change in their work schedules without retaliation. The proposed legislation does not require employers to grant such requests, but they would have to give a reason if they deny a request" (Williams and Boushey, 2010, 70).
5. Improve FMLA (see Table 2.2).
6. Improve child-care entitlements
   - Increase child-care subsidies
   - Increase funding for after-school programs
   - Increase and fund child-care quality regulations
   - Require states to provide state-funded universal pre-K for children beginning at ages 3 and 4; and full-day kindergarten at age 5.
7. Increase the minimum wage to a "living wage" and strengthen anti-discrimination policy (Stone and Kuperberg, 2005).
8. Reform Social Security
   - Give tax credits for caregiving years toward the calculation of Social Security benefits
   - Ease eligibility requirements to reflect real demographic patterns of marriage
   - Increase survivors and divorced partner's benefits
   - Allow eligibility of domestic partners.
9. Modify divorce laws
   - Broaden definition of assets included in settlements: pensions, future stock options, employment termination packages
   - Consider lost earning capacity of caregiver (and enhanced earning capacity of worker) in settlements (Chang, 2010).

Table 2.5

Approaches to Adding Family Responsibility Discrimination to Organizational Policy

Approach	Example
Revise antidiscrimination policy	"It is the Company's policy not to discriminate against any employee or applicant for employment because of race, color, religion, . . . or family responsibility. . . ."
Develop a stand-alone policy	" . . . [T]he company prohibits discrimination against employees and applicants for employment based on their family responsibilities. . . ."

Sources: Von Bergen (2008); originally from the The Center for WorkLife Law, www.worklifelaw.org.

In the meantime, organizations may develop, implement, enforce, and educate employees about family responsibility discrimination. The Center for WorkLife Law offers two approaches for doing so: revise antidiscrimination policy and/or develop stand-alone policy (Table 2.5).

Barriers, Challenges, and Opportunities

Beyond Americans valuing equality, diversity has been shown to strengthen organizational outcomes. This fact offers incredible opportunities if it can overcome the barrier of ignorance surrounding it. Because diversity is something we have to make a conscious effort to avoid, this presents a significant challenge. We all hold implicit biases that lead us to overlook traits and behaviors that are inconsistent with our expectations as well as to notice traits and behaviors that are consistent. These biases compound overtime, resulting in significant disadvantages for women and others. We previously offered Table 1.5 (see page 24) with several suggestions to overcome unconscious biases (opportunities).

Important pieces of legislation have improved the workplace for women and others. When discussing workplace legislative protections, we can think about laws that either (a) protect against discrimination or (b) guarantee benefits. Within both of these categories, Europe appears to have stronger protections for its citizens.

Title VII of the Civil Rights Act prohibits private employers with fifteen or more employees and also state and local governments from discriminating on the basis of race, color, religion, sex, or national origin. Because Title VII does not protect against biological differences in sex (i.e., pregnancy), the Pregnancy Discrimination Act fills that gap by legislating equal protection in the workplace with regard to hiring, promotion, retention, and overtime pay.

Additional antidiscrimination laws attempt to equalize pay between the sexes—the Equal Pay Act of 1963 and the Lilly Ledbetter Fair Pay Act of 2009 require equal pay for the same job. Other policies that would go further to equalize pay have been introduced but not passed, leaving future Congresses an opportunity to strengthen protections. Further worker discrimination protections include the ADA (based on disability) and GINA (based on genetic information).

U.S. workplace guaranteed benefits severely lag behind those in other developed countries, which has important implications for the lives of U.S. workers and their families. The gaps in our policies serve as barriers preventing women from fully participating in the workforce, as well as challenges to changing societal attitudes that are needed to bring about reform. FMLA gives a limited number of U.S. employees' job security if they use twelve weeks of unpaid leave to care for a particular family member for medical issues. When we compare FMLA to policies in most other nations, it appears that most developed countries have leave that is (a) universal, (b) paid, and (c) longer than that offered by the FMLA. Recently, federal law gave protection to women wishing to continue breastfeeding after returning to work.

How a country views child care is a good predictor of how well it is supported with government benefits. As discussed, the United States tends to view children under the "children as pets" notion, in contrast to most industrialized countries that view children as a "public good." Childbearing and childrearing essentially serve the public interest by serving the demographic and economic interests of the nation. In countries like Canada, for instance, residents raising children receive a monthly "baby bonus." The United States offers very limited financial support for families with children (e.g., child-care support). Furthermore, the quality of U.S. child-care facilities is uneven, dependent on a family's ability to pay. The U.S. societal attitude toward children is a significant challenge to changing policy. Added to this is the barrier of having an inadequate safety net in U.S. policy, which tends to disproportionately penalize women across their life span. A list of policies (or opportunities) aimed at shifting the burden of caregiving from women to society is described in the next chapter.

While it is important to lobby for improved policy at the federal, state, and local levels, as future managers you may take the initiative to educate co-workers and superiors on the benefits that businesses reap from implementing workplace protections that go beyond the minimums required by law.

Executive orders and court decisions will be discussed in the next chapter. The U.S. Supreme Court has had the tendency to limit policy aimed at increasing diversity. Simultaneously, the EU and the European Court of Justice have been expanding their reach to improve the representation of women in the workplace (Krstic, 2003).

Key Terms

Americans with Disabilities Act (ADA) of 1990, ADA Amendments Act (ADAA) of 2008
Bona fide occupational qualification (BFOQ)
Child Care and Development Block Grant (CCDBG)
"Children-as-pet" notion
Comparable worth
Disparate impact
Disparate treatment
Employment Non-Discrimination Act (ENDA)
Equal Pay Act of 1963
Fair Paycheck Bill
Family and Medical Leave Act (FMLA) of 1993

Family responsibility discrimination
Genetic Information Non-discrimination Act (GINA) of 2008
Lilly Ledbetter Fair Pay Act of 2009
Pattern of practice
Pregnancy Discrimination Act of 1978
Section 4207 of the Patient Protection and Affordable Care Act of 2010
Tax credits
Title VII
Welfare system

3

Policy, the Executive Branch, and the Courts

Policy affecting women in the workplace goes well beyond the legislation discussed in the previous chapter. This chapter delves into policy in the executive and judicial branches of government. The executive branch actions are divided into actions by the political leadership of the executive branch, such as president and cabinet, and the administrative units of the federal government. The administrative leg of government is involved in women and work policy enforcement. An integration of legislation with executive and judicial policy can be seen in Exhibit 3.1. In this chapter, we discuss the roles of the Department of Labor (DOL) and the Equal Employment Opportunity Commission (EEOC) in issues affecting the status of women in public service organizations. In addition, we briefly describe proactive projects funded by the National Science Foundation (NSF).

The policies made by the political leadership of the executive branch have been important in the area of women's issues. The Obama administration created several task forces to improve pay equity and work–life balance: National Equal Pay Enforcement Task Force, Middle Class Task Force, Council on Women and Girls. An important mechanism for setting policy in the executive branch is through executive orders. Affirmative Action has been a pivotal executive order, but it has been limited over the years.

As the Supreme Court becomes more conservative, Affirmative Action is likely to be struck down by the Roberts Court. The U.S. Supreme Court has played a key role in policy related to women in work. The Supreme Court narrowed the interpretation of affirmative action, the Equal Pay Act, and the ability of workplace discrimination victims to be heard in court, through class-action lawsuits. But, the U.S. Supreme Court broadened

Exhibit 3.1

**Status of Women: Changes in Law,
Implementation, and the Courts**

Year	Act/Court case
1963	Equal Pay Act
1964	Title VII, Civil Rights Act
1965	Affirmative Action (Executive Order 11246)
1967	Age Discrimination Act
1971	*Griggs v. Duke Power Co.*, 404 U.S. 424
1978	Pregnancy Discrimination Act
1986	*AFSCME v. State of Washington*
1987	*Johnson v. Transportation Agency, Santa Clara County, Cal.*, 480 U.S. 616
1990	Americans with Disabilities Act (ADA)
1991	Civil Rights Act of 1991
1993	Family and Medical Leave Act (FMLA)
1996	California's Proposition 209
2000	*EEOC v. Joe's Stone Crab, Inc.* (11th Cir.)
2007	*Ledbetter v. Goodyear Tire and Rubber Co.*
2008	Genetic Information Discrimination Act (GINA)
2008	ADA Amendments
2009	Amendments to FMLA
2009	Lilly Ledbetter Fair Pay Act
2010	Section 4207 of the Patient Protection and Affordable Care Act
2011	*Dukes v. Wal-Mart Stores, Inc.*
2011	*Staub v. Proctor Hospital*

the interpretation of Title VII of the Civil Rights Act in *Staub*. Selected landmark cases will be discussed below.

Policies by Political Leadership of the Executive Branch

Affirmative Action (Executive Order 11246)

The most notable policy of the executive branch has been Affirmative Action (Executive Order 11246). *Affirmative action* seeks to remedy workplace underrepresentation of women and minorities. The federal government and organizations who conduct business with the federal government (i.e., federal contractors and subcontractors) are required to offer equal opportunities for employment regardless of race, color, religion, sex, or national origin. Other private companies voluntarily undertake affirmative action. Employers are required to take steps to ensure that all individuals have equal opportunity. The Office of Federal Contract Compliance Programs (OFCCP) enforces the executive order.

To evaluate affirmative action plans, courts typically apply a three-part test. First, the court looks for evidence that the workforce is segregated (in this case by sex). Second, the court looks for evidence that the plan is temporary and that it is aimed at eliminating segregation. Finally, the court needs to see evidence that the plan does not unreasonably affect the rights of nonprotected individuals? See, for example, *Johnson v. Transportation Agency, Santa Clara County, Cal.*, 480 U.S. 616 (1987).

The Supreme Court has been clear that *quotas* and strong preferential treatment are forbidden. Yet, there continues to be a backlash against affirmative action. Some states have deemed affirmative action to be illegal (e.g., California's Proposition 209, in 1996). With the shift in balance of the Court to the right, affirmative action policies could become obsolete. Opposition to affirmative action frequently charges that it is "reverse discrimination." But treating people "equally" is not always "equitable." In other words, treating people identically may preserve disparities experienced by women and minorities because of our conscious and/or unconscious biases.

As will be discussed in chapter 4, occupational discrimination (i.e., pink-collar work), position segregation (i.e., glass ceiling), and agency discrimination (i.e., glass walls) continue to exist. Prejudice (thought) and discrimination (behavior) may be conscious or unconscious (i.e., implicit bias and institutional discrimination, as discussed in chapter 1). *Affirmative action, then, is important because it may offset these biases and stereotypes about women in the workplace with workplace opportunities* (U.S. DOL, 2002).

Has affirmative action been successful for workers? Systematic reviews of the literature suggest that affirmative action has benefited, at least modestly, women and minorities in several ways (Holzer and Neumark, 2000). There is a higher percentage of women and people of color in the public sector compared to the private sector. Women and minorities are more likely to be promoted in the public sector. There is also a higher percentage of women and people of color working for federal contractors compared to nonfederal contractors. These groups are more likely to be promoted by federal contractors (Crosby, Iyer, and Downing, 2003).

Affirmative action may have a broader social impact. Because affirmative action ushered more women and minorities into the workforce, and at higher levels, affirmative action may create more mentors and expand networking opportunities for women and people of color (Blau and Winkler, 2005).

Has affirmative action been successful for employers? Economists have found evidence that a diverse workforce benefits organizations (Hong and Page, 2001, 2004). Diversity leads to more creative solutions, innovations, and markets. Affirmative action has been shown to have a positive effect on organizational stock prices; it also reduces lawsuits (Crosby, Iyer, and Downing, 2003).

Affirmative action is an important executive order that seeks to increase the presence of women and minorities in organizations. Despite the potential benefits to organizations and underrepresented individuals, there has been quite a bit of backlash as well as narrowing of affirmative action by U.S. courts. Affirmative action in the EU applies only to women. In other words, affirmative action is not used to increase the representation of minorities, which has resulted in continued inequities for men and women of color (Krstic, 2003).

Obama Administration's Leadership

President Obama created a number of task forces to improve pay equity and work–life balance: National Equal Pay Enforcement Task Force, Middle Class Task Force, and the Council on Women and Girls (White House, 2010).

The *National Equal Pay Enforcement Task Force* brings together the *Equal Employment Opportunity Commission (EEOC)*, the Department of Justice (DOJ), the Department of Labor, and the Office of Personnel Management (OPM). The task force made five overarching recommendations:

1. Improve interagency coordination and enforcement efforts to maximize the effectiveness of existing authorities.
2. Collect data on the private workforce to better understand the scope of the pay gap and target enforcement efforts.

3. Undertake a public education campaign to educate employers on their obligations and employees on their rights.
4. Implement a strategy to improve the federal government's role as a model employer.
5. The administration will work with Congress to pass the Paycheck Fairness Act.

(White House, n.d.b)

The Middle Class Task Force (White House, n.d.a) is a White House initiative, chaired by Vice President Biden, that seeks to raise the standard of living for middle-class working families. The Middle Class Task Force's goals include:

- Expanding education and lifelong training opportunities
- Improving work and family balance
- Restoring labor standards, including workplace safety
- Helping to protect middle-class and working-family incomes
- Protecting retirement security

The *White House Council on Women and Girls* was created on March 11, 2009, by an Executive Order. It is composed of the heads of all U.S. cabinet level agencies and White House offices. The mission is to ensure that all federal agencies take into account the distinctive needs of women and girls when developing policy and programs (Gerard, 2009).

The Supreme Court and Landmark Rulings

Over the past few years, the composition of the Supreme Court has shifted from a moderate-liberal–leaning Court to a conservative-dominated Court. Table 3.1 categorizes the leanings of individual justices, the nominating U.S. president, and the new justices' predecessors. While Republican presidents overwhelmingly nominated the *Rehnquist Court*, two of those appointments tended to be more moderate players on the Court—O'Connor and Souter. Moderate-leaning O'Connor was replaced by an ultraconservative. This was an important shift of the Court to the right. Roberts, another ultraconservative, replaced ultraconservative Rehnquist. The *Roberts Court* does not appear to have moderate judges; but this may change as we see the way that the new justices vote (e.g., Kennedy).

In the meantime, we have mostly seen the erosion of policies protect-

Table 3.1

Rehnquist vs. Roberts Court Composition

Rehnquist Court (1986–2005)

Liberal	Moderate	Conservative
John Paul Stevens (Ford, Dem.) Ruth Bader Ginsburg (Clinton, Dem.) Steven G. Bryer (Clinton, Dem.)	Sandra Day O'Connor (Reagan, Rep.) David Souter (Bush I, Rep.)	William H. Rehnquist (Nixon, Rep.) Anthony M. Kennedy (Reagan, Rep.) Antonin Scalia (Reagan, Rep.) Clarence Thomas (Bush I, Rep.)

Roberts Court (2005–present)

Liberal	Moderate	Conservative
Ruth Bader Ginsburg (Clinton, Dem.) Steven G. Bryer (Clinton, Dem.) Elena Kagan (Obama, Dem.) Sonia Sotomayor (Obama, Dem.)		John G. Roberts (Bush II, Rep.) Samuel A. Alito (Bush II, Rep.) Anthony M. Kennedy (Reagan, Rep.) Antonin Scalia (Reagan, Rep.) Clarence Thomas (Bush I, Rep.)

Notes:
Dem. = Appointed by a Democrat
Rep. = Appointed by a Republican

ing women at work (e.g., University of Michigan admissions policies, *Ledbetter v. Goodyear Tire*, and *Dukes v. Wal-Mart*).

Affirmative Action: University of Michigan Admissions Policies

Under the Rehnquist Court, the Supreme Court narrowed the interpretation of affirmative action. In 2003, two lawsuits were heard against the University of Michigan: Law School (*Grutter v. Bollinger*) and undergraduate program (*Gratz v. Bollinger*). The Court ruled in favor of the Law School (5–4), allowing it to continue to consider race to achieve student diversity, as diversity is a broad social value. But, the

Court found that affirmative action should no longer be about redressing past discrimination. Instead, the Court reasoned that having diversity throughout society is a "compelling state interest." Sandra Day O'Connor cast the swing vote in this case. But under the Roberts Court, this ruling will likely be reversed. There is an affirmative action case, *Fischer v. University of Texas*, that was heard in October of 2012 but there has no decision as of yet.

In the undergraduate admissions case, the Court ruled (6–3) that race could not be a prominent part of the decision-making process: the undergraduate point system was unconstitutional. Unlike the Law School admissions policy, the point system was not individualistic enough. The Supreme Court narrowed the interpretation of affirmative action.

Equal Pay Act: Ledbetter v. Goodyear Tire

In 2007, under the Robert's Court, the U.S. Supreme Court ruled that a person must bring a lawsuit within 180 days of the company's original discrimination under the Equal Pay Act of 1963. This ruling would have made it virtually impossible to sue for pay discrimination. In the previous chapter, we discussed how the Lilly Ledbetter Fair Pay Act provided the "fix" for this misinterpretation of the Equal Pay Act.

To discover one is being discriminated against, an employee needs to be privy to other employees' wages. It is not customary for employees to discuss their pay with each other. It is frequently considered confidential information; some employees may even be contractually obligated not to discuss their compensation. Most state governments, however, publish public employee compensation in an effort to operate with transparency on how government dollars are spent.

In *Ledbetter*, the U.S. Supreme Court ruled that a victim of pay discrimination under the Equal Pay Act must discover the inequities within the first six months of employment. This ruling would have made it nearly impossible to sue for pay discrimination. The Lilly Ledbetter Fair Pay Act fixed this Court interpretation.

Implications for Title VII of the Civil Rights Act: Staub v. Proctor Hospital

Despite the Court's moving further to the right, Elena Kagan likely influenced the Court in her arguments when she was U.S. solicitor general;

the vote was 8 to 0, with Kagan abstaining from the case because of her former connection to it. A recent U.S. Supreme Court ruling, *Staub v. Proctor Hospital*, settled different interpretations by lower courts about whether workplace discrimination should focus narrowly on a single supervisor or broadly on other supervisors (*Staub v. Proctor Hospital*, 2010).

The Court interpreted the case broadly: If there is discrimination by one of the persons who influenced the adverse employment decision, in this case firing the employee, then the employer may be held liable, even if there is no bias by the supervisor who fired the employee and the employee was fired for a legitimate reason. Why?

The Court reasoned that, in practice, multiple supervisors might try to influence or actually influence employment decisions. In this case, the decision maker reviewed the employee's personnel file, which contained entries prejudiced by the biased supervisors. The biased actions taken by other supervisors likely contributed to the adverse employment decision. *Staub v. Proctor Hospital* was a victory for minimizing workplace discrimination. The U.S. Supreme Court *broadened* the interpretation of Title VII of the Civil Rights Act in *Staub*. Although *Staub v. Proctor Hospital* relied on the Uniformed Services Employment and Reemployment Act of 1994, which prohibits discrimination against employees because of their military duties, it has implications for Title VII cases.

Dukes v. Wal-Mart

Dukes v. Wal-Mart was the largest civil rights class-action suit in U.S. history. The case alleged that Wal-Mart violated Title VII of the Civil Rights Act by discriminating against women in pay, promotions, and access to training, and by retaliating against women who reported sex discrimination. The case was filed in 2001; it went before the U.S. Supreme Court in 2011.

For more than ten years, Wal-Mart avoided the trial by challenging that the claims were not similar enough to justify a class-action lawsuit. The 9th Circuit upheld the California District Court's ruling that the case may move forward as a class-action suit.

This same question was appealed to the Supreme Court: can the case move forward as a class-action lawsuit—did the group of people experience similar enough discrimination to be combined into one case or should the claims be separated? The Supreme Court ruled that the cases were too dissimilar to be certified as a class, stopping the class-action suit. The cases will be separated; as a result, most cases will probably *not* go to trial. Passage of the Fair Paycheck Act would negate this ruling.

The U.S. Supreme Court again narrowed the ability of victims of workplace discrimination to be remedied. It ruled that the largest civil rights class-action lawsuit in U.S. history could not be heard because the class-action status was not certified. This ruling is a significant setback for victims of workplace discrimination who wish to seek legal remedy.

Sex Equality and Federal Agencies

Agencies within the federal government, including the Department of Labor, the Equal Employment Opportunity Commission, and the National Science Foundation, have the charge to promote workplace equity. Different departments and agencies have played a central role in tackling some of the most stubborn challenges facing equity in representation of women in public service organizations.

Department of Labor

The Department of Labor has two agencies that monitor and enforce EEO laws: the Civil Rights Center and the Office of Federal Compliance Programs (OFCCP). The Equal Employment Opportunity (EEO) laws forbid particular forms of discrimination—age; disability, ethnicity, national origin, color, race, sex, religion; immigrants; and veterans—in certain workplaces. The Department of Labor (DOL) has two agencies that monitor and enforce EEO laws: Civil Rights Center (CRC) and Office of Federal Contract Compliance Programs (U.S. DOL, n.d.c).

The Civil Rights Center ensures nondiscrimination for DOL employees as well as applicants for DOL services (U.S. DOL, n.d.b) The OFCCP enforces affirmative action (Executive Order 11246) and equal employment opportunity required by those who do business with the federal government) (U.S. DOL, n.d.c).

Equal Employment Opportunity Commission

The EEOC enforces federal discrimination law. The U.S. Equal Employment Opportunity Commission is a five-member bipartisan commission appointed by the president. The commission is charged with enforcing

---

Exhibit 3.2

Laws Enforced by the EEOC

- Title VII of the Civil Rights Act
- Pregnancy Discrimination Act
- Equal Pay Act of 1963
- Age Discrimination Act of 1967
- Americans with Disabilities Act, Title I
- Civil Rights Act of 1991, Sections 102 and 103
- Rehabilitation Act of 1973, Sections 501 and 505
- Genetic Information Nondiscrimination Act of 2008

Source: U.S. EEOC (n.d.c.)

---

federal discrimination law for protected groups: race, color, religion, sex (including pregnancy), national origin, age (forty or older), disability, or genetic information (Exhibit 3.2) (U.S. EEOC n.d.c).

The EEOC investigates discrimination charges. If discrimination is found, the EEOC attempts to settle the charge. If no settlement can be reached, the EEOC has the authority to file a lawsuit.

If an individual feels she has been discriminated against in the workplace, based on one or more of those factors, she may file a charge with the EEOC (U.S. EEOC, n.d.b). Typically, charges must be filed within 180 days of the alleged discriminatory act.

The EEOC investigates discrimination charges against employers. If the EEOC finds that discrimination has occurred, the EEOC attempts to settle it. If this is not successful, the EEOC has the authority to file a lawsuit, although the EEOC is not required to exercise that authority (U.S. EEOC, n.d.c). EEOC lawsuits are declining while private lawsuits are rising (Blau, Ferber, and Winkler, 2002). EEOC lawsuits are less expedient than civil lawsuits, and they involve lower financial implications for organizations. This is unfortunate, as lawsuits filed by the EEOC tend to have a greater effect on employment practices than do laws or the lawsuits filed by private law firms.

National Science Foundation

The National Science Foundation is a federal agency that funds about 20 percent of federally supported research at U.S. universities (NSF, 2011).

The NSF funds science and engineering, for example, math, computer science, and social science. NSF does not fund the medical sciences.

The NSF offers programs to increase the participation of underrepresented populations in science and engineering (e.g., women and people of color). Why? Research shows that a diverse workforce leads to more innovations and creative solutions to problems (Page, 2007). The NSF's ADVANCE program seeks to increase the number of women in academic science and engineering by identifying and changing the components of academic culture or institutional structure that inhibit women faculty members from reaching their full potential (ADVANCE at a Glance, http://www.nsf.gov/crssprgm/advance/). The ADVANCE program currently has three projects: Institutional Transformation (IT); IT-Catalyst; and Partnerships for Adaptation and Implementation and Dissemination (PAID). One of the authors of this book is a co-principal investigator on an ADVANCE IT grant.

The ADVANCE program has generated much replicable work. More information can be obtained from the ADVANCE Portal (ADVANCE for the Advancement of Women in Science and Engineering Careers, n.d.). Individual ADVANCE projects can also provide useful materials to help organizations decrease unconscious bias in hiring, promotion, and so on. Three particularly strong programs include those at the University of Rhode Island, Utah State University, and Virginia Tech.

Barriers, Challenges, and Opportunities

A major barrier to reducing employment discrimination is the new composition of the Supreme Court. Affirmative Action is an important Executive Order that seeks to increase the presence of women and minorities in organizations. Despite the potential benefits of affirmative action to organizations and underrepresented individuals, there has been quite a bit of backlash as well as narrowing of it by U.S. courts.

The U.S. Supreme Court has played a key role in policy related to women in work. The Supreme Court narrowed the interpretation of affirmative action, the Equal Pay Act, and the ability of workplace discrimination victims to be heard in court through class-action lawsuits. But the U.S. Supreme Court broadened the interpretation of Title VII of the Civil Rights Act in *Staub*.

At the same time, we are seeing new and extant opportunities. President Obama created several task forces to improve pay equity and work–life balance: the National Equal Pay Enforcement Task Force, Middle Class Task Force, the Council on Women and Girls.

The administrative leg of government is involved in women and work policy enforcement. The Department of Labor has two agencies that monitor and enforce EEO laws: the Civil Rights Center and the Office of Federal Contract Compliance Programs. The EEOC enforces federal discrimination law. These agencies may be more aggressive under Democratic leadership.

The NSF funds projects to increase gender diversity. Research findings and materials developed by grantees may be used by organizations to become more diverse. While a societal goal in the United States is equal opportunity, reducing biases, which allows for a more diverse workforce, has the added benefits of more innovative solutions to problems.

Key Terms

Affirmative action
Dukes v. Wal-Mart
Equal Employment Opportunity
   Commission (EEOC)
Ledbetter v. Goodyear Tire
Middle Class Task Force
National Equal Pay Enforcement
   Task Force

National Science Foundation
   (NSF)
Quotas
Rehnquist Court
Roberts Court
Staub v. Proctor Hospital
The White House Council on
   Women and Girls

4

Social Costs of Career

As dual-income families become the norm in the United States, families find themselves making choices between family and personal responsibilities on one hand and work responsibilities on the other. The term "work–life fit" refers to these choices. However, no one should find him/herself between the "rock" of family and the "hard place" of career. In a workplace that allows for work–life fit, individuals should be able to have both—family life and career success. Unfortunately, however, working families in the United States are often forced to make choices that families in other industrialized countries do not face because of the lack of universal family-friendly workplace policies. This chapter highlights trends in home life that are affected by work. For example the trends of professional women to be unmarried, have fewer children, or be divorced, while carrying a heavy housework burden. The chapter also links these trends to lower pay and lack of career progression.

The chapter explores and critiques workplace policies. It is no wonder that Williams (2010) writes, "The United States has the most family hostile public policy in the developed world" (p. 1). She is concerned that the United States lacks the political will to change the law because business elites dominate the political discussion. At the same time, progressive groups have alienated the white working class, who currently align themselves with the business elites.

Workplace "Choices"

Families in the United States face choices that families in other industrialized countries may not because the United States lacks a robust social safety net. In addition, the composition of American families has changed, as has the important role that women's wages now contribute to a family's subsistence.

Given that individuals in organizations have the need to belong, do women fit in the workplace? The workplace in the United States is structured around the assumptions of an "organization man": an individual who dedicates his time to the organization, without taking breaks or having competing family responsibilities. In reality however, employees do have families. Women (and men) have to make "choices" with regard to work and family, but do employed women in the United States have the ability to make real choices? In this chapter, we argue that no one should have to choose between paying attention to their family and succeeding at work. In fact, we argue that this is the ultimate nonchoice. No man or woman should find him/herself in a position of having to choose between these two life events. Family life should be shared between partners, and work life should accommodate family life, allowing individuals and organizations to prosper.

Social Costs of Career: Trends in Marriage, Divorce, and Children

As discussed in previous chapters, today's women are not choosing to "opt out" or exit the workforce, as their mothers had before them. Nevertheless, women today face the same gender image paradoxes their mothers faced, which makes career progression and pay equity a challenge. This discussion highlights trends in home life that are adversely affected by work, such as the lower likelihood of professional women to be married, have children (or fewer children), be divorced, while carrying a heavy housework burden.

Social costs manifest themselves in marriage and divorce patterns, the "second shift" of housework, and penalties associated with childbearing. Social costs are incurred as a direct consequence of the conventional ideology of working men and *family women*, and the admission of women into the workforce under the terms of this ideology. This ideology rests on assumptions made in an industrialized male-dominated workplace. Fundamentally, men will be "organization men"—fully dedicated to work, while women will be "family women"—fully dedicated to family. The idea of work–life fit is simply nonexistent under this ideology. One is either fully dedicated to work or fully dedicated to family.

Organizational cultures have rested on the primary assumption that workers will be *organization men*. Unfair as this may have been to men who might have wanted to balance family and work needs, or who felt overwhelmed to have the sole responsibility for financially providing for the family, the ideology was manageable because society expected women to care for family. This ideology, however, becomes a serious problem when women, who continue to bear the heavier burden of family responsibilities, are admitted into the workforce under the same terms—which is that they become organization women with full dedication to work, and this dedication becomes a condition for success.

Women tend to incur *social costs* when they are ambitious about their career progression. The conventional ideology of the organization man leaves out, for most women and some men, the possibility of combining family and work commitment. For women, the trade-offs are clear: if you choose your career, you undermine your family life (Tower and Alkadry, 2008), and if you choose family, you undermine your career. In this section, we highlight how the social costs have manifested themselves in the process of integrating women into the workplace.

Historic Patterns

Over the past sixty years, for women, the social costs of having a career have changed. While women were welcomed into the workforce in the 1950s to help with the war effort, they were encouraged to exit the workforce when World War II ended. There were limited opportunities for women to work outside the home. Betty Friedan (1963), in *The Feminine Mystique*, identified the unspoken dissatisfaction among suburban housewives.

Since the 1960s, women have been increasingly entering the workforce, particularly married women with young children. First-time moms were more likely to work during pregnancy, 44 percent in 1961–1965 to 67 percent in 2001–2003 (Johnson, 2008). In fact, by 2002, working women largely stopped exiting the labor force between the ages of twenty-five and thirty-four and reentering between the ages of forty-five and fifty-four; instead, women have a continuous pattern of work that parallels men's (U.S. Bureau of Labor Statistics, 2003).

From 2008 to 2009, male-dominated industries (e.g., construction and manufacturing) shrunk, while female-dominated industries (e.g., health care) grew (Woodring, 2010). More recently, however, there has been a strategy to "end big government." This includes eliminating (a) public-sector jobs, which are more often held by women, (b) public services, which are more often used by women, and (c) unions, from which women often gain more workplace protections and benefits (Abramovitz, n.d.). Increases in women's educational attainment results in a gender gap where women are more likely to keep their job or reenter the workforce, even among married couples.

Yet, the conventional ideology of the organization man persists. Shapiro, Ingols, and Blake-Beard (2008) describe trends that affect the way workers define themselves in relation to their careers (see Table 4.1). It is instructive to note that the *Womb-to-Tomb Employment Model*—long-term employment with a stable organization—has been on its way out for the past twenty years. Because of organizational changes, including the instability of organizations and their workforces, workers may be better served to take control of their own careers, which translates into the *We Are Self-Employed Model*. At the same time, these new generations of workers value time outside of their work, making this new model a better fit for younger workers, who in all likelihood cannot rely on a single organization for career-long employment.

Work continues to take a higher toll on women's personal lives compared to men's. The next several sections describe the effect of employment for women on marriage, divorce, housework, and children.

Marriage and Divorce

Women are delaying marriage or not marrying at all. The average age of marriage has increased by about five years since 1950 (U.S. Department of Commerce, 2011). College-educated women tend to marry four years older, at age thirty, compared to women who did not complete their high school education (ibid.).

Women's decision to delay marriage is influenced by choice, barriers, or both. Women may delay marriage because an individual has not met the right person or because it simply is not a priority. Marriage may also be delayed to attend postsecondary school (Sweeney, 2002), to focus on career success (Bachrach, Hindin, and Thomson, 2000; Hoffnung, 2004), or until a higher income is achieved (Bachrach, Hindin, and Thomson, 2000). Individuals may also delay marriage because they perceive that they cannot shoulder the responsibilities of both work and family simultaneously (Frazier et al., 1996; Sharp and Ganong, 2007).

Compared to previous cohorts, fewer women are married today.

Table 4.1

Trends that Impact Workers' Definition of Career

	"Womb to Tomb Employment" Model	"We Are Self-Employed" Model
Organization changes	Stability in organizations	Unstable organizations: downsizing, outsourcing, bankruptcy
Changes in who directs career path	Workers rely on employer to control career	Workers control own careers. Stay marketable and self-motivated
Definition of employment	Long-term, continuous, employment	Employment as a temporary state
	Employer focused	Project focused
Demographic changes	Homogeneous workforce	Some desegregation of women in the workplace
Changing values	Work as primary; support person at home to take care of family responsibilities	Value having time for family, relationships, and fun
Effect of technology	Traditional workday in the office	Allow work to occur anywhere and anytime
	Import of face time	Import of outcomes
Economic changes	Robust middle class	Increasingly necessary for a family to have two incomes to pay its bills*
		Real wages decreasing**

Sources: Shapiro, Ingols, and Blake-Beard (2008).
*Bartley, Blanton, and Gillard (2005).
**Real wages for professional, middle-, and low-income workers has been declining since the late 1970s (DiPrete, Eirich, and Pittinsky. 2010. p. 1671).

Between 1970 and 2009, the proportion of women who were married dropped from 72 percent to 62 percent. Among women age sixty-five and older, 7 percent were never married in 1970 compared to 15 percent in 2009 (U.S. Department of Commerce, 2011). It is logical that young women desire self-reliance, as they tend to view breadwinning as a component of "good" mothering (Gerson, 2009). These young women believe that self-reliance will allow them to establish a separate identity, while also protecting them against financial hardship from an unstable economy or a divorce as well as against their perception of domestic work as having low status.

From a national data of 1,600 public procurement officials, Tower and Alkadry (2008) reported that men were more likely to be married, while women were more likely to be divorced or single across all study categories of buyer, senior buyer, manager/supervisor, and director. If women have a higher desire to marry than men (Blakemore, Lawton, and Vartanian, 2005) and stay married, then women may be paying a higher social cost for their careers than their male counterparts. The impact of divorce on women tends to hurt them in the long term; in fact, divorced women are five times more likely than married women to be impoverished during retirement (Williams, 2010).

The "Second Shift." The second shift is the phenomenon of women working outside the home for pay and then returning home to carry out the responsibilities of a homemaker (Hochschild, 1989). Because the organization of work tends to be based on social norms for men, which includes a support person (most likely a wife) to concentrate on household tasks, men are able to assume the breadwinner role (Johnson and Duerst-Lahti, 1992; Ranson, 2005). To cope with this "double shift," women may transfer to part-time work that is less stable and less well paid (Guy, 2003).

Women tend to perform housework more frequently and for longer periods of time than men. In households with employed husbands and wives, women spent 2.6 hours conducting household activities and caring for household members, compared to men who spent 1.7 hours (U.S. Department of Commerce, 2011). On an average workday, 87 percent of employed married women compared to 65 percent of employed married men conducted household activities (ibid.). Women spend more days of the week and more time during each day of the week on household activities.

The 22 percent sex difference in completing housework is attributed to the type of housework women and men conduct. Women were more likely to complete time-sensitive chores, such as making dinner, compared to men who were more likely to conduct non–time-sensitive chores, such as home maintenance (ibid.). The frequency and length of time spent on household responsibilities are important, and so is the time-sensitive nature of the chores.

The time-sensitive nature of women's housework appears to limit women's ability to behave as the "organization man" does. For example, if women are responsible for making dinner every night, how can they stay at work after hours? On an average workday, employed married men spent more time in the labor market than employed married women: 8.8 vs. 7.6 hours (ibid.). These men also spent more time in leisure activities than their female counterparts.

While single mothers spent more time in the labor market each day than married mothers (37 minutes), they spent less time than married men (35 minutes) (ibid.). Single women also spent more time doing housework and parenting than men (Perrone, Webb, and Blalock, 2005; Tower and Alkadry, 2008). Having children in the home creates more housework (South and Spitze, 1994). The result of this unequal distribution of housework is that home responsibilities handicap women's career advancement more than men's (Johnson and Duerst-Lahti, 1992).

The Third and Fourth Shifts. Hochschild (1997) describes the third and fourth shifts as those that have emerged for workers trying to maintain work and home responsibilities. The "*third shift*" refers to the emotional work of listening to hurt family members about not being at home as much as their children/spouse would prefer. Time away from family has other implications. Researchers have found numerous benefits of parental involvement in health and educational matters: (a) sick children have fewer symptoms and recover more quickly from illnesses and procedures when parents are involved; and (b) children have higher educational achievement, lower dropout rates, and better behavior when parents are involved (Heymann, Penrose, and Earle, 2006).

While technology has allowed employees more flexibility in where and how work gets done, which can feel empowering, the downside is the extension of the workplace into the home, which can feel intrusive. The "*fourth shift*" is the time late at night, early in the morning, or on weekends spent returning e-mails, writing reports, and engaging in other work-related tasks that may be accomplished electronically. The fast pace of technology has sped up the work environment, particularly for white-collar employees. In one study, academics felt pressure to be accessible and responsive to students and administrators quickly, even on weekends and evenings (Currie and Eveline, 2010). Smartphones allow employees to take calls, respond to text messages, and even respond to e-mails any time. This accessibility intrudes on family time, recreation, and downtime. An important way to maximize the empowerment and minimize the control of e-technology is to set limits around one's accessibility and responsiveness (Currie and Eveline, 2010; Edley, 2001).

The Children Question

Demographics related to whether women have children and when they have children, have changed. First, the percentage of women who have never had a child has increased. Second, women are having fewer children. Third, women are delaying their first child to older ages (U.S. Department of Commerce, 2011).

When women have children, their careers tend to suffer while men may even benefit from having children (Kirchmeyer, 2006; Miree and Frieze, 1999; Wolfinger, Mason, and Goulden, 2010). More specifically, it appears that the number of children and the timing of childbearing affect women's salaries. From longitudinal data, Taniguchi (1999) reported that early childbearing (at ages twenty to twenty-seven) had a 4 percent wage penalty, compared to late childbearing, which had no wage penalty. Early childbearing coincides with a critical time in one's career for gaining experience and networking. Education, however, may reduce the magnitude of the wage penalty.

Although young men may be willing to participate more in caregiving than in the past, men continue to view it as a secondary role to breadwinning (Gerson, 2009). In other words, today's men continue to believe that women may choose to work or not, but it is women who are responsible for finding time to work around caregiving responsibilities.

Another important trend is that today's mothers tend to view the role of mothering differently than previous cohorts, considerably increasing the time, energy, and money dedicated to raising children. Hays (1996) coined the term "*intensive mothering*," to describe a childrearing style that is "child-centered, expert-guided, emotionally absorbing, labor-intensive, and financially expensive" (p. 8), where the mother's needs take a backseat to the needs of the child. Nevertheless, mothers often aspire to, and popular magazines reinforce, this impossible ideal, which is particularly out of reach for less-affluent mothers (Williams, 2010). This trend emerged in the 1990s, perhaps to prepare children for increasingly competitive university admissions (Ramey and Ramey, 2009). Gillespie and Temple (2011) encourage women to define success by focusing on the parts of work and home that matter most to the individual.

It makes sense that women are more likely to delay having children compared to men at the same career levels. Some women may choose not to have children at all. Postponing childbearing for too long may result in forgone fertility (Rindfuss, Guzzo, and Morgan, 2003). In fact, employment decreases the likelihood that women will have a child by 15–16 percent (Budig, 2003).

Women at higher levels of an organization tend to have fewer children or no children at all (Olshfski and Caprio, 1996; Thomas, 2002). In a national study of procurement officers, women at the top of the organizational hierarchy were less likely to have children when compared to their male counterparts and were less likely to have children than women in lower levels of the hierarchy (Tower and Alkadry, 2008).

Then again, because careers are designed to fit male gender roles and the ability of males to be fully dedicated to work, having both family and career can be tricky for women. As a result, some women delay or end their careers (Ranson, 2005; Thomas, 2002). Other women may shift to part-time work, exit and perhaps reenter the workforce, or become entrepreneurs. Table 4.2 offers tips to help women exist successfully in the workforce.

In summary, U.S. workers have less public support for attending to family than do other nations. Although women today are not exiting the workforce as they had in previous cohorts of women, work continues to be organized around the assumption of the "organization man." Because these expectations are inconsistent with women's gender roles, women tend to pay higher social costs for their careers than men. Gender roles are also related to women working shifts beyond the standard workday:

1. Second shift—time spent engaging in household and child-care responsibilities;
2. Third shift—time spent repairing hurt feelings for not being at home as much as children/spouse prefers; and
3. Fourth shift—time spent at home (for example, on weekends and evenings) remotely engaging in workplace tasks.

Table 4.2

Tips to Help Women Exist in the Workforce

Understanding gender-role dynamics	Be aware of double-binds that limit women's career choices. Gauge your behavior on what you can live with, understanding the potential consequences.
	1. Feminine behaviors—may be more liked; may be viewed as less competent.
	2. Masculine behaviors—may be consistent with managerial stereotypes; inconsistent with gender role expectations that may result in sanctions (O'Neill and O'Reilly, 2010).
Self-monitor masculine traits	Adapt your behavior (level of aggressiveness, assertiveness, and confidence) to fit the organizational environment and particular social situation (O'Neill and O'Reilly, 2011).
Challenge norms of ideal worker	Explicitly name the norm; offer alternatives to the norm (Shapiro, Ingols, and Blake-Beard, 2008).
Say "no" by saying "yes"	Take a piece of what is being asked, reframing it as, "This is what I *can* do . . ." (Dean and Simpson, 2010).
Flexible schedules	Whereas part-time or work from home appears to negatively affect wages, flextime does not appear to do so (Glass, 2004).
Flextime	Flextime allows moms to perform time-sensitive caregiving responsibilities (O'Neill and O'Reilly, 2010).
Do NOT exit, before you HAVE to make a choice to exit, stay, or downshift.	In anticipation or hope that you will get married or have children, do NOT hold yourself back regarding career opportunities. Stay on your career trajectory until you MUST make a choice. Otherwise, you may have set yourself up for fewer choices.

While demographic trends change, but workplace expectations do not, additional organizational changes are occurring. The Womb-to-Tomb Employment Model has been shaken, as the We Are Self-Employed Model has become the norm.

Career Costs: Salvaging a Career by Exiting and Reentering, Downshifting, or Entrepreneurship

Because some women's priorities deviate from the image of the "organization man"—unencumbered by personal responsibility and fully dedicated to the workplace—when women do not follow the career path

Table 4.3

Tips for Exiting the Workforce

Tip	Example
Retain career identity	Become active in professional organizations (Shapiro, Ingols, and Blake-Beard, 2008)
Maintain relationships	Stay in touch with business contacts (e.g., send holiday cards)
Stay current	Read trade publications; take courses

of "organization men," what do they do? What are the *career costs*? We answer these questions and also offer tips to minimize the costs; we also argue that it is in the best interest of women workers and the organizations they work for to keep women connected to the workplace.

Exiting a Career and Reentering

Why do women exit the workforce? Women tend to exit the workforce to care for children, elderly family members, or themselves, while men tend to exit the workforce to reposition themselves in the workforce (i.e., switch careers, obtain training, or start a business) (Hewlett and Luce, 2005). This decision is rarely an individual decision, but rather one that partners or a family make together (Chang, 2010).

When professional women exit the workforce, overwhelmingly, they plan to reenter, but are frequently unable to do so. In a nationally representative survey of 2,443 professional women, 93 percent desired to reenter the workforce, but only 40 percent were able to return to full-time professional work (Hewlett and Luce, 2005). As a backup plan, women may downshift to part-time jobs (24 percent) or become self-employed (9 percent). Table 4.3 offers tips that may help reduce the penalties associated with exiting the workforce as well as tips to position oneself to relaunch a career.

Given that most women who have exited a career plan to reenter it, but most are unable to do so, why then do professional women plan to reenter the workforce? Women want to return to the workforce for the additional household income it provides, for the financial independence it brings, and for the satisfaction they experience from their careers. Work gives structure to women's (and men's) lives; it is a source of self-confidence;

it confers status in their communities; for some, it may be a way to give back to society (Hewlett and Luce, 2005).

How do women decide whether to reenter the workforce? Ericksen et al. offer a conceptual framework to explain whether women reenter the workforce or not. They suggest that several "driving forces" motivate a woman to reenter (or not)—financial insecurity, environmental pressure to return to work, self-image that is tied to her professional role, desire to use her skills, and interest in working, as well as "filters" that serve to discourage (or encourage) reentry—family demands, lack of support from family and friends, lower educational levels, experiences, and costs outweighing benefits (Ericksen et al., 2008, pp. 158–160).

Women's decision to return to work appears to be rational, based on measurable costs and benefits (Hotchkiss, Pitts, and Walker, 2008). Women who exit the workforce tend to have lower costs of exiting the workforce, work in shrinking industries, have concerns about their children, or are married. On the other hand, women who do not exit the workforce tend to have higher costs of exiting the workforce, have relatively higher earnings, or are employed in a relatively large firm or industry.

Cohen and Rabin (2007) developed "Seven Steps to Relaunch" a successful career (Table 4.4). The steps spell out the acronym, "RE-LAUNCH." As stated earlier, many women who want to reenter their careers are unable to do so. But for those who are able to, there are career costs. What career costs do women pay when they reenter the workforce full-time? Research shows that women pay a substantial wage penalty when they reenter the workforce. The wage penalty appears to be correlated with the amount of time one remains outside the workforce: being out for less than one year tends to result in an 11 percent wage penalty; three or more years out results in a 37 percent wage reduction (Hewlett and Luce, 2005).

This wage penalty implies that caregivers lose human capital—competencies and skills valued by the labor market—when they are not attached to the workforce. Crittenden (2004), however, argues otherwise, indicating that skills used in caregiving and volunteering *are* useful in the workplace. Again, it is the ideology of the organization man that precludes organizations from recognizing the transferability of these skills. It is debatable that there is a difference in learning curves between caregivers who have exited the workforce and workers who

Table 4.4

Tips for Reentering the Workforce

1.	**Re**	Relaunch or not?	Whether to go back to work or not is an individual decision
2.	**L**	Learn confidence	Project positively on your time at home, value maternal experiences (e.g., interpersonal skills and resiliency), and neither be afraid to say "no," nor take "no" for an answer
3.	**A**	Assess your career options	Flexibility/control, job content, and compensation
4.	**U**	Update	Update your professional and job search skills, and prepare for the interview
5.	**N**	Network	Network, market yourself, and clinch the opportunity
6.	**C**	Channel family support	Prepare your partner, child(ren), and yourself
7.	**H**	Handle the job (or find another one)	Help colleagues, they will return the favor; do not attribute every absence as child-related

Source: Cohen and Rabin (2007).

change their field of employment; yet, the former incurs a wage penalty, while the latter may even garner a wage increase.

Downshifting a Career

Because of the difficulties in reentering the workforce, some women downshift to less well-paid work that does not require long hours, long commutes, or extensive travel. Other women may downshift to part-time work rather than exiting completely. Part-time workers who remain attached to their profession by negotiating a temporary part-time schedule with their employer tend to be professional women who have "good" part-time jobs (Webber and Williams, 2008). These jobs tend to have high wages, benefits, and opportunities for advancement.

Compared to women who exit the workforce entirely, women who work part-time in their career experience advantages. The advantages of this choice may be that it helps them to preserve their professional identity and remain competitive because their skills will not have deteriorated.

Table 4.5

Part-Time in the Workforce: Tips for Women

Frame decision	How does your decision benefit the organization (vs. how it benefits you personally)? (Shapiro, Ingols, and Blake-Beard, 2008)
Challenge norms of ideal worker	Explicitly name the norm; offer alternatives to the norm (Shapiro, Ingols, and Blake-Beard, 2008).
Exercise your "NO!"	Ask yourself: • Must this be DONE? (Who says?) • Must this be done BY ME? (If not me, then who?) • Must this be done RIGHT NOW? • Must this be done THIS WAY? (Why?) • If I say yes to this, what am I saying no to? (Dean and Simpson, 2010)
Flexible schedules	Whereas part-time or work from home appears to negatively affect wages, flextime does not appear to do so (Glass, 2004).

These women also challenge the image of the ideal worker because they have commitments outside of the workplace (Blair-Loy, 2003).

Although there are benefits of *downshifting* to part-time work, part-time schedules have associated career costs. Researchers have found that when professional women reduce their hours to part-time schedules, they are disadvantaged compared to their full-time counterparts. Disadvantages come in the form of slower career progression (ibid.), reduced opportunities (Webber and Williams, 2008), and slower pay growth (Glass, 2004). Changing employers often reduces the wage penalties associated with the use of part-time schedules (ibid.). Table 4.5 offers tips in regard to the decision to transition into part-time work.

Women and their families are not the only ones who benefit by keeping women connected to the workforce. Organizations benefit too. A shortage of talented workers is projected. Therefore, retaining workers who have proved themselves is beneficial to organizations. As baby boomers exit the workforce, there will be fewer numbers of workers to replace them. In addition, women are surpassing men in educational achievement. Women are increasingly earning more college degrees as well as graduate and professional degrees (U.S. Department of Commerce, 2011). In fact, women make up 57 percent of undergraduate enrollment and 59 percent of graduate school enroll-

Table 4.6

Keeping Women Connected: Tips for Organizations

Reduced-hour jobs	Part-time work that is not marginalized. Access to benefits and training.
Daytime flexibility	Flexibility about where, when, and how work is completed. Perhaps time is needed for child-related responsibilities.
Career orientation	Flex careers that allow one to stay on track, skilled, and connected while taking time off. Offer chunks of work that may be completed by telecommuting.
Attitude change	Destigmatize the use of flexible work arrangements.
Alumni program	Stay connected with employees who exit.
Support ambition	To foster women's passion for work, make and provide opportunities for mentoring and networking.

Source: Hewlett and Luce (2005, pp. 7–10).

ment. With fewer workers to choose from, and a higher percentage of them being female, employee retention will undoubtedly be a critical challenge to organizations.

Keeping talented women connected to the company from which they exited helps the organization retain the investment that has already been made in these employees. It will also make it more likely that the employees will want to go back to that organization. Table 4.6 offers tips directed at organizations to help them keep former female employees connected to the organization.

Private firms are reengaging workers by contacting former workers to fill temporary vacancies or offering project work. Firms are also helping women to reduce barriers to reentry by offering lunches, workshops, mentors, and training to help update their skills and maintain professional networks. Ernst and Young has a program to retain women that includes:

1. Focus—created opportunities to network within the company;
2. Leadership Commitment—created an Office of Retention;
3. Policies—equipped all employees for telework and implemented policy that allowed individuals to take it without opportunity penalty;

4. New roles—tracked the progress of women by partners;
5. Learning resources—offered an "Achieving Flexibility" Web site to learn about flexible arrangements;
6. Peer networking—built skills, confidence, and leadership through Professional Women's Networks; and
7. Accountability—evaluated managers, by the employees on their flexibility and inclusivity as well as metrics that show the number of women in the partner pipeline serving on key accounts.

(Hewlett and Luce, 2005, p. 6).

Entrepreneurship

Some women opt for the nontraditional path of entrepreneurship. More than 8.1 million businesses are owned by women in the United States; women-owned businesses account for 29 percent of all enterprises (American Express, 2012). Women-owned businesses are increasing at a revolutionary pace. Between 1997 and 2011, women-owned businesses increased by 1.5 times that of the national average (American Express, 2012).

Why are some women opting for entrepreneurship? Women choose entrepreneurship to avoid various forms of workplace discrimination and/or to gain flexibility in work–life balance (Moore, 2005; Weiler and Bernasek, 2001). Women anticipate that entrepreneurship may allow them to "have it all." Women have reported becoming entrepreneurs because they wanted autonomy and control over workplace issues (e.g., schedule) or to embrace an opportunity that was presented to them (Gill and Ganesh, 2007). In a study of home-based/online female entrepreneurs, Edley (2004) concludes that:

> These work-at-home moms are neither victims nor ball busters. . . . Yet their discourse is filled with images that can be described as third-wave feminist concepts—self-sufficiency, strength, self-pride, healthy balance between work and family, having it all, and instilling respect for women and . . . "girls can be anything" in the next generation. (Edley, 2004, p. 271)

Unfortunately, self-employment may not solve problems related to workplace discrimination or balancing work and family responsibilities. Self-employed women may actually experience greater discrimination than they had in the labor market, from a combination of:

1. Customers' preferences for male-produced goods and services;
2. Discriminatory supplier systems that may favor long-term relationships in terms of timing and delivery of orders; and
3. Prejudiced credit networks that may refuse to extend credit to women-owned businesses.

(Weiler and Bernasek, 2001).

But, women have reported responding to discrimination with determination to succeed, which felt empowering (Gill and Ganesh, 2007). Although women may have been motivated to become entrepreneurs to make balancing work and family easier, women entrepreneurs reported challenges in completing housework, coordinating child care, and finding time to spend with their families on top of the additional responsibilities that entrepreneurship brings (ibid.). Women entrepreneurs do achieve other aspirations for making the switch. Women entrepreneurs have reported feeling empowered, fulfilled, mentally stimulated, and confident (ibid.).

How do women-owned businesses fare? Although the number of women-owned businesses has been growing steadily, it appears that they tend to stay small (fewer than ten employees). These small and midsize companies are keeping pace with the national average, but are unable to grow to 100+ employees or $1 million in revenue (American Express, 2012).

In summary, women are making different choices related to balancing work and family responsibilities. Balance between traditional gender roles and work expectations may not be possible, as women disproportionately experience social costs related to marriage/divorce and children. Professional women are more likely to be unmarried, have fewer children, or be divorced, while carrying a heavy housework burden. At the same time, professional women experience career costs. They are resilient, attempting to salvage their careers in various ways: temporarily exiting and reentering the workforce, downshifting, or becoming entrepreneurs. But, for some professional women, barriers may be too high to surmount.

Part-Time "Bad" Jobs

Of the professional women who wanted to reenter their careers after an initial exit, about a third of them were unable to do so, and therefore had to take part-time jobs (Hewlett and Luce, 2005). This leads us to conclude that too few professional women are able to salvage their careers after exiting. We can also assert that large numbers of U.S. women work part-time, since about 24 percent of employed women work part-time (vs. 11 percent of men) (U.S. Department of Commerce, 2011).

Part-time work tends to be located in the secondary market, which is characterized by having high turnover, low wages, and few benefits or opportunities for upward mobility. The service industry (e.g., retail) is an example of a secondary market. Both uneducated women and some professional women who have not been able to reenter their careers occupy these "bad" jobs. While former professional women preferred to reenter their careers, nonprofessional women preferred to drop out of the labor market completely (Webber and Williams, 2008). This reinforces the low desirability of secondary market work.

However, the association of part-time work with low status and low pay is *not* inevitable. Again, we may look to the European Union (EU) for a framework to challenge the ideal norm of a worker in the United States, that of the "organization man." The EU limits the workweek. Normal, full-time hours are between 35–39 hours per week; 48 hours may not be exceeded in a week (Webber and Williams, 2008). As mentioned earlier, working fewer than 35 hours per week is defined as part-time in the United States, but as full-time in some EU countries.

In addition, the EU requires member countries to expand access to part-time schedules, guarantee the equitable treatment of part-time workers, and improve the quality of part-time work (Webber and Williams, 2008). This could not be more dissimilar to U.S. policy, which may even reinforce disparities between full-time and part-time work. For example, the Family and Medical Leave Act (FMLA), pension benefits (under the federal Employee Retirement Income Security Act [ERISA]), and unemployment insurance (under state laws) do not offer protection to part-time workers (Williams and Cooper, 2004). These laws need to be amended to offer similar protections to full-time and part-time workers. Furthermore, the United States and organizations operating in it should follow EU policy initiatives and make part-time schedules more widely available as well as offer equitable treatment of part-time and full-time workers.

Both professional and nonprofessional women in the United States tend to view their participation in the secondary market as their own "choice." They recognize the costs and take personal responsibility for it (Webber and Williams, 2008). By ascribing blame to themselves, women become unaware of the institutional discrimination that is occurring. Professional women actually feel "lucky" to have a part-time option. To show their appreciation, it sometimes means working extra hours. Women frequently do not recognize the structural constraints in the workplace (Webber and Williams, 2008). *Structural constraints* are implicit rules about how work is organized and rewarded. These taken-for-granted norms serve to exploit and discriminate against working mothers, yet these mothers see their "choices" as a preference.

Work–Life Balance Policies

Work–life balance policies—policies with the goal of helping employees balance their work and family responsibilities—will be explored and critiqued, including family leave, flexible schedules, lactation policy, and child- and elder-care benefits. The presence of work–life balance policies however does not guarantee a family-friendly workplace. In fact, usage of these policies often comes at the cost of career penalties, such as lower salaries; as a result, employees may be uneasy about utilizing work–life balance policies (Blair-Loy and Wharton, 2004). Nevertheless, research shows that employees who take advantage of work–life balance policies, such as flexible hours, experience less work–life conflict (ibid.) with the exclusion of service occupations that have intense client demands (Blair-Loy, 2009).

Workplace culture that supports the use of these policies is necessary for the policies to be fully utilized (Mesmer-Magnus and Viswesvaran, 2006). In fact, a culture that has "organizational understanding" of work–life balance may have more of an effect on a worker's perceptions of her own work–life balance and job satisfaction than any family-friendly policy (Saltzstein, Ting, and Saltzstein, 2001). However, if a workplace does not support the use of such policies, a powerful supervisor may be able to protect the employee from perceived or real career penalties (Blair-Loy and Wharton, 2002). In any event, we have to be on the lookout because cultural change is coming. This is in part from new generations of workers who enter the more unstable workplaces with different values: those living the "We Are Self-Employed" Model.

Family and Medical Leave Act as the Floor

As discussed in chapter 2, the *Family and Medical Leave Act (FMLA)* is a federal law that offers job security for up to twelve weeks of unpaid leave; however, it has exclusions that tend to limit women's (and men's) eligibility for it. Therefore, the FMLA is the minimum benefit that eligible workers can expect. The goals of the FMLA are: (1) to promote gender equality in the workplace; (2) to resolve work/family conflicts; and (3) to ensure some extent of job security. To create equal employment opportunities for men and women, Congress used gender-neutral language in the law. This attempt at equality has *not* turned out to be equitable.

Government policy has the opportunity to do so much more than attempt to legislate gender equity (which has not been achieved). This policy, however, may improve the health outcomes of children, as the lack of universal paid leave in the United States has American mothers returning to work relatively quickly after giving birth. Returning to work less than twelve weeks after having a child is considered a "short leave." Children of mothers returning to work full-time within twelve weeks of birth are likely to have poorer health and developmental outcomes, such as lower rates of breastfeeding, less well-baby care, and possible behavior problems by age four (Berger, Hill, and Waldfogel, 2005). Mothers who took less than twelve weeks of leave also had poorer outcomes for themselves and their family. For example, women returning less than twelve weeks after giving birth experienced higher rates of maternal depression, less knowledge about how their infant was developing, a perception that their child was more difficult, and a perception that the birth had a more negative effect on their self-esteem and marriage (Feldman, Sussman, and Zigler, 2004).

Government policy also has the opportunity to strengthen men's ties to caregiving as well as women's connection to paid employment. The FMLA attempted to do just that. The *earner–carer model* predicts gender equity will be achieved when women and men participate evenly in both unpaid caregiving and paid employment (Ray, Gornick, and Schmitt, 2010). While no country has been successful in achieving gender equity, Finland, Norway, Sweden, and Greece have parental leave policies that simultaneously promote generosity and gender equality. How?

These countries provide couples with a minimum of six months of fully paid leave—offering generosity. In addition, these countries promote gender equality by offering either "use it or lose it" leave time for men (ibid.) or strong incentives for men to take leave. For example, while Finland offers only 8 percent of a couple's total leave to men, women are permitted to transfer up to 65 percent of their leave to men. There is a large financial incentive for fathers to take leave, with a wage replacement rate of two-thirds of their usual salary (ibid.).

U.S. policy is quite limited as it relates to supporting families. The FMLA offers weak protections and has multiple exclusions. Strong public support for families improves health outcomes for children and mothers as well as strengthens men's ties to caregiving and women's ties to employment.

Flexible Schedules

Flexible work arrangements are frequently viewed by organizations as a way to recruit and retain talented women workers. Data on federal workers from the 2004 Federal Human Capital Survey, conducted by the Office of Personnel Management (n = 125,338), show that younger workers and workers in higher pay grades tend to prefer alternative work schedules and are likely to be satisfied with these programs (Kim and Wiggins, 2011). Workers who are able to have better work–life balance ought to be more satisfied with their employment. Table 4.7 lists a number of formal programs for full-time and reduced hours as well as use of informal negotiations.

While flexible work arrangements may help some women, Benko and Weisberg (2007) argue that these programs are ad hoc. Moreover, flexible work arrangements have numerous problems, for example, they do not work with large numbers of employees; it is difficult to manage co-workers' perceptions of fairness; and they are difficult to implement as one progresses up the chain of command. Organizations tend to view individuals who use flexible work arrangements as less committed and may find turnover is still high among women; employees do not use available flexible work arrangements because they anticipate negative consequences to their career. To address these concerns Benko and Weisberg developed the *Mass Career Customization Model* (p. 84). The model is intended to be used by all employees, to alleviate the perceived and real inequities from informal negotiations, and to be reassessed as life circumstances change. The Mass Career Customization Model has four dimensions: Pace (Rate of career progression), Workload (Options for quantity of work), Location/Schedule (Choice about where and when work is completed), and Role (Range in responsibilities and position).

Supportive Lactation Policies and Programs

What is a workplace lactation program? A *workplace lactation program* is a set of policies and practices that support a woman's choice to con-

Table 4.7

Types of Flexible Arrangements

Full-time	Flextime	Office hours that are flexible (arrive, leave, lunch); coupled with hours the employee must be present
	Compressed workweek	Completing work hours in fewer days than the traditional workweek (e.g., 40 hours in 4 days)
	Telecommuting	Completing some work remotely
	Banking of hours	Work hours per day/week are uneven, but over a period of time meet the standard requirement
	Off-cycle hours	Nontraditional schedules (e.g., 7:00 a.m.–3:00 p.m.)
	Vacation hours	Allowing employees to use vacation time in increments of hours vs. days
Reduced hours	Job share	Sharing job responsibilities with another employee(s)
	Part-time	Quality part-time work
	Gradual retirement	Reduced hours prior to retirement
	Leaves/sabbaticals	Unpaid time off from work
Informal negotiations	Idiosyncratic-Deal (I-Deal)	Individually negotiated work arrangement(s) (Rousseau, 2005, p. 8)

Source: Benko and Weisberg (2007, p. 58); Shapiro, Ingols, and Blake-Beard (2008, pp. 321–322).

tinue breastfeeding her child after returning to work. Workplace lactation programs only began appearing in the United States in the late 1980s. Lactation programs are proving to increase the initiation and duration of breastfeeding among women who have access to workplace support programs (Balkam, Cadwell, and Fein, 2011; Ortiz, McGilligan, and Kelly, 2004).

As discussed in chapter 2, organizations with fifty or more employees are required by law to provide a private, nonbathroom space for mothers to express breast milk. Breastfeeding benefits children, moms, employers, and society. How? It is the American Academy of Pediatrics (AAP) position that "breastfeeding ensures the best possible health as well as developmental and psychosocial outcomes" (Gartner et al., 2005,

p. 501). Seven years later, the AAP reinforces its conclusion, stating, ". . . breastfeeding and the use of human milk confer unique nutritional and nonnutritional benefits to the infant and the mother and, in turn, optimize infant, child, and adult health as well as child growth and development" (AAP, 2012, p. e841). For example, breastfed children are less likely to contract ear infections, gastrointestinal infections, asthma, obesity, diabetes, many childhood cancers, and SIDS (sudden infant death syndrome) (AAP, 2012; Ip et al., 2007). Breastfeeding has health benefits for moms too. Women who breastfeed recover faster from childbirth and are less likely to develop breast and ovarian cancers (ibid.).

An ongoing breastfeeding relationship is also good for employers. Benefits include higher morale, productivity, and loyalty; higher employee retention/lower turnover; lower health insurance costs; and reduced absenteeism due to sick children (WomensHealth.gov, 2010b). Women who continue to breastfeed after returning to work miss less time because of baby-related illnesses and have shorter absences when they do miss work, compared with women who do not breastfeed (Spangler, 2000).

Despite the numerous benefits of breastfeeding, women face barriers to breastfeeding when returning to work. Cardenas and Major (2005) characterize these as conflicts of: *time* to fulfill roles as employee and breastfeeding mom, *strain* or *stress* in performing a job as well as being a nursing mom, and *behavior* related to expressing milk or feeding a baby while at work. Table 4.8 lists workplace policies and programs to reduce the conflicts.

A simple example of a program that managers can implement with reasonably low financial effect on workers' productivity is a program to promote sustained breastfeeding at work. The National Women's Health Information Center offers resources including The Business Case for Breastfeeding (WomensHealth.gov, 2010a), which provides the rationale as well as the concrete steps for pursuing such programs.

Nursing programs must meet the needs of employees across the organizational hierarchy. As we have noted throughout the text, women tend to be segregated into lower-level positions that offer less autonomy and flexibility, and lower pay. Based on national databases, Williams and Boushey (2010) revealed different needs of low, middle, and professional income employees. But they also found four crucial policy areas that would benefit all three groups: (a) paid leave—short-term and extended; (b) flexibility at work; (c) affordable child care; and (d) protection against discrimination for having family responsibilities.

Table 4.8

Policies and Programs to Reduce Barriers to Continuing a Breastfeeding Relationship After Returning to Work

Prenatal education	Educate employees on the benefits of breastfeeding as well as realistic expectations about it to reduce strain and conflict.
Lactation programs and equipment	At minimum, provide the space and time required by law. In addition, do not dock pay during milk expression. Provide pre- and postnatal education classes, lactation consultants, and equipment. Reduces time, strain, and behavior conflicts.
Managerial support	When supervisors are supportive, women have less concern about maintaining professionalism or job security (strain and conflict).
Lactation support groups	Employer-sponsored support meetings (lactation consultants may facilitate) for guidance, emotional support, and problem solving. Meetings may also take place via Internet or hotlines.
Job flexibility	Flexible work hours, part-time employment, or telecommuting, adequate duration of paid maternity leave.
On-site child care	Costly to employers, but reduces employee absenteeism costs, may be a recruiting or retention tool, convenient for women to nurse on breaks.

Source: Cardenas and Major (2005, pp. 40–45).

Additional research informs us that specific factors affect whether a mom will be exclusively breastfeeding at six months: registering for a workplace lactation program prior to the birth, using telephone support, participating in a "return to work" consultation that provided advice on how to store milk at the workplace, and using more services were factors that identified women who are more likely to be exclusively breastfeeding at six months (Balkam, Cadwell, and Fein, 2011, p. 4). In sum, breastfeeding has numerous benefits for the worker and her child as well as the employer; and breastfeeding support programs have been studied to the point of offering empirical support and low-cost best practices.

Child-Care and Elder-Care Benefits

Women tend to provide the bulk of caregiving in U.S. families. Because work continues to be organized around the "organization man," child-

and *elder-care* benefits are not the norm. While, child-care benefits tend to be more common, elder-care benefits are a response to changing demographics, with today's worker being "sandwiched" between caring for children and adult relatives. Child and elder-care benefits have been shown to benefit public and private employers in many ways; for example, these benefits may reduce absenteeism and tardiness, increase commitment to the organization, and increase productivity (Major, Cardenas, and Allard, 2004).

The U.S. Office of Personnel Management (OPM) provides leadership on federal leave policies and programs. The OPM develops regulations and policies, allowing each agency to administer its own employee programs. Federal agencies may offer on-site child care, referral services, long-term care insurance, and child-care subsidy programs for low-income employees. Under the provisions of Public Law 100-202, the General Services Administration (GSA) has authority to guide, assist, and oversee the development of child-care centers at federal agencies, for federal employees (USDA, n.d., http://www.dm.usda.gov/employ/worklife/worklife/faq. htm).

Even federal employees are not a homogeneous group when it comes to preferences. Federal employees in lower pay grades tend to be more satisfied with child-care programs than those in higher pay grades; younger workers may be less interested in child-care and benefits related to families because they are unmarried or childless (Kim and Wiggins, 2011). While the lifestyle of a single person may not require these benefits at that time, it is likely that they will have family responsibilities as they age and then such policies will be of value.

Federal employees also have access to dependent care accounts. *Dependent care accounts*—pretax dollars used to pay for caregiving expenses—may be used to offset the cost of child and elder care. Many private companies also offer dependent care accounts (72 percent). A national study of local governments found that child-care benefits and elder-care benefits were the least frequently offered benefit programs in local governments (Roberts et al., 2004).

As per a national survey conducted by the Society for Human Resource Management (2010), the most common types of benefits provided in private companies are found in Table 4.9. The most common type of child-care benefit was the ability to bring a child to work in case of an emergency, followed by a referral service for off worksite child care. A referral service for elder care was the most common type of elder-care benefit.

Table 4.9

Common Child- and Elder-Care Benefits

Child-care benefit		Elder-care benefit	
Bring child to work in emergency	30%	Elder-care referral service	11%
Babies at work	1%		
Child-care referral service	17%		
Child-care center			
Subsidized	4%		
Nonsubsidized	3%		
Consortium with other employers	1%		
On-site lactation/mothers' room	28%		
Lactation support services	4%	Geriatric counseling services to seniors and their families—evaluate needs, identify and coordinate resources for seniors	4%
Access to backup child-care services	4%	Access to backup elder-care services for an unexpected event	2%
Adoption assistance	9%	Elder care in-home assessment	1%
Foster care assistance	1%	Elder care assisted living assessment	1%
Parenting workplace seminars	3%	On-site elder-care fair—an event where organizations that specialize in the well-being of elderly individuals or their caregivers display their products and services to educate participants about what is available in their community. In addition to booths, seminars and other resources may be offered.	1%
On-site vaccinations for infants/children	5%		
529 plan	13%	A college saving account. There are no federal taxes (and sometimes no state taxes) on the growth of the account when used for approved educational expenses (e.g., tuition).	

Research suggests that working parents value "sick care services"—backup care when a child is sick, and thus unable to go to regular child care or school—as one of the most important employer-sponsored child-care benefits, yet these services are uncommon (Major, Cardenas, and Allard, 2004). This service is probably uncommon because it is very expensive to operate. This type of service is even less common for elder care.

Barriers, Challenges, and Opportunities

Families in the United States face systematic barriers that families in other industrialized countries do not because the United States lacks a robust social safety net. Although women today are not exiting the workforce as they had in the previous cohort of women, work continues to be organized around the assumption of the "organization man." Because these expectations are inconsistent with women's gender roles, women tend to pay higher social costs for their careers than men.

Gender role is another barrier, as it is related to women's working shifts beyond the standard workday: (a) second shift—time engaging in housework and child-care duties; (b) third shift—time repairing hurt feelings for not being at home as much as children/spouse prefer; and (c) fourth shift—time at home (e.g., weekends) remotely engaging in workplace tasks. While demographic trends change, but workplace expectations do not, additional organizational changes are occurring. The *Womb-to-Tomb Employment Model* has been shaken, as the *We Are Self-Employed Model* has become the norm.

This chapter highlighted the social costs that women experience because of a successful career: a third barrier. Professional women are more likely to be unmarried, have fewer children, or be divorced, while carrying a heavy housework burden. Professional women are attempting to salvage their careers in various ways: temporarily exiting and reentering the workforce, downshifting, or engaging in entrepreneurship. Workplace policies were explored as well as tips for women wishing to minimize career costs. However, barriers may still be too high for some professional women to surmount. Some professional women are unable to return to previous careers, finding themselves taking part-time jobs that tend to be inferior to full-time employment.

Challenges relate to expanding U.S. worker protections. As has been discussed, U.S. policy is quite limited as it relates to supporting families.

For example, the FMLA offers weak protections and has multiple exclusions. There are considerable opportunities for the creation of work–life policies because families, organizations, and society benefit from them. Such policies have the opportunity to improve health outcomes for mother and child. Moreover, there tends to be strong public support for families. Unfortunately, business elites tend to dominate the political discussion, while progressive groups alienate the white working class, who currently align themselves with the business elites.

Organizational policies and practices offer another opportunity that may impact work–life fit, albeit one organization at a time. Several flexible work arrangements were described. Opportunities for better work–life fit for employees also include lactation programs as well as child-care and elder-care organizational policies.

Key Terms

Career costs
Compressed workweek
Dependent care accounts
Downshifting
Earner–carer model
Elder care
Family and Medical Leave Act
   (FMLA)
Family women
Flextime
Fourth shift
I-Deal
Intensive mothering
Job share

Mass Career Customization Model
Off-cycle hours
Organization men
Second shift
Social costs
Structural constraints
Telecommuting
Third shift
We Are Self-Employed Model
Womb-to-Tomb Employment
   Model
Work–life balance policies
Workplace lactation program

5

Segregation and Representation of Women in Public Organizations

One of the distressing problems facing public managers who seek proper representation of women across public organizations is that of segregation of women in *female-dominated fields*, occupations, and agencies. The segregation issue is a major prerequisite for having representative organizations that actively mirror society. Despite the narrowing gap in educational attainment and experience, women continue to be segregated in certain fields and in certain occupations in private and public service agencies. There are many reasons—individual, societal, and organizational—that may be cited for this continued segregation. Some of these issues were explored in the previous chapter and some will be explored in future chapters.

For purposes of studying the issue of representation of women in public service, we can look at segregation in certain agencies, certain occupations, and certain position levels. In this chapter, we explore the extent of segregation in the past few years in female-dominated agencies, positions, and occupations in local, state, and federal agencies. For each one of these forms of segregation, we address the prevalence of the problem (barriers), its underlying explanations (challenges), and the opportunities to move in the future to a more even representation situation in public service organizations. Before all that, we discuss the role of women in representative institutions and changes in that representation over the past few decades.

Women in Representative Institutions

There is no question that more women are in elected offices today than there were fifty years ago. It is not uncommon for many states now to have a woman governor. State and federal cabinets are populated with many women. For several years now, women have held positions historically reserved for men in the federal cabinet, such as secretary of state. While the inventory of anecdotal evidence that women are now better represented in political institutions has grown substantially over the past years, the overall numbers indicate that women are far away from parity in representation in these institutions.

Perhaps even more alarming is that improvement in the representation of women has slowed down substantially in the past two decades. If the goal is to see more women in elected offices, then one should not worry, as that goal is within reach. If the goal, however, is to achieve parity in representation between women and men in elected offices, then we should be worried about the attainability of this goal given the slower pace of improvements in representation in political institutions over the past decade. The pace of improvement in representation might leave us a century away from parity in representation.

Figure 5.1 shows the pace of improvement in representation of women in the U.S. Congress, statewide elected offices, and state legislatures. In 2011, women held 88 elected congressional offices—16.4 percent of the House of Representatives' 435 seats and 17 percent of the Senate's 100 seats. This is a substantial improvement in the representation of women at the federal level over 1979, when women held only 3 percent of congressional offices. However, in 2013, women continue to be far from holding half of the congressional seats, and more important, the change has been slower in the past fifteen years, considering that women were 10.1 percent of congressional elected officials in 1997 (CAWP, 2011). The deceleration of improvement in the representation of women is alarming because it cannot be explained by budget cuts or layoffs, based on the last-in/first-out principle. These are rather selections by voters and local and state party leaders who choose whom to vote for, and whom to give financial and political support, respectively.

The pace of progress in terms of women's representation in state legislatures has been even slower than that in congressional elected offices. In 2011, women held 23 percent of all state legislative elected seats—or 1,738 of the 7,382 available seats (CAWP, 2011). This is a substantial improvement from 1979 when women held 10 percent of the state legislative elected offices. However, the improvement has been modest in the past 15 years—from 21 percent in 1995 to 24 percent in 2011.

In statewide elected offices (governor, secretary of state, treasurer,

Figure 5.1 **Women in Federal and State Representative Institutions**

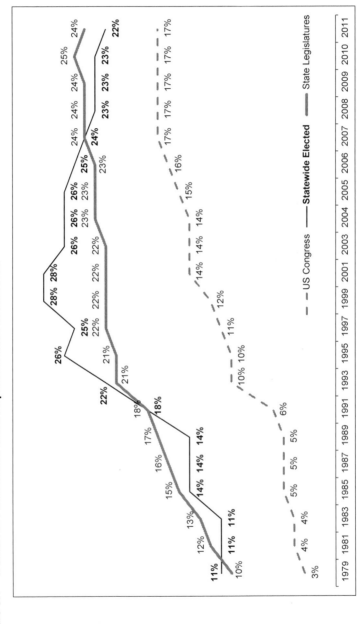

Source: Center for American Women and Politics (CAWP), 2011.

auditor, etc.), improvements were substantial between 1991 and 1997, when women's representation in these offices increased from 14 percent to 26 percent. Since 1997, however, the representation of women declined from 26 percent to 22 percent. In 2011, women held 22 percent of the statewide elective offices compared to 11 percent in 1979. In 2011, there were 6 women governors (12 percent), 11 women lieutenant governors (22 percent), 7 state attorney generals (14 percent), 11 state secretaries of state (22 percent), 6 state treasurer seats (12 percent), 4 state comptroller seats (8 percent), 7 state auditor seats (22 percent), 1 commissioner of labor seat, 4 public service commissioner seats, and 1 public regulation commissioner seat (CAWP, 2011). These numbers again draw a picture showing that while women in these statewide elected offices are present, they continue to be far from achieving parity—meaning 50 percent of these offices. Moreover, the slowing and in this case the reversal of progress in the past decade indicate clearly that representative institutions might not even be on the right track.

At the local level, women held mayoral seats in 8 of the 100 largest cities in the United States. Women held mayoral offices in 11.7 percent of the 256 cities with populations larger than 100,000 and 16.7 percent of the mayoral offices in the 1,163 U.S. cities with populations of 30,000 and higher. The obvious conclusion from these figures is that women are more likely to be elected mayors of smaller cities than larger ones. As we will discuss in later parts of this book, this is consistent with the underrepresentation of women in positions with more responsibility and authority. In their study of chief procurement officers nationwide, Alkadry and Tower (2011) found that female public procurement executives, on average, were supervising half of the number of employees and managing half the budget, compared to their male counterparts. The figures from U.S. cities seem to imply a similar trend. A trend in both the public and private sectors shows that women are more likely to be better represented in leadership positions of smaller organizations, with fewer people to supervise, and less financial responsibilities.

The slow progress toward a proper representation of women and men in elected offices cannot be blamed on mismanagement of these organizations. It also cannot be blamed on any of the traditional *human capital* (i.e., the term used to explain competencies and skills valued by the labor market) reasons that are used to explain disparities between men and women in merit-based, nonelected public offices.

There are three possible explanations for the poor representation of women in elected offices. First, it could be that not enough women are seeking these offices. Cut-throat politics and negative campaign advertising, among other things, might result in keeping potential female politicians away from the adventure of campaigns. Second, the problem may be traced to the lack of support of female candidates by local and state party political leaders. Many candidates need the financial and political support of party leaders to launch a successful campaign. Third, female candidates who are running for office might be less successful than their male counterparts in gaining the confidence of voters. The final reason is very important because it can be traced to gender roles prescribed by society. Perhaps the discussion around Sarah Palin's run for office in 2008 is a case in point. The Alaska governor ran for vice president on the Republican presidential ticket. Many conservative men and women questioned the ability of Governor Palin to balance the needs of her family and those of the office she was seeking. Interestingly enough, such discussions are rarely present in the cases of male candidates (such as Senator John Edwards in 2004 and then Senator Barack Obama in 2008) running on the top ticket.

The slowing progress of women's representation in elected offices signals a need for political parties to have better programs to nominate women for public office. Unfortunately, despite the parade of women leaders at both parties' political conventions in 2012, neither party announced any program to improve the representation of women. Nominating a woman for a congressional seat that is secure for Democrats or Republicans is a sure way to improve representation of women in representative institutions. While understanding the poor progress of women in elected offices is very important, it is better left to another book that deals specifically with voter attitudes and behavior. In contrast to the slowing progress of women in elected offices, the rest of this chapter is dedicated to examining the situation within the public sector's nonelected administrative institutions. At first glance, it appears that the representation of women in the public sector is higher. But a closer look at the situation reveals inconsistencies across different agencies, occupations, and organizational levels. The authors of this book contend that the progress that occurred in nonelected institutions has been very significant at all levels of government. However, the authors also warn that the issue of segregation of women to certain agencies, fields, and position levels continues to be a distressing problem facing public service agencies across the nation.

Overrepresentation and Underrepresentation
in Public Administration

Like a lawn that grows unevenly, the representation of women in the public sector has not been even. Half a decade after outlawing discrimination against women in employment, women continue to be overrepresented in some fields and agencies and underrepresented in others. While the representation of women in most public sector organizations is nearing parity with men, women continue to be concentrated in lower-echelon jobs that pay less and assign less authority and power. Underrepresentation and overrepresentation of women in organizations, occupations, and position levels is deeply rooted in complex social norms, female gender roles in family and culture, as well as human capital variables and discrimination.

Women's strides in educational attainment and work experience/tenure are helping to ease human capital barriers to equitable representation in the workforce. However, social and cultural norms are proving to be the more challenging barriers to employment of women. Cultural change is not so simple and cannot be achieved through modest investments of resources or policy interventions. Discrimination, certainly, may be blamed, in some cases, for the exclusion of women.

While this chapter discusses underrepresentation and overrepresentation in the context of agency segregation, occupational segregation, and position-level segregation, it is important to keep in mind that these issues are sometimes interconnected. For instance, the overrepresentation of women in clerical occupations and in lower-level positions could divert attention from agency segregation. Female-dominated occupations and agencies and obviously female-dominated lower-level positions pay substantially lower wages than male-dominated ones. This signals a clear link between segregation and pay inequity—as will be discussed in chapter 6. The following sections discuss segregation in three contexts: agency segregation, position-level segregation, and occupational or *field segregation.*

Agency Segregation

Are men likely to be found in certain agency types and women in other agency types? For example, are we likely to expect more men than women in the federal or state department of transportation? As another example, are we more likely to find women or men in a department of education, health, or welfare? *Agency segregation*, as the name suggests, refers to the concentration of women in some agencies but not others. According to Lowi (1985), there are three types of administrative agencies: redistributive, regulatory, and distributive. *Redistributive agencies* include all agencies that are concerned with the reallocation of money and provision of services to certain segments of society and include agencies dealing with health, welfare, or education. *Regulatory agencies* are associated with functions such as implementing control and regulatory policies and include environmental agencies, law enforcement agencies, or taxing authorities. *Distributive agencies* deal with the general population and include transportation, parks, and recreation agencies. According to Alkadry, Nolf, and Condo (2002), Kim (2004), Miller, Kerr, and Reid (1999), and Newman (1994), women in public sector agencies are more likely to be concentrated in redistributive agencies. They are substantially underrepresented in regulatory and distributive agencies.

Before discussing the reasons behind agency segregation, it is important to examine the extent to which this underrepresentation is reflected in current data from state, local, and federal agencies. The *Federal Equal Opportunity Recruitment Program (FEORP)* reports that women equaled or exceeded the number of men in 6 of the 18 executive departments listed in Table 5.1 (U.S. OPM, 2009). In the federal government as a whole, women represent about 44.2 percent of the civilian labor force. In the ten regulatory executive departments, women on average represent 41.1 percent of the labor force. In the two distributive departments, women on average represent 32.9 percent of these two agencies. Finally, in the four redistributive executive departments, women on average represent 62.4 percent of these departments' workforces.

Here, it is very important to note that agency segregation may be concealed by other forms of segregation, such as occupational and position level. For example, while 45.6 percent of employees in the Department of Commerce are women, these women might primarily hold clerical and/or lower echelon positions. Similarly, while nearly 26 percent of employees in the Department of Education are men, they may primarily be in senior positions. We will discuss this issue more when we get to the occupational and position-level segregation.

The picture at the state and local level was not much better in terms of segregation of women. The Equal Employment Opportunity Commission (EEOC) requires state and local government jurisdictions to report on

Table 5.1

Representation of Women in Executive Departments at the Federal Level

Type	Department	Percent
Regulatory	Air Force	30.2
	Agriculture	43.9
	Army	37.1
	Commerce	45.6
	Defense	49.6
	Justice	39.5
	Treasury	62.6
	Homeland Security	32.2
	Interior	39.9
	Navy	29.9
	Average	41.1
Distributive	Transportation	27.0
	Energy	38.7
	Average	32.9
Redistributive	Education	63.6
	Health and Human Services	64.8
	Housing and Urban Development	61.5
	Veterans affairs	59.8
	Average	62.4
	Government-wide	44.2

Source: U.S. OPM (2009).

the composition of their current workforce as well as the composition of their incoming class of employees. Table 5.2 includes data for all agencies that could be distinguished in the three Lowi classifications. The table includes data from 6,081 reporting units.

There are three important things to consider when looking at Table 5.2. First, the number of full-time employees by agency function reflects the current composition of the labor force in these agencies. This is a reflection of the extent to which women are concentrated in some agency types, but not others. The 192,215 female employees in distributive agencies represent 22 percent of the labor force in these agencies. The 532,178 female employees in regulatory agencies represent 31 percent of the labor force in these agencies. The 1,016,967 female employees in redistributive agencies represent 75 percent of the labor force in these agencies.

In a nutshell, women continue to be segregated in redistributive agencies and to be underrepresented in distributive and regulatory agencies (see Table 5.1). Of the 3,918,569 employees who work full-time, in 6,081

Table 5.2

Agency Segregation in State and Local Government Organizations

	Reporting units	Total full-time female	Total part-time female	Total female new hire
Distributive				
Streets and highways	564	65,651	6,313	3,860
%		21	33	19
Utilities and transportation	656	107,687	9,771	8,154
%		25	40	27
Sanitation and sewage	438	18,877	1,382	1,774
%		17	29	19
Distributive totals	1,658	192,215	17,466	13,788
%		22	36	23
Regulatory				
Police protection	1,208	188,925	21,878	15,906
%		29	47	33
Fire protection	599	17,600	1,330	1,356
%		9	17	11
Natural resources	566	79,703	85,613	12,947
%		35	47	47
Corrections	507	245,950	10,470	27,350
%		39	49	42
Regulatory totals	2,880	532,178	119,291	57,559
%		31	46	37
Redistributive				
Public welfare	470	302,081	19,804	29,173
%		78	74	78
Hospitals and sanatoriums	534	418,372	114,417	50,318
%		74	79	75
Health	486	255,818	40,525	29,700
%		73	74	73
Employment security	53	40,696	5,469	3,975
%		63	72	63
Redistributive totals	1,543	1,016,967	180,215	113,166
%		75	77	74
All				
Totals	6,081	1,741,360	316,972	184,513
%		44	59	50

Source: U.S. EEOC (2009).

reporting state and local units, 44 percent were women. Women made up 75 percent of the redistributive units (including employment security, health, hospitals and sanatoriums, and public welfare), 31 percent of regulatory units (including corrections, natural resources, police protection, and fire protection), and 22 percent of distributive units (including streets and highways, utilities and transportation, and sanitation and sewage). Therefore, in 2009, women continue to be clearly segregated in redistributive agency types at the local and state levels. Women continue to be substantially underrepresented in distributive and regulatory agencies. This picture is a textbook example of segregation of women in redistributive agencies and their underrepresentation in distributive and regulatory agencies.

Second, the number of part-time employees is also important, as women historically tend to occupy part-time positions. Although not close to parity with men, the percentage of women among part-time employees is slightly better than their percentages among full-time employees. The same segregation pattern that is discussed above is obvious in the case of part-time employment. Of the 540,842 employees who worked part-time in 2009, in the 6,081 reporting state and local government units, 59 percent were women. This is a higher percentage than that among full-time workers—which is consistent with the trend that women are represented at higher rates in the part-time workforce than in the full-time workforce. This is consistent with Young's (2010) analysis of responses from the National Survey of the Changing Workforce, which included 3,504 individuals. Young concludes that even when men and women have equivalent levels of education and work experience, men tend to earn higher wages and are less likely to work part-time.

Third and more important, the percentage of women among *new hires* in each of the agencies gives us an indication of the effort made by local and state agencies to correct any imbalance in the workforce. Although women are being hired almost at parity with men, the new hires tend to gravitate to female-dominated agencies, where women were traditionally segregated. Although 50 percent of the newly hired employees were women, 74 percent of the newly hired employees in redistributive agencies are women; 37 percent of newly hired employees in regulatory agencies are women; and 23 percent of newly hired employees in distributive agencies are women. In other words, new hiring tends to conform to existing segregation in redistributive agencies and underrepresentation in distributive and regulatory agencies. This information is valuable if one is trying to gauge the largely unfounded argument that men are being discriminated against in the hiring process because there is a preference for women.

Representation of women in state and local agencies is not uniform across all levels of government. While women seem to be represented at levels close to parity with men at the state, county, and special district

Figure 5.2 **Representation of Women in State and Local Agencies, 2009**

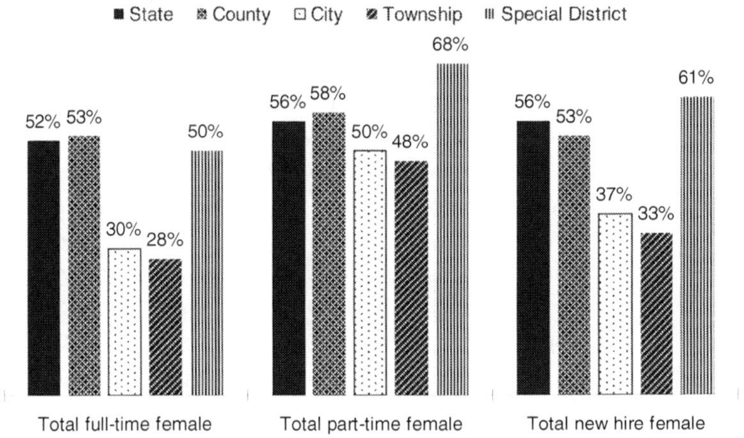

■ State ▩ County ▢ City ▨ Township ⫼ Special District

Source: U.S. EEOC, 2009.

levels, it substantially lags behind the city and township levels (see Figure 5.2). The proportions of women working full-time in reporting cities and townships are 30 percent and 28 percent of the respective full-time workforces. This same disparity in representation of women is consistent with new hiring records where 37 percent and 33 percent of new hires are women at the city and township levels, respectively. Among the part-time workforces in city and townships, parity exists among men and women. It is difficult to determine the reasons behind this variance among different government levels in overall representation of women in their workforces, part-time employment of women, and the representation of women among new hires. Public administration researchers have done little to gauge these disparities and conducted very little theoretical and empirical research.

Women's concentration in redistributive agencies comes with a major disadvantage to women's compensation. Departments that are female-dominated tend to have lower salaries than those that are male-dominated. In chapter 4, we discussed the problem of segregation, not only in female-dominated agencies but also in female-dominated occupations and lower-echelon positions, as a substantial contributor to the pay gap between men and women (Budig, 2002; Miller, Kerr, and Reid, 1999; Orazem and Mattila, 1998; Riccucci, 2009).

The above findings are not far from Newman's (1994) study, which found that more than half of the women who worked in the public sector were concentrated in redistributive agencies, while a third were in regulatory agencies and an eighth of the women in her sample worked in distributive agencies. Since then, numerous studies have reported the same trend: the overrepresentation of women in redistributive agencies and their underrepresentation in distributive and regulatory agencies (Alkadry, Nolf, and Condo, 2002; Cornwell and Kellough, 1994; Lewis and Nice, 1994; and Miller, Kerr, and Reid, 1999). It is troubling that segregation continues despite our clear identification of the problem.

Why are women overrepresented in redistributive or female-dominated lower-paying "caring" agencies? Redistributive agencies tend to be characterized as having more caring functions (and also tend to be lower paid). Why are women concentrated in caring agencies? One often-cited reason is that women tend to receive education in areas of social work, education, and other *caring fields*, rather than science, engineering, and fields that are associated with better-paying agencies. This is a valid reason, although women are becoming increasingly better represented in these traditionally *male-dominated fields*. If an agency has more social workers than engineers, and women are more likely to be social workers and less likely to be engineers than men, then men end up being concentrated in transportation departments while women end up being concentrated in social service agencies. If this reason is driving the overrepresentation of women in redistributive agencies and their underrepresentation in other agency types, then as one can imagine, the progress of women toward parity in representation across all agencies will be a tough road. Issues at stake would be societal gender roles, individual choices, and socialization of girls into these roles and choices.

A less studied reason for agency segregation is the possibility that women are excluded from male-dominated agencies not because they are disinterested as many people claim, but rather because they are being discriminated against by the dominant gender in these agencies. That issue is easy to pinpoint for each agency. If the number of qualified women in an applicant pool is 50 percent of all applicants, and only 20 percent of the new hires are women, then one could flag discrimination as a source of the disparity. Women might also gravitate toward redistributive agencies because they feel more comfortable working with women than men.

Figure 5.3   **Employment of Women in Federal Government in GSR and SES Levels, 2009**

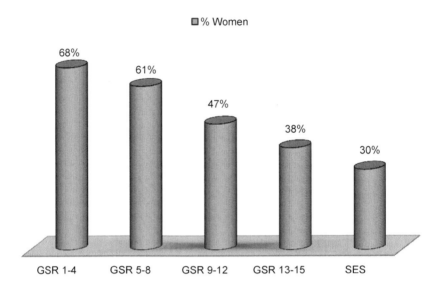

□ % Women

Source: U.S. OPM, 2009.

Position Segregation

For many reasons, women enter at lower levels of the hierarchy than men, they advance through the ranks slower than men, and they reenter the workforce after childbirth and caregiving at lower levels too. *Position segregation* occurs when women are concentrated in lower-echelon positions in organizations. Research shows that women tend to be concentrated in lower levels of organizations, in positions such as administrative support and clerical positions (Alkadry, Nolf, and Condo, 2002; Hsieh and Winslow, 2006; Meier and Wilkins, 2002). Compared to men, women are more likely to occupy jobs that are part-time, lower paid, and have less job security (Young, 2010).

A case in point is the percentage of women in the federal government, by level. Women represented 68 percent of all employees in *General Schedule (GSR)* levels 1 through 4 in the federal government in 2009. As we ascend the ladder, we find that women represent smaller and smaller proportions of the workforce (see Figure 5.3 and Figure 5.4). In GSR levels 5–8, 9–12,

Figure 5.4   **Representation of Men and Women in GS and SES Levels, 2010**

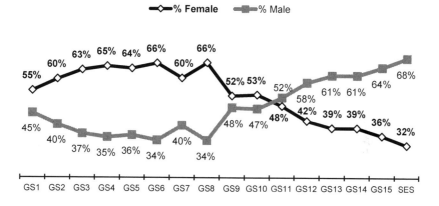

and 13–15 and in SES (Senior Executive Service) levels, women represent 61 percent, 47 percent, 38 percent, and 30 percent, respectively, of these workforces. As we climb higher up the hierarchy women are less and less represented—from 68 percent in lower-level positions to 30 percent in the highest senior civil-service positions (see Figure 5.3).

Women represent half of the workforce in the reported GSR 1–15 and SES levels. Of the 714,155 women who work in Office of Personnel Management categories of GS 1-15 and Senior executive service, 7 percent work in GSR 1–4, 32 percent work in GSR 5–8, 40 percent work in GSR 9–12, and 21 percent work in GSR 13–15. Only 0.4 of female federal employees work in the Senior Executive Service. By comparison, of the 728,854 men who work at the same levels, 4 percent work in GSR 1–4, 19 percent work in GSR 5–8, 46 percent work in GSR 9–12, 33 percent work in GSR 13–15, and 1 percent work in the senior executive service positions. *The problem with representation of women is not simply their overall numbers, but rather how these numbers are distributed across the different hierarchical levels.* Figure 5.5 shows that position level segregation is also a problem in the private sector. These findings are supported by a history of women accessing the public sector through lower ranks (Guy, 1993; Naff, 1994; Newman, 1994). Figures 5.6 and 5.7 show how women consistently outnumber men in positions below GS10, while men outnumber women also consistently in positions above GS10. The 2010 data are not particularly encouraging for managers and

Figure 5.5   **Occupational Segregation in the Private Sector**

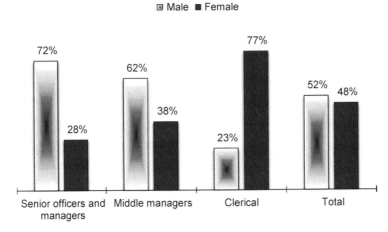

Source: U.S. EEOC, 2009.

Figure 5.6   **Percentage of Women in Different Occupations by Level of Government, 2009**

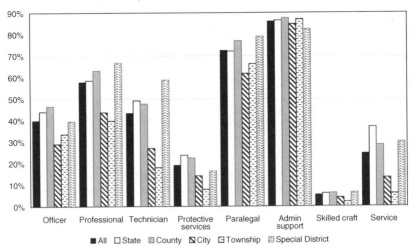

Source: U.S. EEOC, 2009.

advocates who are working to achieve parity in representation across all levels of the organization.

As one studies the status of women in public organizations, it is very

Figure 5.7   **Percentage of Women Among New Hires by Government Level, 2009**

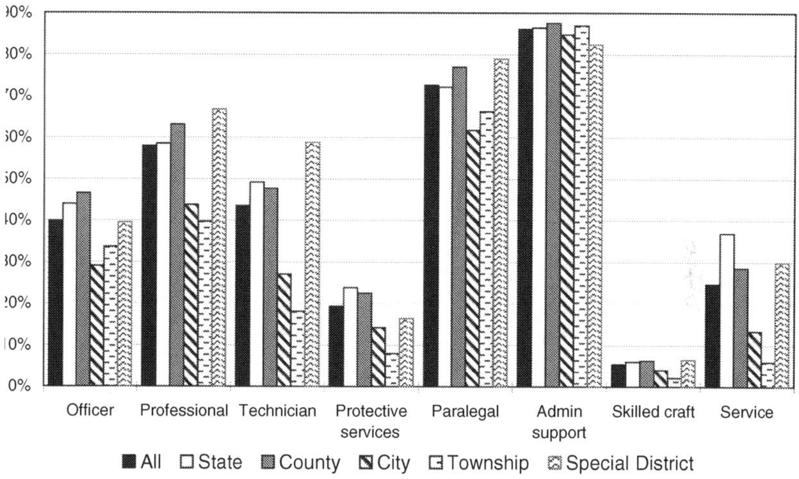

Source: U.S. EEOC, 2009.

helpful to consider the status of women in private organizations too. In terms of segregation in lower-echelon positions, women have not done particularly better in the private sector than they have in the federal government. Figure 5.5 shows how the problem of women being concentrated or segregated in lower level positions is also prevalent in the private sector. As we move from clerical positions, where women are concentrated, we see women become less represented in middle management, and even less represented in senior management ranks. In the data reported to the EEOC in 2009, 72 percent of senior officers and managers, and 62 percent of middle managers in the private sector were men, and only 23 percent of clerical positions in the private sector were occupied by men. The concentration of women in lower-echelon clerical positions in the private and the public sectors is also a textbook case of position-level segregation.

Why are women segregated in lower-level positions? There are many reasons that act separately or together to paint the picture presented in the above data. Some of the reasons are organizational, some are personal and sociocultural, and some are human capital reasons. Women are graduating from college at a faster pace and with higher degrees than men. This signals a change in human capital differential between men and women. In the past, people resisting affirmative action programs used to argue that men get higher positions and/or earn more because they are better educated. These people can no longer make such a claim—in fact, a reverse claim might be in order. As human capital differences between men and women seem to resolve themselves, it becomes even more important to focus on the other reasons behind the overrepresentation of women in lower-level positions.

Women enter the public service through lower-echelon positions or into certain occupations and stay there. Once in these lower-level positions, women move up the ladder more slowly than men (Guy, 1993; Hsieh and Winslow, 2006; Kelly et al., 1991; Meier and Wilkins, 2002; Naff 1994) and face more barriers to career advancement than men (Newman, 1994). Women who are promoted tend to have higher performance ratings compared to their male counterparts (Lyness and Heilman, 2006).

Advancement into leadership positions may also be affected by what Stivers (1993) labeled as *"gender images,"* whereby women are not always associated with images of leadership and management profiles. If women are portrayed in sociocultural images as weak, and managers need to be assertive, then women are less likely to be seen as good candidates for promotions into higher levels of the organization. While Stivers makes a good case based on this image problem, it is obvious that society is increasingly becoming more receptive to the idea of women holding leadership positions. But men and women alike hold implicit biases toward women (see chapter 1). Women's entrance into nontraditional female occupations and into management positions continues to be challenged, particularly in male-dominated jobs or agencies (Maume, 1999; Newman, 1994; Padavic and Reskin, 1994). When we see women in management ranks, they tend to be concentrated in management ranks in female-dominated agencies, such as departments of education and human services, and in service-oriented, intra-agency departments, such as personnel and administrative support (Orazem and Mattila, 1998).

Occupational Segregation

Women also tend to be overrepresented in certain occupations, such as social services, education, and nursing, and underrepresented in traditionally male-dominated occupations, such as engineering and finance. The concentration of women in female-dominated occupations is referred to as *occupational segregation*. This sort of representation has serious implications for pay disparities, as female-dominated occupations tend to pay lower wages than male-dominated occupations. In this section, we discuss the representation issues facing women in *occupational categories* and in occupations. The first refers to the segregation of women into certain occupational categories (clerical/administrative support, professional, technician, etc.) as reported in the Equal Employment Opportunity Commission data. Women tend to be more concentrated in service, clerical, and sales positions than in professional, technical, and operational categories.

Representation in EEOC Occupational Categories

Public and private organizations are required to report the representation of women and minorities in different occupational categories or classes of employment. Under Public Law 88–352, Title VII of the Civil Rights Act of 1964, as amended by the Equal Employment Opportunity Act of 1972, all state and local government employees with a workforce of more than fifteen employees are required to report diversity data (including race, sex, and ethnicity) on a regular basis. The EEOC report typically includes data on the representation of women in eight categories: Officials and Administrators, Professionals, Technicians, Protective Service Workers, Paraprofessionals, Administrative Support (includes clerical and sales positions), Skilled Craft Workers, and Service-Maintenance Workers. Exhibit 5.1 provides descriptions for each of these categories.

Table 5.3 provides data on the representation of women in these categories, as reported to the EEOC in 2009, in five types of entities: state, county, city, township, and special district. Overall, there were 13,367 reporting units in the above five types of jurisdictions or entities. These reporting units had a total of 5,980,305 employees—46 percent of whom were women. Among the nearly 6 million employees, women were the highest represented in administrative support categories (86 percent of employees were women), followed by the paraprofessional category (73 percent), and then professionals (58 percent). This picture is consistent across the different government levels or entity types, in the case of the overrepresentation of women

Exhibit 5.1

EEOC Description of Job Categories

a. *Officials and Administrators:* Occupations in which employees set broad policies, exercise overall responsibility for execution of these policies, or direct individual departments or special phases of the agency's operations, or provide specialized consultation on a regional, district or area basis. Includes: department heads, bureau chiefs, division chiefs, directors, deputy directors, controllers, wardens, superintendents, sheriffs, police and fire chiefs and inspectors, examiners (bank, hearing, motor vehicle, warehouse), inspectors (construction, building, safety, rent-and-housing, fire, A.B.C. Board, license, dairy, livestock, transportation), assessors, tax appraisers and investigators, coroners, farm managers, and kindred workers.

b. *Professionals:* Occupations that require specialized and theoretical knowledge that is usually acquired through college training or through work experience and other training that provides comparable knowledge. Includes: personnel and labor relations workers, social workers, doctors, psychologists, registered nurses, economists, dietitians, lawyers, systems analysts, accountants, engineers, employment and vocational rehabilitation counselors, teachers or instructors, police and fire captains and lieutenants, librarians, management analysts, airplane pilots and navigators, surveyors and mapping scientists, and kindred workers.

c. *Technicians:* Occupations that require a combination of basic scientific or technical knowledge and manual skill that can be obtained through specialized postsecondary school education or through equivalent on-the-job training. Includes: computer programmers, drafters, survey and mapping technicians, licensed practical nurses, photographers, radio operators, technical illustrators, highway technicians, technicians (medical, dental, electronic, physical sciences), police and fire sergeants, inspectors (production or processing inspectors, testers and weighers), and kindred workers.

d. *Protective Service Workers:* Occupations in which workers are entrusted with public safety, security and protection from destructive forces. Includes: police patrol officers, firefighters, guards, deputy sheriffs, bailiffs, correctional officers, detectives, marshals, harbor patrol officers, game and fish wardens, park rangers (except maintenance), and kindred workers.

e. ***Paraprofessionals:*** Occupations in which workers perform some of the duties of a professional or technician in a supportive role, which usually require less formal training and/or experience normally required for professional or technical status. Such positions may fall within an identified pattern of staff development and promotion under a "New Careers" concept. Includes: research assistants, medical aides, child support workers, policy auxiliary, welfare service aides, recreation assistants, homemakers' aides, home health aides, library assistants and clerks, ambulance drivers and attendants, and kindred workers.

f. ***Administrative Support*** *(including clerical and sales):* Occupations in which workers are responsible for internal and external communication, recording and retrieval of data and/or information and other paperwork required in an office. Includes: bookkeepers, messengers, clerk-typists, stenographers, court transcribers, hearing reporters, statistical clerks, dispatchers, license distributors, payroll clerks, office machine and computer operators, telephone operators, legal assistants, sales workers, cashiers, toll collectors, and kindred workers.

g. ***Skilled Craft Workers:*** Occupations in which workers perform jobs that require special manual skill and a thorough and comprehensive knowledge of the process involved in the work, which is acquired through on-the-job training and experience or through apprenticeship or other formal training programs. Includes: mechanics and repairers, electricians, heavy equipment operators, stationary engineers, skilled machining occupations, carpenters, compositors and typesetters, power plant operators, water and sewage treatment plant operators, and kindred workers.

h. ***Service-Maintenance:*** Occupations in which workers perform duties that result in or contribute to the comfort, convenience, hygiene, or safety of the general public or that contribute to the upkeep and care of buildings, facilities, or grounds of public property. Workers in this group may operate machinery. Includes: chauffeurs, laundry and dry cleaning operatives, truck drivers, bus drivers, garage laborers, custodial employees, gardeners and groundskeepers, refuse collectors, construction laborers, park rangers (maintenance), farm workers (except managers), craft apprentices/trainees/helpers, and kindred workers.

Source: U.S. EEOC, 2003 EEOC Form 164, State and Local Government Information (EEO-4) Instruction Booklet, http://www.eeoc.gov/employers/eeo4survey/e4instruct.cfm.

Table 5.3

Percentage of Women Among All Full-Time (FT) and New Hires (NH) in States, Counties, Cities, Townships, and Special Districts, 2009

	All employees	Women (All)		State		County		City		Township		Special district	
		FT	NH	FT	NH	FT	NH	FT	NH	FT	NH	FT	NH
Officials and administrators	382,627	40	42	44	45	47	44	29	34	34	40	39	49
Professionals	1,593,351	58	64	59	63	63	67	44	57	40	57	67	70
Technicians	474,191	43	53	49	58	48	55	27	37	18	26	59	67
Protective services workers	1,237,028	19	25	24	34	23	25	14	17	8	9	16	21
Paraprofessionals	388,506	73	70	72	69	77	75	62	59	66	63	79	81
Administrative support	898,422	86	80	86	83	88	82	85	74	87	73	82	84
Skilled craft workers	430,041	5	9	6	7	6	12	4	7	2	1	7	14
Service-maintenance	576,139	25	34	37	45	29	32	13	29	6	21	30	37

Percent women

Source: U.S. EEOC (2009).
Note: 13,367 reporting units.

in the administrative support categories, but much different in the case of professionals. While women make up 59 percent of professionals in state agencies and 63 percent of professionals in county agencies, they make up only 44 percent of city professionals and 40 percent of township professionals.

Table 5.3 also shows that women are underrepresented in top management positions such as officials and administrators. Women represent 44 percent, 47 percent, 29 percent, 34 percent, and 39 percent of current full-time officials and administrators in state, county, city, township, and special districts, respectively. Women consistently represent less than 7 percent of skilled craft workers and less than 25 percent of protective services workers in these agencies. Women seemed to have broken the barriers in the technician category in state and county agencies, where women represent 49 percent and 48 percent, respectively, of technicians in these reporting agencies. However, they still lag behind in cities and townships where 27 percent and 18 percent, respectively, of technicians are women.

One of researchers' main arguments in the area of occupational segregation is that although the historical trends tend to leave women overrepresented in some fields and underrepresented in others, data on new hires should reflect a more even distribution across the different categories and across the different levels of government. Table 5.3 shows that in state and local jurisdictions, women were hired at a higher rate in categories where they were historically underrepresented (officials and administrators, professionals, technicians, protective services workers, skilled craft workers, and service-maintenance workers) and they were hired at a slower pace in categories where women were historically segregated (paraprofessionals and administrative support categories). This is a positive development that suggests, to some extent, new hiring patterns are likely to make modest improvements in the overall gender composition of the workforce in the state and local jurisdictions.

The segregation of women into clerical positions is something that also happens at the federal level. Women hold almost 70 percent of all clerical positions, and 45 percent of all professional and administrator/ official positions. Figure 5.8 reflects that distribution.

In the private sector, of the 241,356 reported organizations, with nearly 50 million employees, women were in parity with men in the professional and technician categories. Women slightly outnumbered men in the sales

Figure 5.8   **Percent of Women in Federal Civil Service**

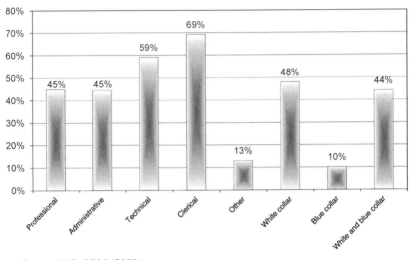

Source: U.S. OPM (2009).

Table 5.4

Occupational Segregation in the Private Sector

Occupational class	Percent	Percent	Percent male	Percent female
Professional	9,116,675	19	46	54
Technology	2,795,481	6	50	50
Sales	5,392,792	11	45	55
Clericals	6,439,391	14	23	77
Craft	2,899,017	6	92	8
Operational	4,936,510	10	75	25
Laborers	3,550,338	7	67	33
Service	7,182,027	15	41	59
Total	47,466,290	100	52	48

Source: U.S. EEOC (2009).

and service categories. Women, however, were more concentrated in clerical positions where 77 percent of employees were women, underrepresented in craft (8 percent women), operational (25 percent women), and laborer (33 percent women) categories (Table 5.4).

There is a great deal of variance in how women are represented in one category—say administrators and officials—in different agency types.

In regulatory and distributive agencies the percentage of women in the official and administrator category can be as low as 7 percent; whereas in redistributive agencies women's representation in the same category ranges from 49 percent to 66 percent. Table 5.5 presents a different picture that intersects occupational segregation with agency segregation. Data for new hires do not reveal the same optimism as above. For the most part, there is not a consistent promise in the new hire data to suggest that things are improving across the board. Representation is improving in some cases, and in other cases, new hires are reinforcing segregation.

Underrepresentation of Women in Science and
Engineering Fields and Their Segregation in
Caring Fields

In the federal government female scientists and engineers make up 27 percent of all scientists and engineers. Women make up 20 percent of the scientists and engineers in the federal senior executive service, while they make up 27 percent of the scientists and engineers in non-SES ranks. Table 5.6 represents the distribution of women and male scientists in the federal civil service.

The issue of the intersection of occupational segregation and position-level segregation is an important one. Women in female-dominated occupations also tend not to be in positions of authority at the same rate as men, even after controlling for human capital variables (Huffman, 1995; Huffman and Cohen, 2004; Kraus and Yonay, 2000). Huffman (1995) labels this phenomenon as *occupational-level gender composition*. The fact that women scientists and engineers are more prevalent in nonsenior executive service positions (27 percent) than in SES positions (20 percent), as shown in Table 5.6, is consistent with this occupational-level segregation.

Women also continue to be underrepresented in fields such as criminal investigators and law enforcement in general, but that pattern is changing. In a study that tracked the progress of women between 1980–1982 and 1990–1992, the percentage of women in the criminal investigator category nearly doubled in that decade in four major law enforcement agencies. Figure 5.9 shows the distribution of women in that field in the four agencies.

Table 5.7 confirms what research has consistently reported about

Table 5.5

Percentage of Women Among All Full-Time (FT) and New Hires (NH) in States, Counties, Cities, Townships, and Special Districts, 2009

| | All employees | Distributive agencies | | | | | |
| | | Streets and highways | | Utilities and transportation | | Sanitation and sewage | |
		FT	NH	FT	NH	FT	NH
Male dominated							
Officials and administrators	40	21	22	22	29	18	28
Technicians	43	18	17	20	22	20	28
Protective services worker	19	15	11	20	19	21	23
Skilled craft workers	5	4	6	5	4	4	4
Service-maintenance	25	8	9	22	21	7	8
Female dominated							
Paraprofessionals	73	57	42	54	57	50	55
Administrative support	86	77	69	70	68	80	71
Neutral							
Professionals	58	28	31	36	37	34	34

Regulatory agencies

	Police protection		Fire protection		Corrections		Natural resources	
	FT	NH	FT	NH	FT	NH	FT	NH
Male dominated								
Officials and administrators	23	24	7	4	38	41	30	34
Technicians	35	60	17	24	53	66	28	37
Protective services worker	17	19	4	5	27	33	12	19
Skilled craft workers	8	9	7	6	8	8	6	17
Service-maintenance	33	34	7	5	37	42	23	51
Female dominated								
Paraprofessionals	67	47	32	23	50	47	55	54
Administrative support	85	69	78	72	89	85	85	78
Neutral								
Professionals	39	52	9	26	52	58	39	45

Redistributive agencies

	Hospitals and sanatoriums		Health		Employment security		Public welfare	
	FT	NH	FT	NH	FT	NH	FT	NH
Male dominated								
Officials and administrators	66	60	60	59	49	46	66	64
Technicians	74	76	66	68	49	53	76	75
Protective services worker	26	27	34	40	15	54	68	71
Skilled craft workers	21	42	17	25	11	5	24	26
Service-maintenance	64	65	58	53	49	50	55	62
Female dominated								
Paraprofessionals	78	79	78	75	78	73	83	81
Administrative support	90	88	92	88	85	74	89	87
Neutral								
Professionals	78	76	72	76	62	62	77	78

Source: U.S. EEOC (2009).

Table 5.6

Federal Scientists and Engineers, by SES Status and Gender, 2009

Gender	All scientists and engineers		Senior executive service (SES)		Non-SES	
	No.	%	No.	%	No.	%
Both sexes	235,110	100%	1,483	100%	233,627	100%
Female	64,107	27%	292	20%	63,815	27%
Male	171,003	73%	1,191	80%	169,812	73%

Source: National Science Foundation/Division of Science Resources Statistics, tabulations from data provided by the Office of Personnel Management.

Table 5.7

Federal Scientists and Engineers, by Agency and Gender, 2009

All agencies	All	Females	% Female
Female, all agencies	235,110	64,107	27
Department of Defense	102,195	20,080	20
Department of Transportation	6,486	1,307	20
Nuclear Regulatory Commission	2,463	488	20
Department of Energy	4,817	1,071	22
National Aeronautics and Space Administration	11,494	2,554	22
General Services Administration	784	185	24
Department of Agriculture	20,104	6,128	30
Department of Commerce	11,769	3,505	30
Department of the Interior	14,672	4,409	30
Department of Homeland Security	4,819	1,509	31
Department of the Treasury	4,321	1,522	35
Department of Housing and Urban Development	268	97	36
Environmental Protection Agency	9,918	4,011	40
National Science Foundation	550	221	40
Department of Veterans Affairs	10,600	4,356	41
Social Security Administration	2,409	1,020	42
Department of Health and Human Services	12,557	5,652	45
Department of Justice	6,650	3,032	46
Department of Education	359	169	47
All other agencies	7,875	2,791	35

Source: National Science Foundation/Division of Science Resources Statistics, tabulations from data provided by the Office of Personnel Management.

Figure 5.9   **Percentage of Women Criminal Investigators in Four Law Enforcement Agencies and in the Entire Civil Service**

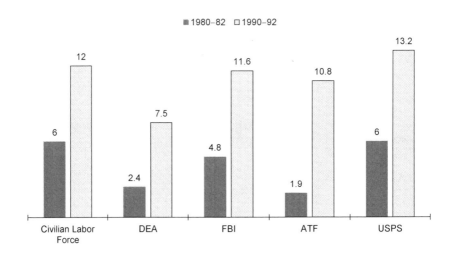

Source: U.S. GAO (1995).

the intersection of occupational and agency segregation. Women in redistributive agencies, which tend to be female-dominated, are almost as likely to occupy science and engineering jobs as men. In the Department of Veterans Affairs, Social Security Administration, Department of Health and Human Services, and Department of Education, women make up 41–47 percent of all the scientists and engineers. In distributive and regulatory agencies, where women were historically underrepresented, women constitute as little as one-fifth of the scientists and engineers. In the Department of Defense, Department of Transportation, the Nuclear Regulatory Commission, the Department of Energy, and the National Aeronautics and Space Administration, women make up 20–22 percent of all scientists and engineers.

Women, however, are not underrepresented in all science fields. It seems that the "softer" the science, the more likely it is that women would be well represented. Table 5.8 shows that women make up 46 percent of all social scientists in the federal government, while they make up only 26 percent of all physical scientists and 15 percent of

Table 5.8

Federal Scientists and Engineers, by Occupation and Gender, 2009

	All scientists and engineers	All scientists	Computer and mathematical scientists	Life scientists	Physical scientists	Social scientists	Engineers
Male and Female, no.	235,110	142,243	49,650	39,534	24,399	28,720	92,876
Female, no.	64,107	50,324	16,223	14,512	6,427	13,163	13,782
%	(27)	(35)	(33)	(37)	(26)	(46)	(15)

Source: National Science Foundation/Division of Science Resources Statistics, tabulations from data provided by the Office of Personnel Management.

engineers. These statistics show how gender typing remains relevant in today's workforce.

However, the situation is getting better in the federal government. As Table 5.9 shows, the proportion of women in the public sector increased from 21.2 percent in 2000 to 27.2 percent in 2009. Many programs, especially through the National Science Foundation, aim to improve the representation of women in fields of science, engineering, and mathematics.

What if women have chosen to be in these occupations where they are concentrated? Employers would argue that they should not be blamed for women's deliberate choice of occupations. If women voluntarily choose to work in caring fields and occupations, then organizations should not be blamed for these choices. Gender theorists, however, argue that the "segregation" of women into occupations traditionally defined as "women's work," such as providing health care and other services for children and the poor, is not entirely independent of historic gender discrimination (Adler, 1993; Maume, 1999; Newman, 1994). Girls tend to be socialized into these caring positions; by the time they are ready to choose an occupation, their choice set has been limited (Heilman et al., 2004; Stivers, 1993). Do women continue to be segregated in female-dominated occupations? Most researchers point to evidence of the persistence of occupational segregation (Escriche, 2007; Kmec, 2005; Kmec and Gorman, 2010; Orazem and Mattila, 1998).

As shown above, female federal employees who are willing to venture into male-dominated occupations such as science and engineering are more likely to end up in female-dominated agencies. This might be a factor of choice where women choose an agency in which they perceive more support (Taylor, 2010). It could also be a matter of discrimination, where leaders and human resources recruiters in male-dominated occupations are indeed making an effort to keep the organizations that way. That is a tough question to answer without looking at each situation independently. We propose to look at applicants versus job offers. If women are not applying for these positions, then it is difficult to blame the agency for anything other than poor outreach practices. However, if enough qualified women are in the applicant pool, but are not being hired, then there is a reason to question the hiring practices of these agencies. We suspect that there is a "pool" issue in some cases, but there is also a discrimination issue in others.

Table 5.9

Federal Scientists and Engineers, by Gender, 2000–2009

Year	All federal scientists and engineers (number)	Female (%)	Male (%)
2000	187,396	21.2	78.8
2001	193,448	22.0	78.0
2002	206,182	22.9	77.1
2003[a]	206,620	23.9	76.1
2004[a]	209,994	24.5	75.5
2005[a]	209,747	24.9	75.1
2006	215,929	25.7	74.3
2007	219,383	26.2	73.8
2008	223,189	26.8	73.2
2009	235,110	27.2	72.8

Sources: National Science Foundation/Division of Science Resources Statistics, tabulations from data provided by the Office of Personnel Management; Defense Manpower Data Center for Department of Defense agencies, 2003; Central Personnel Data File (CPDF) of the Office of Personnel Management, 2005.

Notes: Percentages may not add to 100 percent due to rounding. Total includes unknown sex not shown separately.

[a] Data for 2003 to 2005 may not be strictly comparable to data for other years.

Barriers, Challenges, and Opportunities

As mentioned throughout this chapter, it is difficult to pinpoint one reason behind the segregation of women in certain agencies, fields, and position levels. Many reasons may be commissioned to explain the segregation of women. Discrimination is one of these reasons. In our political culture we refer to the barriers as glass walls or glass ceilings. Putting the first crack into these ceilings and walls is perhaps as much of a barrier to a more even representation of women in the workforce as the discrimination that prevents women from ascending to the top of organizations, or to be in certain agencies and occupations. This barrier varies, and it would be unfair to argue that discrimination underlies every segregation problem everywhere. But discrimination—overt discrimination, institutional discrimination, or implicit bias—is probably a major barrier to women's equal representation.

Some of the most compelling challenges facing an even representation of women in organizations are sociocultural in nature. First, there is a challenge of getting women interested in nonfemale-oriented occupations. Employers complain about the so-called pool factor—meaning that if fewer women are in the applicant pool, then even fewer of them would make it into these open positions. The solution to this pool problem is to change the perception of education and employment fields. How do we let girls think about jobs our society reserves for boys only? A second compelling challenge is the fact that women are often driven into lower-echelon positions after reentry into the workforce after a maternity event. Women who leave their careers to have babies reeenter the workforce at lower levels. This is very problematic, but could be improved by a more decent form of maternity/paternity leave system.

The third challenge facing parity in representation of women in all agencies, occupations, and levels is the lag time. No one expects women to be elevated into positions that men are forced to leave. This has to occur naturally. As men leave positions of power, women can be hired or elevated to these positions. Women would rather compete for positions that are vacant because men received another job, retired, or passed away. Given the size of the public sector, it will take several decades to change the composition in a system that is so large. However, this challenge gives rise to the foremost opportunity to correct this imbalance.

The public sector today faces a great opportunity to capitalize on the many retirements that are scheduled to occur over the next decade in order to correct the imbalance in representation across government's many levels, agencies, and occupations. The public sector, at the federal, state, and local levels, has an aging workforce—more so than the private sector. Of all federal, state, and local government employees, 38.9 percent, 34.2 percent, and 36.1 percent, respectively, are scheduled to retire within 15 years. Another 30 percent, 26 percent, and 27 percent are scheduled to retire within the following 10 years. If women are given an equal opportunity to be admitted into these positions, this should become a serious opportunity to alter the misrepresentation or segregation of women in all agencies, position levels, and occupations across all levels of government.

Key Terms

Agency segregation
Caring fields
Distributive agency
Federal Equal Opportunity
  Recruitment Program
  (FEORP)
Female-dominated fields
Field segregation
Gender images
General Schedule
Human capital

Male-dominated fields
Masculine images
New hires
Occupational categories
Occupational-level gender
  composition
Occupational segregation
Position segregation
Redistributive agency
Regulatory agency
Senior executive service

6

Equal Pay

What does pay equity mean? Pay equity is essentially about paying people equally for equivalent work, regardless of demographic traits such as gender, race, ethnicity, national origin, or age. Equal work does not mean the same work—rather, it means work of equal value. Two jobs have equal value if they require the same type of skills, have similar responsibilities, require the same amount of effort on the job, and have similar working conditions. They do not have to be in the same field, and they do not need to be in the same classification system. In the context of gender, one could then compare the value of the work done by a social worker—a field dominated by women and historically paid less than other fields—to the value of the work done by an engineer—a field dominated by men. If the two jobs have similar conditions, require the same type of skills, have similar responsibilities, have similar work conditions, and require similar academic qualifications and certifications, then one could reasonably compare a social worker's pay to an engineer's pay.

Do men earn more money than women? In 2009, on average, women earned 80 percent of what men earned. The pay gap has narrowed since 1979, when it was 62 percent (U.S. Department of Commerce, 2011). This percentage varies significantly across the United States—it is as high as 89 percent in the District of Columbia and as low as 66 percent in Wyoming and Louisiana. According to projections by the Institute for Women's Policy Research (IWPR) (Hayes, 2011), women will not achieve the same earnings as men until 2056—nearly a century after the removal of discriminatory laws related to employment conditions and pay.

The U.S. Bureau of Labor Statistics (2011) reports data from the Current Population Survey of Households and Individuals on a quarterly basis. In the first quarter of 2011, the average median weekly earnings were $749—the median female earnings were $683 weekly, which is

82.4 percent of the median men's earnings of $829. Hispanic and African American women, on average, earn 90.4 percent and 95 percent of their respective male counterparts, while white and Asian women earn 81.7 percent and 90.4 percent of their respective male counterparts.

An often-made comparison of American data is that to the members of the Organization for Economic Cooperation and Development (OECD), originated in the Marshall Plan more than 50 years ago. The OECD works with governments to "improve the economic and social well-being of people around the world" (OECD, 2011a). The OECD has expanded from the original 20 country members to 34 member countries. Of OECD member countries, the gender pay gap ranges from as low as 1.3 percent in Italy to 38.8 percent in Korea, with an average pay gap of 16 percent. The U.S gender pay gap falls below the average, at 20.1 percent (see Figure 6.1), placing the United States eighteenth out of twenty-six countries in gender gap (OECD, 2011b).

There is no question that women have historically been, and continue to be, paid less than men. This historic inequity is not specific to the private or the public sector. It spans different fields and sectors of employment. Yet, when one states this fact, one or more of the following responses are often heard:

- But, "things are getting better"
- But, women have not been in the workforce long enough
- But, women have less education than men
- But, women have babies and that means:
  - time-off work (reentry into the workforce)
  - unpaid family leave
  - less ability to work overtime
  - more likely to work part-time
  - and more important, less ability to get promoted into higher-level positions
- But, women tend to work in occupations that do not pay as well
- But, women tend to occupy lower positions that pay less

While the above reasons may be valid in some cases, they ultimately fail to justify the totality of pay inequity. The authors of this book regard these reasons themselves as issues that need to be strategically addressed to reduce pay inequity. Data show that things are getting better. However, the pace of this improvement, particularly in recent years, is

Figure 6.1   **Gender Gap in Median Earnings of Full-Time Employees, 2008**

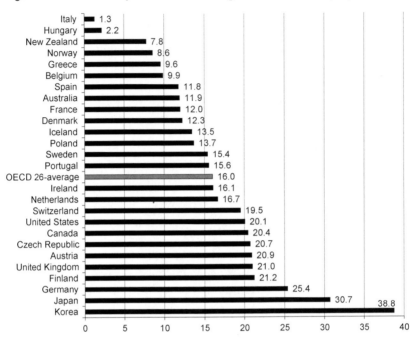

Source: OECD Employment Outlook (2010).

inadequate in the area of *pay equity* as much as it is inadequate in the area of representation (discussed in the previous chapter). Pay parity is not expected until 2056 (Hegewisch, Williams and Zhang, 2011). Is 2056 an acceptable date for parity to be achieved? This might seem to be a very normative question, but it is fundamentally a very political one, involving policymakers and administrators alike.

The reasons given for pay inequity are also worth some analysis. It might be fair for people working at lower levels to get paid less, but one has to question why women end up in these positions, particularly as more women than men are graduating from colleges and universities. Is it fair that a social worker or teacher (female-dominated fields) gets paid less than an engineer or a data analyst (male-dominated fields), even though the teacher or social worker spent more time in college to prepare for these positions? Is it fair for women to suffer a greater burden from childbearing and childrearing? However, how can we explain the fact that women earn less than men within ten years of working after graduating from college (American Association of University Women [AAUW], 2012)? We also question the assumption that women have less experience and/or less education. There is no reason for women today to be concentrated in female-dominated, lower-level positions. In other words, while the above are ways to explain the pay gap between men and women, these explanations need to be examined closely to ensure that they are not driven by discrimination. The bottom line is that pay inequity results from many factors that will be investigated in this chapter.

Nature of Work and Pay

Historically, women assumed jobs in "caring" fields while men assumed jobs in bureaus and fields with less "caring" requirements. This segregation is largely blamed on sociocultural images. Women are perceived as caring, they are given caring jobs, and caring jobs tend to pay less. This leads to women earning less on average than men. The sociocultural bases of the segregation of women in caring fields cannot be ignored. While there are other reasons, the sociocultural images of women have contributed substantially to the segregation of women in lower-paying, caring positions and agencies. The *gender-typing* of women into positions with caring responsibilities has been the subject of much scholarly writing.

Mary Wollstonecraft (1787) traces the role of women from the days when productive work was shared between the two sexes, to the days when middle-class women traded in their liberty and virtue for the prestige, pleasure, and power provided by their husbands. Wollstonecraft argues that women's social and political conditions were both socially constructed and biologically inherent. In her critique of Jean-Jacques Rousseau, Wollstonecraft suggests that Sophie (representing Rousseau's female student) should receive the same education as Emile (Rousseau's male student). Instead of training Sophie to be caring and sensitive and Emile to be sensible, Wollstonecraft suggests that Sophie needed to make sensible decisions when raising her future children (Tong, 2008). In the *Enfranchisement of Women, Harriet Taylor-Mill* (1851) also argues against the social construction of inequality. She affirms that women's biggest enemy was not human nature, but rather traditions and norms. She calls for equal education, economic partnership, and political rights for women. She argues that women should earn an income outside their homes in order for them to be considered as partners in their relationships.

In the twentieth century, *Betty Friedan* (1963) frames her book, *The Feminine Mystique*, by arguing that the subjugation of women in society has split it into two classes: the powerful sex, or males, and the powerless sex, or females. *The Feminine Mystique* is a product of women's domestic environment and her involvement within the home and little outside it. The solution to dealing with this mystique is for women to get involved outside the home. A woman's moral and normal priority is her marriage and motherhood first, and her profession and career second. In doing this, Friedan seems to have addressed the experience of the bourgeoisie women who were still suffering from the social syndrome described originally by Wollstonecraft.

In the world of public service literature, *Camilla Stivers* (2000), in *Bureau Men, Settlement Women*, shows how at the turn of the century men have historically approached public reform in a scientific way, while women approached the same problems with a concern for vulnerable poor citizens. Women were more interested in carnage from administrative actions than men. The backdrop to this story is that women were historically relegated to caring "settlement"-like functions while men were given "bureau"-like positions. The dominance of women and men in gendered occupations is largely explained by this history of segregation.

In *Gender Images in Public Administration: Legitimacy and the Administrative State*, Stivers (1993) also reaches into the deeply rooted reasons behind the segregation of women into female fields and position levels and men in male fields and position levels. At the heart of this segregation is an irreconcilable clash of images between societal images of gender roles and societal and professional images of leadership. The socially constructed masculine images of leadership make it much more difficult for women, who are viewed as feminine, to shatter the glass ceilings and walls that keep them in lower-echelon positions and occupations, respectively. Images of expertise, leadership, and virtue have historically been associated with masculine features that "help keep in place or bestow political and economic privilege on the bearers of culturally masculine qualities at the expense of those who display culturally feminine ones" (Stivers, 1993, p. 4). According to Stivers, this masculinity "contributes to, and is sustained by, power relations in society at large that distribute resources on the basis of gender and affect people's life chances and their sense of themselves and their place in the world" (p. 4).

In *Emotional Labor: Putting the Service in Public Service*, Guy, Newman, and Mastracci (2008) compare types of work performed in an Office of the Public Guardian and a Department of Corrections: *emotional labor* compared to cognitive labor. Based on their comparisons, they contend that emotional work tends to be performed by women. Emotional work requires person-to-person transactions (e.g., customer service), rather than person-to-object work. They explain that performing emotional work requires the employees to actively engage with the entire job and the agency's mission. As a result, the authors suggest a new paradigm in how work is defined from (a) *task-in-job related work*—which separates the individual from her/his skills and cognitive abilities used to perform the job tasks, to (b) *person-in-job related work*—which maintains that the individual is connected to the job tasks by bringing "dignity, courage, maturity, respect for citizens" in how the employee interacts with the citizen. More specifically, in emotional work, the employee "must intuit the other's state of mind and make split-second adjustments in words, tone, or body language" (p. 187). Emotional work, therefore, requires managers to give more autonomy to the employee, as a manager cannot control an employee's perceptions and responses within a person-to-person transaction.

Gender-typing contributes to the segregation of women in certain fields, occupations, and agencies. This segregation is driven not by biological or intellectual limitations, but by sociological ones. The fundamental question in this chapter on equal pay is: "What do gender images have to do with pay equity?" The answer is that historically, female-dominated caring fields offered lower wages than male-dominated bureau fields. Women in these positions are usually as qualified as men in bureau positions, and they usually have equivalent, if not more demanding requirements in their positions. Yet, women are paid less. There is hardly a reasonable explanation for a bus driver earning more than a social worker in some cases, or an engineer earning substantially more than what a social worker earns. But there is evidence that emotional work continues to be less well-compensated in both the private and the public sectors. Men tend to earn more than women in the same occupation, but they earn even more in male-dominated occupations compared to female-dominated occupations.

New management concepts emphasize participatory and caring management skills. Such management skills include the involvement of subordinates in the decision-making process. Participatory management, caring, or emotional work skills were historically associated with women, but have now become mainstream theories. Assertive skills, which were often associated with masculine images, are now largely considered a form of bull-headedness that often results in wrong decisions and poor morale. Can we then say that new management reforms are moving the dominant management practice from what traditionally was known as a male style of leading to what traditionally was associated with women's way of leading?

Occupational, Agency, and Position-Level Segregations

In chapter 5, we discussed the chronic problem of segregation of women into female-dominated occupations, agencies, and position levels. The least complicated of these segregations, but the toughest to remedy through workforce policies, is the impact of position-level segregation on pay. Employees working in lower levels earn less than those working at higher levels. Higher-level positions require more education, more skills, and more experience than ones at lower levels. Therefore, it would make sense that these positions offer higher pay. What makes less sense is the fact that women are segregated in these lower positions while they are underrepresented in higher positions.

The General Schedule (GS) is a personnel classification system used by the federal government for nonexecutive-level personnel. There are fifteen GS classifications, and pay within each follows a step system. In 2011, the starting salary of employees entering at the lowest GS level in the federal government was $17,803 while that of employees entering at the GS-15 level was $99,628 (see Figure 6.2). This means that entry at the top of the General Schedule pays 5.6 times more than entry at the lower levels. If more women were entering and/or staying at lower levels, then this would explain the overall pay gap. Figures 6.2 and 6.3 tell the story. Women outnumber men at ranks lower than GS 10/11, which is where men start outnumbering women. Only 32 percent of members of the Senior Executive Service at the federal level are women. In years of teaching, our experience is that Figure 6.3 shows the most powerful picture of the segregation of women in lower-echelon positions in the federal public sector.

Female-dominated occupational categories tend to pay less than the male-dominated technician and officials/administrators category. To demonstrate this point, we looked at all 18,833 employees in the state of West Virginia. The average pay for all state employees in West Virginia in 2008 was $30,072. The average for the administrative sup-

Figure 6.2   **Federal Salary Table 2011, Annual Rates by Step and GS Grade**

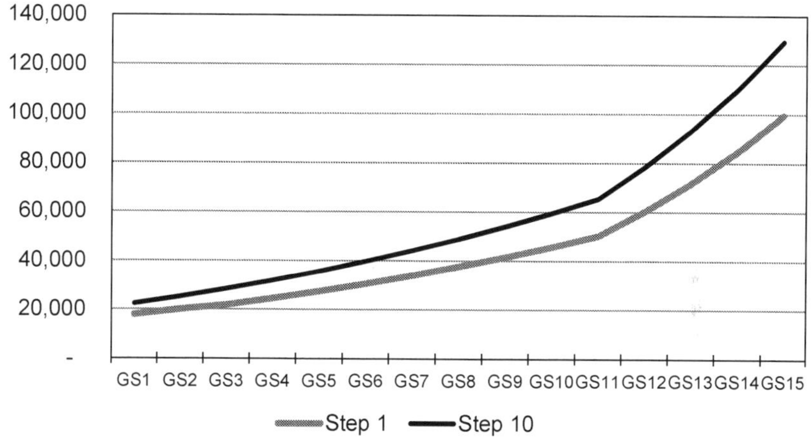

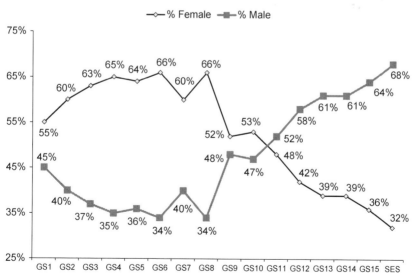

Source: Office of Personnel Management (2011). Salaries and Wages: Salary Table 2011-GS. Washington, D.C. http://www.opm.gov/policy-data-oversight/pay-leave/salaries-wages/2011/general-schedule/2011-gs-annual-rates-by-grade-and-step/.

Figure 6.3   **Representation of Men and Women in GS and SES Levels, 2010**

Source: Data from the U.S. Office of Personnel Management, Office of Planning and Policy Analysis, 5/13/2011.

Figure 6.4 **Do Female-Dominated Occupational Categories Pay Less?
West Virginia State Government, 2008 (18,833 Employees)**

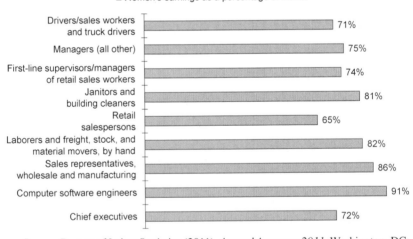

Source: Alkadry and Tower (2013).

Figure 6.5 **Women's Earnings in 10 Most Common Occupations for Men**

Source: Bureau of Labor Statistics (2011). *Annual Averages 2011.* Washington, DC: U.S. Bureau of Labor Statistics, Department of Labor.

port category, which is 86 percent women, was $24,894 or 83 percent of the average. The average for the paraprofessionals category, which is 79 percent women, was $27,189 or 90 percent of the average. The average for the officials/administrators category, which is 41 percent

Figure 6.6   **Women's Earnings in 10 Most Common Occupations for Women**

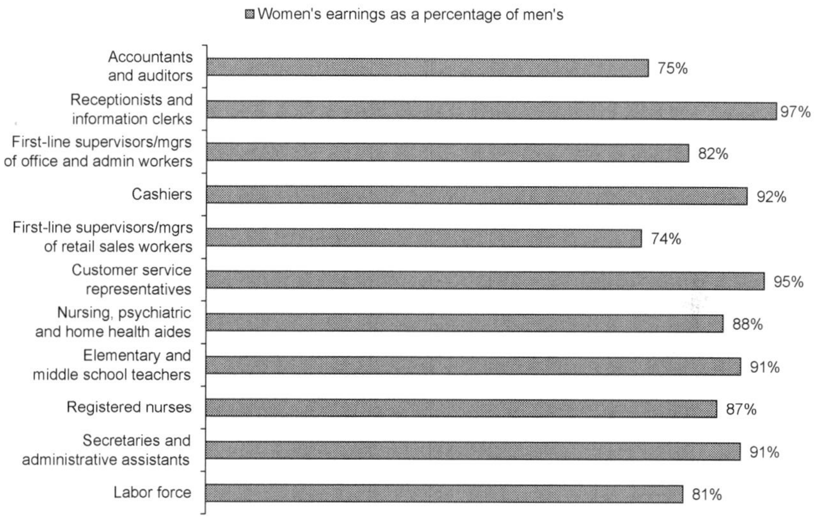

☒ Women's earnings as a percentage of men's

Occupation	Percentage
Accountants and auditors	75%
Receptionists and information clerks	97%
First-line supervisors/mgrs of office and admin workers	82%
Cashiers	92%
First-line supervisors/mgrs of retail sales workers	74%
Customer service representatives	95%
Nursing, psychiatric and home health aides	88%
Elementary and middle school teachers	91%
Registered nurses	87%
Secretaries and administrative assistants	91%
Labor force	81%

Source: Bureau of Labor Statistics (2011). *Annual Averages 2011.* Washington, DC: U.S. Bureau of Labor Statistics, Department of Labor.

women, and the average for the technicians category, which is only 30 percent women, was 171 percent and 114 percent of the overall average, respectively (see Figure 6.4). There are some exceptions to this rule, particularly among service/maintenance workers, who were only 76 percent of the overall salary average and among protective services workers who were only 93 percent of the overall average salary. Certain occupational categories tend to pay more than others, and if women are concentrated in lower-paying occupational categories, then they might be at a pay disadvantage.

The effect of occupational segregation on the gender pay gap is as clear in the private sector as it is in the public sector. In the first quarter of 2011, the U.S. Bureau of Labor Statistics (2011) reported that the highest median earnings were among people working full-time in management, professional, and related occupations (see Figures 6.5 and 6.6). The median weekly salary was $1,266 for men and $939 for women. In service occupations, the median weekly salary was $565 for men and $431 for women. In sales and office occupations (62 percent women), the median salary for men was $736 while it was $607 for women. In natural resources, construction, and maintenance occupations (4.5 percent women), the median weekly salary of men was $743

Table 6.1

Men's and Women's Earnings in the Most Common Occupations for Women and Men

	Men's median weekly earnings	Women's median weekly earnings	Women's earnings as a percentage of men's	Percentage of women in occupation
Labor force	$824	$669	81.2	45
Ten most common occupations for women				
Secretaries and administrative assistants	$725	$657	91	96
Registered nurses	$1,201	$1,039	87	91
Elementary and middle school teachers	$1,024	$931	91	81
Nursing, psychiatric and home health aides	$488	$427	88	87
Customer service representatives	$614	$586	95	66
First-line supervisors/managers of retail sales workers	$782	$578	74	46
Cashiers	$400	$366	92	72
First-line supervisors/managers of office and administrative workers	$890	$726	82	67
Receptionists and information clerks	$547	$529	97	93
Accountants and auditors	$1,273	$953	75	59
Average	$794	$679	85	
Ten most common occupations for men				
Drivers/sales workers and truck drivers	$691	$492	71	3
Managers, all other	$1,395	$1,045	75	37
First-line supervisors/managers of retail sales workers	$782	$578	74	46
Janitors and building cleaners	$494	$400	81	29
Retail salespersons	$651	$421	65	42
Laborers and freight, stock, and material movers, by hand	$508	$419	82	16
Construction laborers	$569	*	*	2
Sales representatives, wholesale and manufacturing	$983	$842	86	24
Computer software engineers	$1,590	$1,445	91	21
Chief executives	$2,217	$1,598	72	26
Average	$988	$804	81	

Source: Hayes (2011); *Earnings data are made available only where an occupation has an estimated minimum of 50,000 workers.

compared to $446 for women. In production, transportation, and material moving (18.5 percent women) occupations the median weekly salaries were $653 for men and $491 for women. These figures reflect variance not only across Equal Employment Opportunity Commission (EEOC) occupational categories but also across gender lines within EEOC occupational categories.

In 2010, the U.S. Bureau of Labor Statistics collected information from 111 occupations and found that women earned more than men in only four of those occupations (see Table 6.1). Women tend to work in female-dominated occupations, such as nursing and social work, which tend to pay less on average than male-dominated occupations. To make things even worse, even in the female-dominated occupations, women earned less than men (Hayes, 2011).

Part-Time vs. Full-Time Work

There are two fundamental questions to be asked here, do more women than men work part-time? How does part-time employment affect pay? In the United States, women are more likely to work part-time than men. In 2009, 24 percent of employed women worked part-time while only 11 percent of men worked part-time (U.S. Department of Commerce, 2011). If more women are working part-time (they are), and if part-time work is compensated at lower rates (it is), then women have yet another pay disadvantage.

Women are more likely to be employed in part-time positions than in full-time positions. Table 6.2 shows that in government levels where men and women are equally represented (such as special districts) in the full-time workforce, women represent two-thirds of the part-time population in the same government level. Women are far more overrepresented in part-time employment than they are in full-time employment in state, county, city, township, and special district government administrations.

In the United States, the percentage of women working part-time has risen, even at times of economic prosperity. Between 2001 and 2009, the proportion of women working part-time increased by 1.6 percent. This is also a worldwide problem. With the exception of eleven countries reporting these figures, all other nations seemed to witness a rise in the percentage share of women's part-time employment rates during the same period.

It is important to note that part-time employment drives women's earnings down and provides them with lower job security and advancement

Table 6.2

Full-Time and Part-Time Employment in State and Local Jurisdictions

	State	County	City	Township	Special district
Reporting units	617	5,639	5,701	524	850
Total full-time male	1,056,057	735,986	1,085,495	63,051	290,419
%	(48)	(47)	(70)	(72)	(50)
Total full-time female	1,133,274	814,452	470,239	24,161	292,385
%	(52)	(53)	(30)	(28)	(50)
Total part-time male	103,409	136,429	218,459	31,448	42,434
%	(44)	(42)	(50)	(52)	(32)
Total part-time female	130,550	191,380	220,857	28,893	92,095
%	(56)	(58)	(50)	(48)	(68)

Source: U.S. EEOC (2009).

opportunities. Women work part-time for many reasons—but mostly as a consequence of family obligations. As discussed in this book, family obligations create an uneven burden for women compared to men, and that burden puts women in the tough position of choosing family over work obligations. Does part-time employment translate into lower pay for women? Yes. But, does it have to? No! As we will discuss in chapter 7, the association between part-time work and "bad" jobs is not inevitable. The European Union (EU) limits the normal workweek for full-time workers to between 35–39 hours per week, with a maximum of 48 hours per week. Moreover, the EU guarantees the equitable treatment of part-time workers (Webber and Williams, 2008).

Better working conditions and human resources-oriented family-friendly practices on one hand, and a fairer distribution of family responsibilities between partners living in the same household on the other could make it easier for women to hold full-time jobs and balance work and family.

Entry and Reentry: "The Mommy Track"

"Our organization is an equal opportunity employer" is a statement that decorates many institutional letterheads and job advertisements. For women, this means that the laws and policies governing the hiring of women are not discriminatory. It does not mean that the workplace is free of discrimination. It also does not mean that the workplace will be a family-friendly workplace. In fact, studies show that women who enter the workplace are often expected to show the same kind of dedication and commitment to work that men with stay-at-home wives once did in the past.

The issue is not quite as simple for women as it is for men. Women continue to bear a heavier burden of family responsibilities than men. Women rarely have the luxury of relying on a househusband to take care of family issues while they dedicate themselves to the workplace. When both men and women work, women tend to bear that bigger burden of caring for the family. The workplace is "greedy," in that even when it wants female employees, it wants them all to itself. Combined with family responsibilities, women often find themselves in the unenviable position of having to choose between compromising their family life or compromising their commitment to work.

The very important issue of social costs of career progression was discussed in chapter 4. The issue directly affects women's pay, particularly their propensity to end up in part-time jobs. The matter of choice here is a tricky one. While some women may prefer to work part-time while their children are young, it is likely that this choice is driven by the lack of any other option. Part-time employment is likely to be seen by women as a way to reconcile work and family at the expense of women's career future. In other words, it is likely that women are forced to make the only choice that they have.

In 2007, the Pew Research Center conducted 2,020 telephone interviews of a representative sample of women. This was a follow-up to another survey conducted in 1997. The survey in both years asked mothers who have children under the age of eighteen the question: "considering everything, what would be the ideal situation for you, working full-time, working part-time, or not working at all outside of the home?" Forty-eight percent of working mothers chose part-time work in 1997, while 60 percent chose the same thing in 2007. Twenty percent of working mothers preferred to stay at home in both years. When stay-at-home mothers were asked the very same question, 39 percent of them preferred not working at all in 1997, while 48 percent of them preferred not working in 2007. What is remarkable in these responses is that women seem to be less enthusiastic about the ability to balance work and family without compromising either.

While only 21 percent of working mothers believe that full-time employment is the ideal situation for them, 72 percent of working fathers had the same preference. In the same survey, working mothers who are employed full-time gave themselves lower parenting marks than those working part-time or not employed at all.

Human Capital Factors

A common response to pay inequity claims is that women have less experience and/or have less education. Experience and education are examples of human capital. *Human capital* is the term used to explain competencies and skills valued by the labor market. While claims of disparate human capital between men and women might have been true in the 1960s, this is no longer the case. Research has shown repeatedly that there remains little or no difference in human capital variables between men and women (Huffman and Cohen, 2004; Smith, 2002). Several studies across many fields of the public and private sectors show that even after controlling for education and experience, women continue to suffer a wage gap (Alkadry and Tower, 2006; Meier and Wilkins, 2002; Ng et al., 2005). Claiming human capital explanations for pay inequity is also questionable when women now make up the majority of college graduates as well as the students in graduate and professional programs. In fact, as data presented earlier in this book show, women surpassed men in four-year degree attainment in 1995 (35 percent of women held bachelor degrees compared to 27 percent of men). In the late 1990s, women also surpassed men in completing masters-level degrees—8.8 percent of women held masters-level degrees while only 6.1 percent of men did.

In this section of our discussion on pay equity, we explore the traditional lineup of factors that can affect one's salary—aside from issues of occupational, positional, and agency segregation. The main question is "what drives salaries?" rather than "what drives women's salaries?" Our strategy is to look at factors driving people's salaries, and then to look at research that has shown the effect of gender on salaries, after controlling for all these factors.

Over the years, researchers, including the authors of this book, have identified a number of factors that affect pay. These include industry type, organization type and size, years of experience, education, and authority level. Other variables relate to geographic factors such as labor market

Table 6.3

Pay Disparities in Different Procurement Positions

Position	Average male salary including bonuses	Average female salary including bonuses	Female salary as a percentage of male salary	Pay gap (significance)
Head of purchasing unit	$70,741	$61,164	86.5%	$9,577 (< 0.0005)
Managers and supervisors	$58,809	$51,323	87.3%	$7,486 (< 0.0005)
Buyers	$45,262	$39,474	87.2%	$5,788 (< 0.0005)
All classifications	$58,106	$47,712	82.1%	$10,394 (< 0.0005)

Source: Alkadry and Tower (2006).

competitiveness and cost of living. Some researchers have also linked race, gender, and age to pay. Alkadry and Tower (2006) conducted one of the recent studies on this subject of human capital and gender effects on salary. The study involved a survey of 1,600 public procurement professionals, and the data were analyzed for three occupational levels: directors, supervisors and managers, and buyers. In this study, Alkadry and Tower found that gender and human capital variables predicted 36.5–to 54 percent of variance in the pay of professionals in these three occupational levels (see Table 6.3).

Organization Type and Industry

Public-sector and nonprofit professionals tend to earn less than their private-sector counterparts. Organization type affects pay in the public (Leenders and Fearon, 1997) and private (Ogden, Zsidisin, and Hendrick, 2002) sectors. A manager in local government might be doing the same work that a manager in the federal government does, yet the pay of the federal manager might be much higher. Similarly, a financial officer in the service industry might well earn much less than a financial officer in a manufacturing organization. Same tasks can well mean different pay for jobs in different industries.

The size of the organization also matters. In the private sector, employees are paid more than they would be paid if they worked in the public sector. A survey of public and private procurement professionals shows that employees of larger organizations made about 11 percent more than those of smaller organizations (Engstrom et al., 2006). Others have also found a positive relationship between organization size and salaries of employees (Langer 2000; Santere and Thomas, 1993).

Years of Experience

It is somewhat reasonable and logical to assume that those with more work experience should earn more money. Ng et al. (2005) looked at the relationship between experience and salaries in 140 different studies and found that experience had a positive effect on salary. This is consistent with other research that found the relationship to be significant (Holzer, 1990). A handful of studies have found the relationship to be insignificant (e.g., Yeh, Suwanakul, and Lim, 1998). In their study Alkadry and Tower (2006) found experience to be statistically significant to directors, managers and supervisors, and buyers. Experience very much affects the ability of individuals to attain a job or a position, and generally affects the starting salary of individuals. If there is any step program for raises and promotions, as is typical in many public-sector administrations, then experience will also play a role in determining annual pay raises. However, absent a step-based personnel system and collective bargaining, experience seems to matter little for pay raises.

Collective Bargaining

Collective bargaining also tends to play a role in employee salaries. Organizations with active unions not only see better wages but also tend to have a smaller wage gap (Currie and McConnell, 1992; Kearney, 2003; Moore and Raisian, 1987; Rees, 1993). Collective bargaining agreements often favor experience and seniority of employees. Research has repeatedly shown that experience with one employer has a positive effect on salaries of public and private employees (Holzer, 1990; Ng et al., 2005). People who work longer in an organization become more familiar with the work processes and develop loyalty toward the organization (Trommer, 1995), and therefore, they are rewarded with better pay. This is obviously not always the case—some employees are given money as incentives to retire. This is a factor that is difficult to capture in the public sector, where money is not always used to define how employees and their work are valued.

Education and Pay

The cliché that "education pays" tends to hold true and is what motivates many people to pursue higher education. Research does not always support this seemingly logical assumption. Although much research shows that education and higher education are associated with increased pay (Engstrom et al., 2006; Fitzgerald, 1998; Morgan, 1997; Ng et al., 2005; Ramoni-Perazzi and Bellante, 2007), the consistent exception to that maxim is the pursuit of a doctorate. Often, earning a doctorate translates into less pay than earning a master's degree. In their study Alkadry and Tower (2006) found that education was statistically significant in explaining variance in pay of directors, managers, and buyers.

Authority Pays!

Employees who supervise others or have management responsibilities would normally earn more money than those without such responsibilities (Huffman and Cohen, 2004; Hopcroft, 1996; Wright, Baxter, and Birkelund, 1995). In their study of procurement chiefs, Ogden, Zsidisin, and Hendrick (2002, p. 36) report that "Chief purchasing officers with more than 100 employees reporting to them are 7.0 times more likely to have above average compensation levels. Chief purchasing officers with less than 50 people reporting to them are 6.2 times more likely to have below average compensation levels." The closer an individual is to the top of the organizational hierarchy, the more likely that he/she will earn more. If a director reports to the city manager directly, he/she will likely earn more money than if he/she reports to another person who in turn reports to the city manager. In their study Alkadry and Tower (2006) found that budget size and the number of people supervised was statistically significant in explaining variance in pay of directors, managers, and buyers in their study.

Age

Should age affect salary? In theory, age alone should not affect how much one earns, but it tends to affect the number of years of experience one has. It could also be a factor in educational attainment. One simply is not likely to have twenty years of experience if she is thirty years old. Likewise, one is not likely to have a masters degree if he is twenty years old. Age tends to correlate with more experience, more job tenure, and more educational and continuing education opportunities. Since age drives many factors that relate to pay, it is difficult for researchers to hone in on its true effect on pay. Therefore, while some research points to age as a factor contributing to pay, other research does not find that relationship between pay and age to be statistically significant. Alkadry and Tower (2006) found that age was not statistically significant in explaining variance in pay of directors, managers, and buyers, because they controlled for years of experience, educational attainment, and other covariates of age.

Merit and Cost of Living

An equitable merit pay system may also drive salary, with employees who earn higher merit scores receiving higher raises (Becker, 1999; Stewart et al., 1996). Likewise, cost of living also affects pay. The cost of living in some cities far exceeds that in others, and as a result, salaries tend to follow cost-of-living concerns (DuMond, Hirsch, and Macpherson, 1999; Engstrom et al., 2006; Kearney, 2003).

Gender

Gender continues to influence pay, even while controlling for human capital variables. Alkadry and Tower (2006) looked at whether or not pay inequity continues (see Table 6.4). After controlling for the above variables (e.g., education, organizational type, merit, and cost of living), they found that pay differences between women and men persisted. Gender was a significant predictor of pay at all of the levels studied. About 10 percent of the variance in pay was consistently predicted by gender compared to experience, supervisory responsibilities, education, organization size, and cost of living. In other words, for the 1,500 procurement professionals surveyed by Alkadry and Tower, gender does affect salary. Education, experience, supervisory responsibilities, and other factors of human capital and cost of living also tend to affect salary differences between men and women, but so does gender. In fact, gender plays as large a role as experience and education for some of the studied occupa-

Table 6.4

Percentage of Variance in Pay Predicted by Gender and Other Human Capital Variables Among Procurement Professionals

	Executives	Managers/ supervisors	Buyers
Female yes/no	10	12	10
Total years with current employer	11	12	20
Total years of experience in purchasing	8	12	20
Number of subordinates	16	15	14
Number of years of education	14	17	14
Hierarchy	0	0	−11
Annual procurement volume	0	0	0
Number of staff in purchasing unit	14	0	0
Age	0	0	0
Certified yes/no	0	0	0
Median household income	16	21	0
Median housing value	10	11	33

Source: Alkadry and Tower (2006).

tions. It is legitimate for experience and education to drive one's salary. If she wants more salary, an employee would seek more experience and education. However, she will find herself helpless in trying to control for gender's effect on salaries.

A New Glass Ceiling

Gender affects authority by hindering women's progress into positions of authority. Authority affects salary in that people in positions of authority earn more money than those in nonauthority positions. A recent study by Alkadry and Tower (2011) shows that even when women make it into positions of authority, their supervisory and budgetary responsibilities tend to be lower than those of men in the same positions. For example, on average, male chief procurement officers supervise more than double the number of employees and manage more than double the budget than female chief procurement officers.

Women are not as likely to occupy top positions (Jacobs, 1992; McGuire and Reskin, 1993) in the private and public sectors. Women are less likely to make it to the top, even after controlling for human capital variables (Alkadry and Tower, 2006; Mitra, 2003). Smith (2002) argues that: "First, gender difference in workplace authority, and in the processes that lead to authority, constitute an important source of gender inequality that is obscured when traditional indicators of occupational status are used to measure inequality. Second, earnings models that do not include measures of job authority are apt to significantly underestimate the gender gap in earnings" (p. 530).

This new glass ceiling is not defined by the position level that women occupy in the hierarchy, but rather by the responsibilities that are assigned to these positions. Does gender influence the authority profile of male and female executives? Is the supervisory and financial authority associated with the positions attained by men comparable to that attained by women? The ultimate question posed by Alkadry and Tower (2011, p. 743) is: "Are women being recruited to fill leadership positions that have less supervisory and financial authority than men?"

After merging two national data sets to create a pooled cross-sectional time series, Jacobs (1992) determined whether more women in top positions translated into a better supervisory profile for these women. The number of women in management positions increased from one in six managers in 1970, to two in five managers in 2000. However, less than 3 percent of top executives of Fortune 500 companies are women. This suggests that while women are being admitted into management ranks, their advancement in larger companies, with more authority and responsibilities, remains constrained.

In response to the newly introduced requirements by the EEOC, some organizations modified the job titles of many positions without changing the job responsibilities. So, some secretaries became office managers without having their responsibilities substantially altered (Jacobs, 1992). This phenomenon is labeled the "glorified secretary" phenomenon and is prevalent in companies with more than 100 employees, which are required to report their data to the EEOC. Smith and Welch (1984) also studied this glorified secretary phenomenon and arrived at similar results.

In their 2011 study, Alkadry and Tower (2011) also found that while supervisory responsibilities and budget responsibilities had a very large effect on a chief procurement officer's salary, gender seemed to trump all other human capital variables in predicting the variance in salaries for the 384 chiefs in the study (see Table 6.5). In other words, gender has a larger effect than experience and education in predicting the number of subordinates these chiefs had. Furthermore, on average, females supervised less than half and about 40 percent of the budget that males supervised. In the conclusion of that study, Alkadry and Tower state that:

Table 6.5

Beta/Effect Size of Human Capital, Organizational, and Individual Factors on the Authority Level of Male and Female Chief Procurement Officers

	Subordinates	Budget
Years with employer	0.0868	
Years in purchasing		
Number of certifications		
Years of education	0.1146	
Agency staff	0.2519	0.2984
Male dummy	0.1573	0.1447
Age in years		
White dummy		−0.0982

Source: Alkadry and Tower (2011).

[G]ender affects the salaries of women indirectly by influencing the amount of women's authority and the direct effect of that authority on one's salary. While authority level and gender drive salaries, gender drives authority level—thus playing an indirect role in predicting pay through authority variables. In this study the indirect effect on pay through the intervening authority variables was almost equal to the direct effect of gender on pay. This makes the analysis of indirect effects imperative in future research on the role of gender in predicting pay differences between men and women.

The findings . . . beg the question of whether authority variables are concealing another dimension of the glass ceiling. Women can become chief procurement officers, but it is likely, based on the analysis of mean differences, that they will supervise fewer than half the number of people and be in charge of less than half the money than their male counterparts. In other words, as women work hard and incur many social costs to break the glass ceiling by attaining higher-level positions, they find themselves facing yet another glass ceiling, albeit more covert, limiting the amount of authority entrusted in them. And, the less authority women have, the less they can expect in pay. (Alkadry and Tower, pp. 747–748)

Barriers, Challenges, and Opportunities

Barriers to equal pay begin with historical patterns and gender roles that are perpetuated by current pay systems. Pay disparities are reinforced in fields, occupations, and agencies. Dealing with pay equity is complicated and requires dealing with issues outside organizations. There is a need to attract women to better-paying jobs even if they are outside our gender comfort zones. How do we start moving women into engineering and science fields that pay better?

Along with significant barriers to eradicating pay inequities, women's gender roles in society are extremely difficult to change. It is likely that women will continue to carry a heavier burden of domestic responsibilities than their partners. This is an issue that may be influenced by law (e.g., by offering paid paternity leave), but also by sociocultural factors. This drives women into lower-income part-time positions and lower-ranked positions. Better working conditions and more family-friendly workplaces would help alleviate some of these problems by making full-time employment less stressful on women.

The challenge facing organizations involves workplace policies that make it easier for women to climb the ladder into better paying leadership positions. Organizations are also challenged to conduct their own *comparable worth* research within their organizational bounds to pay men and women equally for comparable work. The school board that continues to pay its teacher less than it pays its computer scientist or network engineer is faced with the important challenge of comparing these positions and taking appropriate actions.

While significant barriers and challenges exist, there are extraordinary opportunities. As women's education surpasses men's, and male baby boomers leave vacant high-level positions, there is an opportunity to hire women into these positions. Family-friendly policies are needed for women (and men) to better juggle work and life. Mentoring may also assist women in preparing for these positions.

Key Terms

Bureau men
Comparable worth
Emotional labor
Entry and reentry
Betty Friedan
Gender-typing
Human capital

Mommy Track
Pay equity
Settlement women
Camilla Stivers
Harriet Taylor-Mill
Mary Wollstonecraft

7

Women in Organizations:
From Mentoring to Bullying

Unfortunately, there continue to be significant barriers to safety for women in the workplace: workplace bullying, sexual harassment, and physical violence. This chapter discusses these issues as well as strategies to reduce the incidence of these deleterious activities. Despite various forms of bias in the workplace, women may have opportunities to bolster their careers through mentoring and negotiating. Mentoring is often promoted as a solution to fix workplace inequities, such as position segregation and pay inequity. The section on mentoring will focus on the different types of mentoring as well as the strengths and limitations of each. Different career- and psychosocial-related mentoring functions will also be discussed in this chapter.

Negotiating in the workplace and in the home is affected by gender role expectations and associated uneven bargaining power. Research on negotiation has revealed patterns in negotiation outcomes that are related to the sex of the negotiator. Differences occur because of "*gender triggers*." This chapter also contains tips for women to use when negotiating as well as suggestions that organizations can implement to level the playing field for women.

Bullying and sexual harassment are actions targeted against women by co-workers and supervisors. These two issues affect women negatively and present a challenge to organizations to educate men and women about their own rights. The two issues are also important in educating supervisors and co-workers about appropriate workplace behavior. If co-workers, supervisors, and employees themselves understand the implications and dangers of bullying and sexual harassment, then it makes sense to work on educating everyone who could possibly be involved, including both victims and offenders.

Mentoring

Mentoring is often promoted as a solution to fix workplace inequities. Why? Individuals with mentors tend to have better career outcomes (e.g., salary and promotions) and career satisfaction (Allen , Eby, Potect, Lentz, and Lima, 2004, p. 132; Eby, Allen, Evans, Ng, and DuBois, 2008). Furthermore, mentors may increase the retention of their protégées as well as help them envision success in the organization (Singh, Ragins, and Tharenou, 2009). Mentors also benefit from the relationship. Benefits to mentors include: fulfilling the role of organizational citizens and broadening their perspectives (Giscombe, 2007).

Informal vs. Formal Mentoring

There are different types of mentoring. Mentoring can be informal or formal. Informal relationships happen organically between two intrinsically motivated individuals to help the protégée in career development and beyond (Chao, 2009). Organizations have been implementing *formal mentoring* programs to increase the number of employees who benefit from a mentor. But formal mentoring may not be as effective as *informal mentoring* (Baugh and Fagenson-Eland, 2007), because it lacks the intensity, long duration, and broad focus.

Formal mentors may not have the same level of intensity or investment in their protégée. Research has shown that when an organization has a formal mentoring program, allowing the mentor and protégée to have input in regard to whom they are matched with makes both individuals more likely to invest in the relationship (Allen, Eby, and Lentz, 2006).

Unlike informal mentoring, formal mentoring tends to have specific time limits and foci for the protégée. Frequently, formal mentoring programs last about one year. Goals of a mentoring program may include organizational socialization and networking, skill acquisition, leadership development, succession planning, connecting geographically dispersed units of the organization, or combining work cultures as a result of mergers or acquisitions. Formal mentoring programs may also target recruiting, retaining, and advancing underrepresented individuals.

Formal mentoring may offer important benefits to organizations. It extends mentoring opportunities to women and minorities; it utilizes the potential of mentoring for leadership development; and it incorporates mentoring into the organizational culture (Baugh and Fagenson-Eland,

Table 7.1

Mentoring Functions

Functions

Career-related	Support focused on building a career, including securing resources, clearing organizational obstacles, offering exposure and visibility, providing organizational information, backing the individual, offering protection, and giving challenging work
Psychosocial	Support focused on emotions and well-being, including having acceptance and confirmation, having a confidant, friend, and role model, and achieving work–life balance

2007). Formal programs also have unique advantages over informal mentoring, for example, dedicated resources and mentor training (Giscombe, 2007). Sexual themes may cause conflict within a mentor/protégé relationship, particularly when the mentor is male and protégée is female (Bushardt, Fretwell, and Holdnak, 1991). Formal mentoring programs may help legitimize cross-gender dyads (Giscombe, 2007).

Mentoring Functions

Mentoring functions may be *career-related, psychosocial* in nature, or both (see Table 7.1). And, these functions can influence outcomes. Women may benefit more than men from career-related mentoring functions, because women have more obstacles to overcome in an organizational hierarchy than men do (Tharenou, 2005, p. 101).

Negotiating

Negotiating takes place in the workplace and in the home. Although there may not be a lot of room for salary negotiation in government agencies or in unionized workplaces, negotiations can lead to other important work-related rewards. Workplace negotiations can include one's starting salary, or asking for a raise, promotion, office space, resources, project management, or benefits (e.g., leave). Negotiations in the home may be related to who picks up the children, makes dinner, or picks up the dry cleaning. If we recall that women conduct more housework as well as more time-specific housework, and that this type of housework tends to affect women's careers more adversely than men's, then there may be room in the home to negotiate a better situation that can also reduce stress and penalties in the workplace. The following sections discuss differences between the sexes in negotiating in the workplace and in the home.

Negotiations, within the workplace and home, are not immune to gender role expectations. Theorists have speculated that women have less success negotiating because of gender roles and bargaining power:

1. Childhood differences in play, assigned chores, and experiences.
2. Less comfort with negotiating because of this inexperience or socialization to be "nice" or put others first.
3. Not being familiar with the enormous economic costs of not negotiating.

(Babcock and Laschever, 2010)

In the Workforce

Women and men do not negotiate at the same rates (Bowles, Babcock, and Lai, 2007) or with the same effectiveness (Stuhlmacher and Walters, 1999). Some researchers suggest that if women negotiated more frequently, more skillfully, or valued the outcomes of negotiations more, negotiation could be a key to reducing problems such as position segregation or the pay gap (Stuhlmacher and Walters, 1999). But will negotiations solve these problems? Small differences in starting salaries can lead to substantial salary gaps in the future. But, researchers have also found that women tend to be penalized for negotiating (e.g., Bowles, Babcock, and Lai, 2007). Short-term gains in salary may result in long-term obstacles to working relationships.

When attempting to negotiate higher salaries, women encounter more social resistance than men. They tend to be judged as "not nice" and "overly demanding" (p. 91). And, men are less likely to want to work with women who negotiate for higher salaries (Bowles, Babcock, and Lai, 2007).

Women and men come to the negotiation table with different beliefs. These beliefs may contribute to the higher rewards achieved by men through negotiations. Men tend to "know their worth" and attempt to demonstrate their value from previous successes, during the negotiation process itself; whereas women tend to let the employer determine their worth during the negotiation and once on the job, anticipate salary increases as they prove themselves, (Barron, 2003). Understand that these beliefs are consistent with gender roles.

Managers may even expect women to accept lower levels of compensation and be less likely to negotiate. Research has shown that men and women will offer less money to women because they believe women will accept it (Solnick, 2001). Moreover, researchers have shown that men tend to believe they are "entitled" to more than others, while women are more likely to believe they are entitled to the same things as others (Barron, 2003, p. 643). Entitlement for men is rewarded in negotiations because it is consistent with male gender roles. When women have an attitude of entitlement, which is counter to expected feminine behaviors, they are evaluated negatively (Bowles and Babcock, 2008).

Researchers have found that certain situational factors favor men's negotiating outcomes. In negotiations with high ambiguity—unclear standards of agreement on an outcome (e.g., starting salary ranges)—men tend to achieve more (Bowles, Babcock, and McGinn, 2005; Pradel, Bowles, and McGinn, 2005). In negotiations with high levels of competition, men also tend to have more favorable outcomes (Pradel, Bowles, and McGinn, 2005). Competition may be defined as situations where resources are distributed by comparing the relative performance of the individuals. Why do these situational factors favor men?

In situations with high ambiguity and competition, *gender triggers* manifest. Gender triggers are situational cues that seem to activate differences in the ways men and women behave (ibid.). In other words, unconsciously, men may react to certain circumstances, for example high competition, and perform better than usual, while women may underperform under the same circumstances. Gender triggers, then, influence negotiation behavior and outcomes. There is one gender trigger, however, that may favor women: advocating for others. When women advocate for others (vs. themselves), research suggests that their outcomes are much higher. One study found an 18 percent increase in negotiated compensation (Pradel, Bowles, and McGinn, 2005). Women can minimize gender triggers with preparation and state of mind (see Table 7.2).

It is important for organizations to minimize gender differences in negotiations. Because women may be disadvantaged by high ambiguity negotiations, organizations may tie clearly articulated performance indicators to salaries, bonuses, promotions, and other benefits (Pradel, Bowles, and McGinn, 2005). Offering employees the opportunity to negotiate their compensation packages, in conjunction with their annual performance evaluation, opens the door to more regular negotiations for women, without the social costs associated when women initiate negotia-

Table 7.2

Reducing the Impact of Gender Differences in Negotiating

Talk to others	Talk to others, particularly those beyond your immediate social network (e.g., men in male-dominated industries).
Research norms	Research precedents and industry norms.
Research what is available	Gather information on negotiable resources (e.g., administrative assistant, flexible schedules, assignments, career development opportunities).
Identify gender-role "triggers"	Ambiguity and high competition may trigger gender stereotypes or expectations that negatively affect women's salaries or reputation. Visualize that you are representing a colleague.
Name gender biases	Make bias explicit in an effort to avoid it.
Prioritize	Understand your priorities. What do you want? What will you give up?
Frame request communally*	Show cooperation and concern for the organization. Desire to stay with the organization. Emphasize the personal importance of relationships (vs. acting demanding or entitled).
Justify*	Show an outside offer for more money, but do not give the impression it was leverage seeking.
Understand the process	What is your personal negotiation style? What is the style of the person you will be negotiating with?
Practice	Anticipate responses. Role-play with a trusted mentor.
Document	Send a follow-up e-mail summarizing the negotiation. This leaves "a paper trail" and also ensures mutual understanding.
Negotiate over time	Negotiation is a process. Continue to establish rapport; be polite.

Sources: Bowles and McGinn (2008a, 2008b); Pradel, Bowles, and McGinn (2005); Sarfaty et al. (2007).
*Using both strategies simultaneously negated individual effectiveness.

tions. Regular negotiations would alleviate women from weighing the social costs against the economic benefits of initiating negotiations. More specifically, women would not be in the difficult position of initiating negotiations that, while they might increase pay, could also alienate them from management and hurt their career trajectory.

Research also shows that jobs with more women workers are less likely to offer incentive bonuses (Elvira and Graham, 2002). In addition, when women receive incentive bonuses, the amounts tend to be much lower compared to those of men. One study revealed a 25 percent difference (ibid.). The same study found no difference in merit pay between men and women. Therefore, organizations that remove less formalized pay structures (e.g., bonuses) and replace them with more formalized pay structures (merit raises) will have less gender disparity in compensation.

Women and men do not negotiate at the same rates. They have different beliefs about negotiating and encounter different social responses to negotiating. While negotiating has been touted as a forum for women to try to reduce position segregation or pay inequities, penalties associated with women's negotiating may negate that benefit or even put them in a worse position. It also shifts the responsibility for overcoming discrimination onto the one being discriminated against, rather than onto organizational structures, unconscious biases, and other factors undergirding discrimination.

Gender-role expectations and uneven bargaining power influence negotiations in the workforce. Men tend to have an advantage in negotiations that are characterized as high ambiguity or high competition. But women may have an advantage in negotiations when they are advocating for others. Tips for minimizing gender triggers when negotiating are listed in Table 7.2. Organizational practices can also minimize gender difference in negotiating.

In the Home

Women also have the opportunity to negotiate housework and child-care responsibilities in the home. As discussed earlier, women tend to assume more of these responsibilities and more time-specific responsibilities. In addition, these responsibilities result in a higher wage penalty.

Similar to negotiating in the workplace, gender roles and bargaining power affect negotiation outcomes in the home. Gender roles may influence a higher load of household responsibilities as well as limit women's job aspirations (Bowles and McGinn, 2008b). Bargaining power should be drawn from economic contributions to the household. Researchers, however, have found a reverse trend. Economic theory predicts that as women's earnings increase, they have the power to negotiate performing less housework. Housework appears to be more fairly distributed when wives' economic contributions increase from 0 to 50 percent of household income. But researchers have found a curvilinear relationship between relative earnings and performance of housework, with husbands' household labor decreasing as their wives' incomes increase from 51 percent to 100 percent (Bittman et al., 2003; Brines, 1994; Greenstein, 2000). It seems that when wives earn more than their husbands, they compensate with a more traditional gender distribution of housework.

Workplace Violence

Organizational climate is the environment or atmosphere of the organization, how it feels to work at the organization, or the culture of an organization. If we think in terms of Maslow's *hierarchy of needs theory*, we are motivated to have our most basic needs met before we seek to fulfill a higher-level need (i.e., physiological → safety → belonging → self-esteem → self-actualization). Individuals with jobs likely have their most basic physiological needs met for food, water, shelter, and so on. Unfortunately, some women in organizations may be stuck in trying to have their safety needs met, due to *bullying, sexual harassment,* or *physical violence* in the workplace.

Bullying

Workplace bullying affects men and women in the workplace. Schat, Frone, and Kelloway (2006) report that 41 percent of workers experience some form of psychological aggression at work. Bullying is also widely documented in EU countries. Unlike workplace violence in general, bullying tends be characterized by persistence—that is, of frequency and duration—and to occur between individuals who know each other (Lutgen-Sandvik and Tracy, 2012). From a review of the bullying literature, Rayner and Hoel (1997) categorize bullying behaviors as follows:

1. threat to professional status (e.g., belittling opinion, public professional humiliation, accusation regarding lack of effort)
2. threat to personal standing (e.g., name-calling, insults, intimidation, devaluing with reference to age)
3. isolation (e.g., preventing access to opportunities, physical or social isolation, withholding of information)

4. overwork (e.g., undue pressure, impossible deadlines, unnecessary disruptions)
5. destabilization (e.g., failure to give credit when due, meaningless tasks, removal of responsibility, repeated reminders of blunders, setting up to fail)

(Rayner and Hoel, 1997, p. 183)

Bullying is a problem because it can catastrophically affect employee well-being (e.g., posttraumatic stress disorder or depression) as well as devastate organizational productivity (e.g., reduced productivity).

Research on bullying gives us some insight into bullies. Bullies tend to hold a higher rank in the organization than their victims (e.g., manager). In many instances of bullying, multiple individuals are involved: the perpetrator, *passive accomplices* (e.g., individual[s] who laugh at a bully's joke or side with the bully), inaction by upper management, and silent witnesses who do not intervene to help (Namie and Lutgen-Sandvik, 2010). Research has also found that men may be more likely to bully. This could be explained by men's greater frequency at the higher levels of organizations, social norms, or both.

While bullying is not yet illegal in most states, bullying behaviors can be counter to workplace culture. Organizational efforts to deter bullying can include encouraging an organizational culture of respect and civility (vs. a win-at-any cost business model) that is modeled by upper management; developing and enforcing antibullying policies; offering training related to communication skills; and giving voice to marginalized workers. For example, during meetings at the Veterans Administration, the practice of the "talking stick" or passing a stick to the individual who is speaking at a meeting reminds the rest of the group to listen without interruption (Keashly and Neuman, 2009). Workplace bullying policy may be added to the broader context of harassment, such as sexual harassment, or discrimination policies.

Sexual Harassment

Sexual behaviors in the workplace tend to be problematic. Sexual behaviors may be categorized as:

1. *Ambient sexual behavior* (ASB): sexual language, jokes, and materials, or
2. *Direct sexual behavior* (DSB: sexual comments or advances directed at an individual.

(Berdahl and Aquino, 2009)

Even when employees report enjoying sexual behaviors at work (only 10 percent of women vs. 40 percent of men), the more sexual behaviors experienced at work, the lower employees' work-related and psychological outcomes (ibid.). It appears that even when sexual behaviors are welcome, which is infrequently the case for female workers, it negatively impacts productivity.

Sexual Harassment Defined

What is sexual harassment? According to the U.S. Supreme Court, there are two forms of illegal sexual harassment:

1. *Quid pro quo* or "this for that"—unwelcome, gender-based conduct that results in an employment outcome (e.g., a sexual favor in exchange for not being fired) or
2. *Hostile work environment*—unwelcome, gender-based conduct that is pervasive and severe.

(U.S. EEOC, 1990)

While common forms of sexual behaviors may not meet the high standards set forth in legal definitions, organizations have a moral and financial obligation to prevent them.

Sexual harassment is common in the workplace. Extensive research shows that men are more likely to perpetrate sexual harassment than women, but keep in mind that most men do not engage in sexual harassment (O'Leary-Kelly, Bowes-Sperry, Bates, and Lean, 2009). While men are more likely to commit sexual harassment, women are more likely to be the target. Approximately half of women will experience sexual harassment during their education or work lives (Fitzgerald, 1993).

Women who deviate from traditional gender roles—exhibiting masculine personality traits or working in male-dominated occupations—may be more likely to experience sexual harassment than feminine women and women who work in female-dominated occupations (Berdahl, 2007). Sexual harassment may be understood as a social mechanism for punishing those who violate traditional gender roles.

Sexual Harassment Rarely Reported

Sexual harassment is rarely reported. Why? Women may fear retaliation, blame for the incident, or that the complaint will not be taken seriously or kept confidential (Marshall, 2005); women are also skeptical that the complaint can be resolved. Women workers are correct to have these concerns. Many studies show that reporting sexual harassment is frequently ineffective and may even hurt the worker's career (O'Leary-Kelly et al., 2009).

Although grievance systems are the most common process for resolving workers' rights complaints, including sexual harassment, Marshall (2005) warns: "grievance procedures may actually be more effective at protecting employers from liability than they are at protecting employee rights" (p. 85). Managers may discourage women from complaining by minimizing the complaint and perhaps encouraging them to drop it; interpreting sexual harassment policy too narrowly, or taking the side of or advocating for the perpetrator (Marshall, 2005; O'Leary-Kelly et al., 2009).

Sexual Harassment Harms Individuals and Organizations

Sexual harassment has negative consequences. A recent meta-analysis showed that sexual harassment victims experience (a) negative job-related outcomes (e.g., lower job satisfaction, tendency to withdraw, and poor performance), (b) negative psychological outcomes (i.e., lower psychological well-being and higher psychological distress), and (c) negative physical outcomes (lower health satisfaction and physical symptoms) (Chan, Lam, Chow, and Cheung, 2008; Willness, Steel, and Lee, 2007). Sexual harassment perpetrated by clients/customers has also been shown to have these detrimental consequences (Gettman and Gelfand, 2007).

Sexual harassment is also problematic for organizations. Beyond the obvious—employers may be held legally and financially liable for sexual harassment perpetrated in the workplace—sexual harassment has been shown to increase turnover and decrease productivity (Willness, Steel, and Lee, 2007). Sexual harassment not only negatively affects the work of the victim, but also may negatively affect how a team functions and how a team ultimately performs (Raver and Gelfand, 2005). In summary, it makes "business sense" for an organization to eliminate sexual harassment: legally, financially, and morally.

Reducing Sexual Harassment

To reduce sexual harassment, focus needs to be placed on prevention and appropriate intervention. EEOC guidelines suggest that employers "take all steps necessary to prevent sexual harassment from occurring" (U.S. EEOC 1990). These include:

1. Clearly communicating that sexual harassment is prohibited—for example, train employees and supervisor;
2. Establishing complaint procedures—for example, establish a grievance process that thoroughly, impartially, and confidentially investigates all claims; and
3. Responding immediately and appropriately to complaints—for example, take corrective action, as warranted (*Faragher v. City of Boca Raton*, 524 U.S. 775 [1998]).

To reduce sexual harassment, managers must be aware of the *organizational climate* surrounding sexual harassment, which is defined as an employer's perceived tolerance of sexual harassment. It includes the policies and procedures of the organization and how these are implemented, and researchers have found that it is the most important predictor of sexual harassment in the workplace (Willness, Steel, and Lee, 2007). Therefore, having, communicating, and following clear policies and procedures is critical to reducing sexual harassment in organizations. Eliminating sexual harassment can raise productivity and lower costs.

A sexual harassment prevention policy should be well distributed (see Exhibit 7.1). The policy ought to be given annually to each employee, posted around the workplace and, as appropriate, on the Web site; and reviewed and distributed at new employee orientations. Periodic training may also be provided. In addition, it is important to ascertain that all managers understand what behaviors are acceptable or unacceptable. Finally, the policy must be followed.

Physical Violence

Approximately 20 employees are killed and 18,000 are assaulted each week while at work (National Institute for Occupational Safety and Health [NIOSH], 1996). NIOSH defined workplace violence broadly, from offensive language to murder, "violent acts, including physical assaults and threats of assault, directed toward persons at work or on duty" (NIOSH, 1996). NIOSH (2006) categorized four types of workplace violence:

Exhibit 7.1

Components of Sexual Harassment Prevention Policy

1. Clear statement that the organization will not tolerate sexual harassment
2. Identification of inappropriate behaviors
   - Uninvited physical contact (e.g., pinching, leaning in close to another, hugging, or patting)
   - Repeated sexual flirtation or propositions
   - Jokes, remarks, pictures, objects of a sexual nature
   - Obscene gestures or sounds
   - Extended staring
   - Comments about an individual's body
3. Process for making complaints to a designated person(s)
4. Process for investigating alleged complaints (promptly, impartially, thoroughly, and confidentially)
5. Clear statement that anyone who files a complaint will not be subject to retaliation, regardless of the complaint outcome
6. Clear statement that anyone found guilty of harassment will be subject to discipline, including discharge

---

1. Criminal intent (85 percent of cases)—robbery, shoplifting, trespassing, and terrorism;
2. Worker-on-worker (7 percent of cases)—past or present employee perpetrates violence against a past or present employee;
3. Customer/client (3 percent of cases)—a consumer perpetrates violence while being served; and
4. Personal relationships (5 percent of cases)—the perpetrator has a past or present relationship with the employee.

Workplace violence has deleterious effects on both female and male employees. Wieclaw et al. (2006) found that exposure to violence at work increases the risk of stress related disorders and depression in both men and women. They explain that perception of a threat or a possible risk of violence in the workplace may "create a state of chronic alertness" (p. 774). This state of chronic alertness may contribute to workers developing stress, depression, or both.

The risk of work-related rape is more common when workers are isolated from co-workers and the public. In a study of work-related rapes,

85 percent of rapes occurred when the victim/survivor was alone (Alexander, Franklin, and Wolf, 1994).

Managers should develop and implement a workplace violence prevention policy and program. Resources are available from NIOSH and other groups. For example, *Workplaces Respond to Domestic and Sexual Violence National Resource Center* allows individuals to create a policy on its Web site (http://www.workplacesrespond.org/).

Barriers, Challenges, and Opportunities

Despite various forms of bias in the workplace (barriers), women may have opportunities to bolster their careers through mentoring and negotiating. Mentoring is often promoted as a solution to fix workplace inequities, such as position segregation and pay inequity. The section on mentoring described informal and formal mentoring as well as the associated strengths and limitations. There are also different mentoring functions: career related and psychosocial related.

Negotiations within the workplace and home are not immune to gender-role expectations. This is quite a challenge. Theorists have found that women have less success negotiating because of gender roles and the concomitant bargaining power. Nevertheless, opportunities are still available. Whereas certain gender triggers favor negotiation outcomes for men (i.e., ambiguity and competition), women have an advantage in negotiations when advocating for others. We discussed tips women can use to minimize gender triggers that negatively affect their negotiations as well as practices organizations can employ.

Women in organizations may experience additional barriers: bullying, sexual harassment, or physical violence in the workplace. Bullying can catastrophically impact employee well-being as well as devastate organizational productivity. Sexual harassment harms both individuals and organizations. Yet, sexual harassment is rarely reported, which is a significant challenge. The U.S. Supreme Court defines two types of sexual harassment: quid pro quo and hostile work environment. Sexual harassment may be reduced by appropriate prevention and interventions. Physical violence in the workplace is another serious issue that impacts both female and male employees. Workplace prevention policies and programs are opportunities to help reduce workplace violence.

Key Terms

Ambient sexual behavior (ASB)
Career-related function
Direct sexual behavior (DSB)
Formal mentoring
Gender trigger
Hierarchy of needs theory
Hostile work environment
Informal mentoring

Organizational climate
Passive accomplice
Physical violence
Psychosocial-related function
Sexual harassment
Quid pro quo
Workplace bullying

8

Conclusion: Barriers, Challenges, and Opportunities

As we were putting final touches on our book manuscript, the airwaves witnessed a discussion of an article written by Anne-Marie Slaughter (2012) titled "Why Women Still Can't Have It All." The then dean of Princeton's Woodrow Wilson School of Public and International Affairs left her deanship to take a senior position in Secretary Hillary Clinton's Department of State in Washington, DC. Slaughter soon found herself overwhelmed by the demands of her position and her inability to effectively juggle work and family responsibilities. The trouble, as we pointed out earlier, was not the demands of the conventional ideology of working men and family women (Johnson and Duerst-Lahti, 1992). Unlike many partners, her partner was willing to be the family man. But her role as an organization woman took a toll on her children—a price that she was not willing to pay for a career. She was capable of being a career woman, but the choice between family and work is not a fair choice for anyone. She had the luxury of choosing between a relatively family-friendly academic career and a non–family-friendly public-service career. Many women do not have the same choice.

In fact, in this conclusion we would like to protest the fact that many women have to choose between work and family. The problem is equally important for men, working or organization men, who often find themselves excelling at work at the expense of their family lives. Slaughter points to the examples of the New Jersey governor Christine Todd Whitman, and many public officials whose careers came at the expense of spending time with their children. This book has two authors—a man and a woman—each with a reasonably successful career, a partner, and children. This book's authors contend that the choice between family and career tests our human rights as individuals. The problem lies not with the choices that we make, but rather that we have to choose between family and career. Injustice occurs the moment we are forced to make the choice.

The answer that we tried to argue for in this book is a revision of work expectations for men and for women. There are many reasons why it is important for men and women to have the ability to balance work and life demands. First, for women to have lower work expectations would be to relegate women to second-class workplace-citizenship status. That is precisely how women ended up segregated in positions that have less authority and responsibility. Effectively, we have second-class workplace citizens who are able to juggle work and family. That is why workplace expectations need to be modified for everyone. A reasonable workweek is forty hours—not sixty, seventy, or eighty hours. Flexible schedules could be reasonable for men and women. Paid parental leave should be available to all workers. This is the only way to ensure that men and women are equal in the workplace and that hiring a female executive, manager, or supervisor is not a liability in the workplace.

Second, as mentioned earlier, parenting involves many responsibilities and also many rewards. Fathers should have the same opportunity to spend time with their children as mothers. Children also have the right to spend more time with both of their parents—if two parents are around. Some parents may choose not to spend more time with their children, and some children may only have one parent involved in their lives. But these are the choices that people should be making. Choosing to be involved or not is humane. Being forced to choose between work and family is not.

As we have argued throughout the book, among the main barriers to the advancement of women and their ability to balance life and work are societal images and expectations. Equality at work has to be matched with equality at home or within the family. Workplace policies should not start from and enforce societal images. For instance, maternity leave without paternity leave causes women to carry a heavier burden of family responsibilities. Admittedly, there is a very compelling physiological reason why women carry a bigger burden of pregnancy and delivery than men. However, once a child arrives, and the mother recovers medically from delivery issues, there is no reason why care for the baby could not be shared by mother and father. Therefore, workplace policies should treat men and women equally regardless of society's images and expectations. Instead of enforcing societal images, the workplace could establish policies that would become the tools to empower women not only in the workplace but also in society. If women and men have the same rights to parental leave, a woman will inevitably find herself arguing to her partner that she who earns the most in the household is entitled to be back at work sooner. Or, he whose career is likely to suffer the least from a parental leave should take a parental leave.

So, with respect to Slaughter's question in the aforementioned article, we propose a friendly amendment. The title should not be "Why Women Can't Have It All," but rather: "Why People with Families Can't Have It All." This is because men who are "defaulted" into the role of working men and not family men do not have it all. This is not to argue that they suffer the same consequences as women when they dedicate themselves to work and not to family. They often do not, but dedication to work results in missing important milestones such as their children's first steps, the opportunity to be a class parent, children's doctors' appointments, piano practice (not just recitals), soccer practice, and other day-to-day interactions with their children that we all cherish and whine about at the same time.

Barriers

There are many barriers to a workplace friendly to women. Perhaps the most important barrier is the political environment, which creates problems for the advancement of women. While gender equality and women-friendly policies are rarely discussed in the context of conservatism and liberalism in other nations, it seems that our political culture has successfully politicized gender issues. Advocacy for women's issues such as representation, pay equity, and family-friendly workplace policies are somehow associated with Democrats. Republicans tend to stay away from these issues. This is particularly dangerous for women's rights especially given that our political system has fragmented power at the national level.

It is rare to see the president, the House of Representatives, and the Senate affiliated with the same political party. Even when it does happen, we are seeing the increased use of the filibuster. The Supreme Court, which appears to be moving to the right on most social equity issues, is another player that might or might not concur with the political leadership. The Lilly Ledbetter Act is a case in point. A fix to a major existing law on gender equity was passed in a partisan vote. It seems difficult for a political party to articulate an argument against protecting women from pay discrimination—as the Lilly Ledbetter Act did. Yet, it did. The opposition Republicans argued that the law costs businesses more money, consequently thwarting job-creation efforts. There is little but irony in blaming a law that corrects a blatant structural injustice for the economy's ills and its lack of recovery.

A major barrier that was presented throughout the book is the mismatch between societal gender-role expectations and the demands of the workplace. Working women tend to endure a "second shift"—caregiving and homemaking, "third shift"—listening to hurt family members complain about their long working hours, and even "fourth shifts"—conducting work electronically from home (Hochschield, 1997). Women, on average more educated than men, cannot and should not be constrained by a larger share of family responsibilities. These responsibilities have to be better synchronized with employment and performance potential in the workplace. As repeated throughout the book, reversing the conventional ideology of working men and family women (Johnson and Duerst-Lahti, 1992) requires a reversal of both the idea of "working men" and the idea of "family women." While organizations can do little to cause a reversal of the idea of "family women," they can do plenty to turn around the idea of "working men." This shift is particularly important given projected demographic trends of a shrinking workforce who have largely shed the *Womb-to-Tomb Employment Model* replacing it with the *We Are Self-Employed Model*.

Barriers to equal pay begin with historical patterns and gender roles that are perpetuated by current pay systems. Pay disparities are reinforced in fields, occupations, and agencies. Dealing with pay equity is complicated and requires dealing with issues outside organizations. There is a need to attract women to better-paying jobs even if they are outside our gender comfort zones. How do we start moving women into engineering and science fields that pay better?

The lack of a robust social safety net and the lack of universal national women's rights that would include paid paternity/maternity leave emphasize the mismatch between society's prescribed gender roles and workplace expectations. Women tend to pay higher social costs for their careers than men. These social costs affect career women in that they are less likely to be married, more likely to have fewer or no children, more likely to get divorced, and more likely to carry a heavy housework burden.

Challenges

There are many reasons for the segregation of women in certain fields, occupations, and agencies. While the book explores challenges and opportunities in this area, it also cites discrimination as a major barrier to the representation of women in public service.

Presented as the father of all challenges, the issue of representation is a serious issue that could be overcome by public organizations. Women continue to be underrepresented in higher ranks of organizations, and segregated in lower echelon positions. Will issues of representation of women in public organizations self-correct over time? There are many pieces of evidence that would create doubt about the efficacy of time alone to correct the mismatch. First, according to data presented in this book, about 80 percent of federal public servants, 60 percent of state workforces, and 63.5 percent of local workforces are over the age of 40. Assuming that this figure is reasonably constant, public organizations would shed their workforces every 25 years or so. It has been more than 25 years since women started graduating from universities with undergraduate and graduate degrees at a similar or higher pace to that of men. If time solves representation problems, then it is about time we hold time accountable for its failure to do so. If education was the problem, then parity in educational achievement along with 25 years should have solved the problem. Yet, time and educational parity did not solve it. Another indication that time alone is not enough is the fact that data from new hires reflect no better picture than that of the past.

The relationship between work and family is another important juncture for public and private workplaces. Quality men and women employees may also be interested in work–life satisfaction, rather than solely prioritizing excellent work performance at the cost of work–life fit. Absent a change of culture that promulgates work–life satisfaction policies and supports, good male and female employees will continue to be forced into choosing between dedication to work and dedication to family.

Another challenge facing the equitable participation of women in public organizations relates to expanding U.S. worker protections. As has been discussed, U.S. policy is quite limited as it relates to protecting individuals against discrimination as well as guaranteeing benefits for workers and their families. As an example, the FMLA offers weak protections and has multiple exclusions. Work–life satisfaction policies have the opportunity to improve health outcomes for mother and child. When we compare the FMLA to policies in most other nations, it appears that most developed countries have leave that is (a) universal, (b) paid, and (c) longer than that offered by the FMLA.

While there tends to be strong public support for families, inadequate family support remains the norm in the U.S., in part because children are largely viewed under the "children-as-pet" notion rather than "public good" notion. Unfortunately, business elites tend to dominate the political discussion, while progressive groups alienate the white working class, who currently align themselves with the business elites.

Perhaps the most compelling challenges facing the equal representa- tion of women in organizations are sociocultural in nature. First, there is a challenge of getting women interested in male-dominated occupa- tions. Employers complain about the so-called pool factor—meaning that if fewer women are in the applicant pool, then fewer of them would make it into these open positions. The solution to this pool problem is to change the perception of education and employment fields. How do we help girls think about jobs our society reserves primarily for boys? A second compelling challenge is the fact that women are often driven into lower-echelon positions after reentry into the workforce after a maternity or other caregiving event. This career penalty associated with taking time out of the workplace to perform a caregiving role is very problematic, but could be preempted with an improved form of maternity/paternity leave system, as is the norm in the industrialized world.

A challenge facing organizations involves workplace policies that make it easier for women to climb the ladder into better paying leader- ship positions. Organizations are also challenged to conduct their own comparable worth research within their organizational bounds to pay men and women equally for comparable work. The school board that continues to pay its teacher less than it pays its computer scientist or network engineer is faced with the important challenge of comparing these positions and taking appropriate actions.

Today women are not exiting the workforce, but are still discriminated against for caregiving responsibilities. More covertly, women and people of color experience implicit bias, or small unconscious penalties against them, that accumulates overtime. Furthermore, how work is organized and rewarded tends to favor already privileged groups, also referred to as institutional discrimination.

In response to the challenges women experience in the work environment, married middle-class women, as a family decision, may choose to downshift their career, take the nontraditional path of entrepreneurship, or work part-time. These options all come with significant costs. Both policy change and individual behavior (e.g., negotiation) can reduce these costs. An important policy change could be modeled after the European Union, which recognizes that part-time work does not have to be associated with low status, pay, and opportunities for advancement. This books offers tips to minimize the costs women experience when they exit the workforce, downshift a career, reenter the workplace after having children, or shift to part-time work.

Negotiations within the workplace and home are not immune to gender-role expectations. This is quite a challenge. Theorists have found that women have less success negotiating because of gender roles and the concomitant bargaining power. Nevertheless, opportunities are still available. Whereas certain gender triggers favor negotiation outcomes for men (i.e., ambiguity and competition), women have an advantage in negotiations when advocating for others. We discussed tips that women can use to minimize gender triggers that negatively impact their negotiations as well as practices organizations may employ.

Sexual harassment harms both individuals and organizations, yet sexual harassment is rarely reported, and this is a significant challenge. The U.S. Supreme Court defines two types of sexual harassment: quid pro quo and hostile work environment. Sexual harassment can be reduced by appropriate prevention and interventions. Physical violence in the workplace is another serious issue that affects both female and male employees. Workplace prevention policy and programs are opportunities to help reduce workplace violence.

Opportunities

As more employees retire from the public sector, there will be a golden opportunity for administrators and political leaders to attain better representation in institutions. Federal, state, and local governments face the realities of an aging workforce. Within 15 years, 36 percent of the local government workforce, 34.2 percent of state government workforce, and 39 percent of the federal government workforce will retire. With high rates of retirees exiting the government workforce, coupled with the demographic shift in which women become the majority of college graduates and holders of graduate degrees, the public service faces the unprecedented and enormous opportunity to create more representative organizations that will meet the current and future demands of a diverse citizenry.

At the same time, we are seeing new and extant opportunities. President Obama created several task forces to improve pay equity and work–life balance: National Equal Pay Enforcement Task Force, Middle Class Task Force, and Council on Women and Girls. The administrative leg of government has involvement in women and work policy enforcement. The Department of Labor has two agencies that monitor and enforce Equal Employment Opportunity laws: the Civil Rights Center and the Office of Federal Contract Compliance Programs (OFCCP). The Equal Employment Opportunity Commission enforces federal antidiscrimination law. These agencies may be more aggressive under Democratic Party leadership.

The National Science Foundation funds projects to increase gender diversity. Research findings and materials developed by grantees may be used by organizations to become more diverse. While equal opportunity is a societal goal in the United States, reducing biases, which allows for a more diverse workforce, has the added benefit of more innovative solutions to problems. A more diverse workforce offers the opportunity to strengthen organizational outcomes. Likewise, there is the opportunity to involve more men in the campaign to increase gender equity in public and organizational policy, as men have much to gain. We offer strategies to recruit male allies.

Organizational policies and practices offer another opportunity that may affect work–life fit, albeit one organization at a time. We offer suggestions to organizations. Several flexible work arrangements are described. Tips to keep women who exit or downshift their careers connected to the organization as well as tips to minimize implicit bias in evaluating new employees will help increase the ranks of women in the workforce. In addition, lactation programs as well as child-care and elder-care organizational policies are opportunities for better work–life fit for employees.

The public sector today faces a great opportunity to capitalize on the many retirements that are scheduled to occur over the next decade in order to correct the imbalance in representation across government's many levels, agencies, and occupations. If women are given an equal opportunity to be admitted into these positions, this will become a serious opportunity to alter the misrepresentation or segregation of women in all agencies, position levels, and occupations across all levels of government.

However, the data presented throughout this book on new hires to government positions has shown that the new hires, for the most part, have been emulating the existing composition of the workforce. Parity in gender representation among new hires would be the best way to ensure that parity will be achieved after a certain period of time.

While significant barriers and challenges exist, there are extraordinary opportunities. As women's education surpasses men's, and male baby boomers leave vacant high-level positions, there is an opportunity to hire women into these positions. Family-friendly policies are needed so that women (and men) can better juggle work and life. Mentoring can also assist women to be prepared for these positions.

Last Words

This book intended to present the case that many issues affect women in public service. Some issues are framed as women's issues, but do they exclusively affect women? For example, when a woman is systematically paid less than a male counterpart, her family's income is lower, potentially affecting her ability to help support her current or future partner, child(ren), or parents. Other issues affect women disproportionately but are not necessarily women's issues. However, such issues are often framed as women's issues. In this conclusion, we will deal with some critical questions.

It is clear in this book that what happens with women at work cannot be separated from gender roles and the role that women play in society and at home. As mentioned earlier in this conclusion, organizations can resist these unfair gender roles. Some of the policies that organizations enact will not reverse gender roles, but the effects of these gender roles do not have to enforce these roles. A simple example is access to paternity leave policies, which makes it easy for men to assume the role of co-primary caregiver for the first few months in a baby's life. At the same time, such policies implicitly denounce the assumption that only women can assume that role.

While there are significant barriers and challenges to changing assumptions that underlie how work is organized and rewarded, we hope that we have identified those assumptions (e.g., the ideology of the "working men" and "family women") and offered alternatives. Simultaneously, demographic trends—impending retirements of baby boomers and shifting attitudes about work, held by Generation Y who are replacing them—will also demand changes in the workplace. We look forward to the moment when organizations will take advantage of these important opportunities for change.

References

Abramovitz, M. n.d. Triple jeopardy: Women lose public sector services, jobs, and union rights. http://www.cswe.org/File.aspx?id=54067.

Adler, Marina A. 1993. Gender differences in job autonomy: The consequences of occupational segregation and authority position. *Sociological Quarterly* 34(3), 449–465.

Administration for Children and Families. 2011. Office of Head Start: About. http://www.acf.hhs.gov/programs/ohs/about.

ADVANCE at a Glance. http://www.nsf.gov/crssprgm/advance/index.jsp.

ADVANCE for the Advancement of Women in Science and Engineering Careers. n.d. http://www.portal.advance.vt.edu/.

Alexander, B. H., G. M. Franklin, and M. E. Wolf. 1994. The sexual assault of women at work in Washington state, 1980 to 1989. *American Journal of Public Health* 84(4), 640–642.

Alkadry, M. G. 1997. The feminine mystique of public administration. *Administrative Theory and Praxis* 19(1), 106–112.

———. 2007. Democratic administration in a multicultural environment. In *Democracy and Public Administration,* ed. R. Box, 150–168. Armonk, NY: M.E. Sharpe.

Alkadry, M. G., and L. E. Tower. 2006. "Unequal pay: The role of gender." *Public Administration Review* 66, 888–898. doi: 10.1111/j.1540-6210.2006.00656.x.

———. 2011. Covert pay discrimination: How authority predicts pay differences between women and men. *Public Administration Review* 71(5), 740–750.

———. 2013. Steady and Very Slow Progress: Women in West Virginia State Administration. *Public Administration Quarterly* 37(2): 201–231.

Alkadry, M. G., K. Nolf, and E. Condo. 2002. Pay equity in West Virginia state government. *Public Affairs Reporter* 19(2), 1–6.

Allen, T. D., L. T. Eby, and E. Lentz. 2006. Mentorship behaviors and mentorship quality associated with formal mentoring programs: Closing the gap between research and practice. *Journal of Applied Psychology* 91(3), 567–578.

Allen, T. D., L. T., Eby, M. L., Poteet, E., Lentz, and L. Lima. 2004. Career benefits associated with mentoring for protégés: A meta-analysis. *Journal of Applied Psychology* 89(1), 127–136.

American Academy of Pediatrics (AAP). 2012. Section on breastfeeding and the use of human milk. *Pediatrics* 129(3), e827-e841.

American Association of University Women (AAUW). 2007. *Behind the Pay Gap*. Report, April. Washington, DC: AAUW Educational Foundation.

————. 2012. *The Simple Truth about the Gender Pay Gap* (2012 Edition). Washington, DC: AAUW Educational Foundation.

American Express. 2012. The State of Women-Owned Businesses Report. http://smb.blob.core.windows.net/smbproduction/Content/State_of_Women-Owned_Businesses-Report_FINAL.pdf.

American Federation of State, County, and Municipal Employees, AFL-CIO (AFSCME) et al., Plaintiffs-Appellees, v. State of Washington et al. 770 F.2d 1401 (9th Cir. 1985). http://ftp.resource.org/courts.gov/c/F2/770/770.F2d.1401.84-3590.84-3569.html.

Americans with Disabilities Act (ADA). 2009. Americans with Disabilities Act of 1990, as Amended. U.S. Department of Justice. http://www.ada.gov/pubs/ada.htm.

Appelbaum, E., and R. Milkman. 2011. *Leaves That Pay: Employer and Worker Experiences with Paid Family Leave in California*. Washington, DC: Center for Economic and Policy Research. http://www.cepr.net/documents/publications/paid-family-leave-1-2011.pdf.

Armenia, A., and N. Gerstel. 2005. Family leaves, the FMLA and gender neutrality: The intersection of race and gender. *Social Science Research* 35, 871–891.

Arnault, J. E., L. Gordon, D. H. Joines, and G. M. Phillips. 2001. An experimental study of job evaluation and comparable worth. *Industrial and Labor Relations Review* 54(4), 806–815.

Association for Women in Science (AWIS). 2001. www.awis.org.

Babcock, L., and S. Laschever. 2010. Women don't ask: Negotiation and the gender divide. PowerPoint presentation, Louisiana Tech Advance Paid Program, September 23. http://www.advance.latech.edu/pdf/Women_Dont_Ask_.pdf.

Bachrach, C., M. J. Hindin, and E. Thomson. 2000. The changing shape of ties that bind: An overview and synthesis. In *The Ties that Bind: Perspectives on Marriage and Cohabitation,* ed. L. J. Waite, 3–16. Hawthorne, NY: Aldine de Gruyter.

Baker, M., and N. M. Fortin. 2004. Comparable worth in a decentralized labour market: The case of Ontario. *Canadian Journal of Economics* 37(4), 850–878.

Balkam, J. A. J., K. Cadwell, and S. B. Fein. 2011. Effects of components of a workplace lactation program on breastfeeding duration among employees of a public-sector employer. *Maternal Child Health Journal* 15, 677–683.

Barron, L. A. 2003. Ask and you shall receive? Gender difference in negotiators' beliefs about requests for higher salary. *Human Relations* 56(6), 635–662.

Bartley, S. J., P. W. Blanton, and J. L. Gillard. 2005. Husbands and wives in dual-earner marriages: Decision-making, gender role attitudes, division of household labor and equity. *Marriage and Family Review* 37, 69–94.

Baugh, G. S., and E. A. Fagenson-Eland. 2007. Formal Mentoring Programs. A "Poor Cousin" to Informal Relationships. In *The Handbook of Mentoring at Work: Theory, Research, and Practice*, ed. B. R. Ragins and K. E. Kram, 249–271. Los Angeles: Sage.

Becker, William E. 1999. Turning merit scores into salaries. *Journal of Economic Education* 30(4), 420–426.

Bell, M., I. Chopin, and F. Palmer. 2007. Developing anti-discrimination law in Europe: The 25 EU member states compared III. Migration Policy Group, July 1. http://www.migpolgroup.com/publications_detail.php?id=161/.

Benimadu, P., and R. Wright Paulsen. 1992. *Implementing Employment Equity: A Canadian Experience.* Ottawa: Conference Board of Canada.

Benko, C., and A. Weisberg. 2007. *Mass Career Customization.* Boston: Harvard Business School Press.

Berdahl, J. L. 2007. The sexual harassment of uppity women. *Journal of Applied Psychology* 92(2), 415–437.

Berdahl, J. L., and K. Aquino. 2009. Sexual behavior at work: Fun or folly? *Journal of Applied Psychology* 94(1), 34–47.

Berger, L. M., Hill, J., and Waldfogel, J. 2005. Maternity leave, early maternal employment and child health and development in the US. *Economic Journal* 115 (February), F29–F47.

Bertrand, M., and S. Mullainathan. 2004. Are Emily and Greg more employable than Lakisha and Jamal? A field experiment on labor market discrimination. *American Economic Review* 94(4), 997–1013.

Bittman, M., P. England, N. Folbre, L. Sayer, and G. Matheson. 2003. When does gender trump money? Bargaining and time in housework. *American Journal of Sociology* 109, 186–214.

Blair, I. V., J. E. Ma, and A. P. Lenton. 2001. Imagining stereotypes away: The moderation of implicit stereotypes through mental imagery. *Journal of Personality and Social Psychology* 81, 828–841.

Blair-Loy, M. 2003. *Competing Devotions: Career and Family Among Executive Women.* Cambridge, MA: Harvard University Press.

———. 2009. Work without end? Scheduling flexibility and work-to-family conflict among stockbrokers. *Work and Occupations* 36(4), 279–317.

Blair-Loy, M., and A. S. Wharton. 2002. Employees' use of work-family policies and the workplace social context. *Social Forces* 80(3), 813–845.

———. 2004. Mothers in finance: Surviving and thriving. *Annals of the American Academy of Political and Social Science* 596, 151–170.

Blakemore, J. E., C. A., Lawton, and L. R. Vartanian. 2005. I can't wait to get married: Gender differences in drive to marry. *Sex Roles* 53(5/6), 327–335.

Blau, F. D., and A. E. Winkler. 2005. Does affirmative action work? *Regional Review* Q1, 38–40.

Blau, F., M. Ferber, and A. Winkler. 2002. Models of discrimination. In *The Economics of Women, Men and Work*, 4th ed., 219–235. Upper Saddle River, NJ, Prentice Hall.

Bobbitt-Zeher, D. 2011. Gender discrimination at work: Connecting gender stereotypes, institutional policies, and gender composition of workplace. *Gender and Society* 25, 764–786.

Borland, J. 1999. The equal pay case: Thirty years. *Australian Economic Review* 32, 265–272.

Bornstein, S., and R. J. Rathmell. 2009. *Caregivers As a Protected Class? The Growth of State and Local Laws Prohibiting Family Responsibilities Discrimination.* Report, December. San Francisco: Center for WorkLife Law, University of California, Hastings. http://www.worklifelaw.org/pubs/LocalFRDLawsReport.pdf.

Bowles, H. R., and L. Babcock. 2008. *When Doesn't It Hurt Her to Ask? Framing and Justification Reduce the Social Risks of Initiating Compensation Negotiations.* Working Paper. Cambridge, MA: Kennedy School of Government, Harvard University.

Bowles, H. R., and K. L. McGinn. 2008a. Gender in job negotiations: A two-level game. *Negotiation Journal* (October), 393–406.

————. 2008b. Untapped potential in the study of negotiation and gender inequality in organizations. In *Academy of Management Annals*, ed. J. P. Walsh and Al Brief. New York: Routledge.

Bowles, H. R., L. Babcock, and L. Lai. 2007. Social incentives for gender differences in the propensity to initiate negotiations: Sometimes it does hurt to ask. *Organizational Behavior and Human Decision Processes* 103, 84–103.

Bowles, H. R., L. Babcock, and K. L. McGinn. 2005. Constraint and triggers: Situational mechanics of gender in negotiation. *Journal of Personality and Social Psychology* 89(6), 951–965.

Brines, J. 1994. Economic dependency, gender, and the division of labor at home. *American Journal of Sociology* 100, 652–688.

Budig, M. J. 2002. Male advantage and the gender composition of jobs: Who rides the glass escalator? *Social Problems* 49(2), 258–277. doi: 10.1525/sp.2002.49.2.258.

————. 2003. Are women's employment and fertility histories interdependent? An examination of causal order using event history analysis. *Social Science Research* 32(3), 376–401.

Burn, M., and A. Z. Ward. 2005. Men's conformity to traditional masculinity and relationship satisfaction. *Psychology of Men and Masculinity* 6, 254–263.

Bushardt, S. C., C. Fretwell, and B. J. Holdnak. 1991. The mentor/protégé relationship: A biological perspective. *Human Relations* 44(6), 619–639.

Cardenas, R. A., and D. A. Major. 2005. Combining employment and breastfeeding: Utilizing a work-family conflict framework to understand obstacles and solution. *Journal of Business and Psychology* 20(1), 31–51.

Center for American Women and Politics (CAWP). 2011. *Women in the U.S. Congress 2011*. New Brunswick, NJ.

Chan, D. K-S., C. B. Lam, S. Y. Chow, and S. Cheung. 2008. Examining the job-related, psychological, and physical outcomes of workplace sexual harassment: A meta-analytic review. *Psychology of Women Quarterly* 32, 362–376.

Chang, M. L. 2010. *Shortchanged: Why Women Have Less Wealth and What Can Be Done About It*. New York: Oxford University Press.

Chao, G. T. 2009. Formal mentoring: Lessons learned from past practice. *Professional Psychology* 40(3), 314–320.

Cohen, C. F., and V. S. Rabin. 2007. *Back on the Career Track. A Guide for Stay-at-Home Moms Who Want to Return to Work*. New York: Warner Business Books.

Cornwell, C., and J. E. Kellough. 1994. Women and minorities in federal government agencies: Examining new evidence from panel data. *Public Administration Review* 54(3), 265–269.

Council Directive. 1975, Article 1. ttp://eur-lex.europa.eu/LexUriServ/LexUriServ.do?uri=CELEX:31975L0117:EN:HTM.

Crittenden, A. 2001. *The Price of Motherhood: Why the Most Important Job in the World Is Still the Least Valued*. New York: Henry Holt.

————. 2004. *If You've Raised Kids, You Can Manage Anything: Leadership Begins at Home*. New York: Penguin.

Crosby, F. J., A. Iyer, and R. A. Downing. 2003. Affirmative action: Psychological data and the policy debates. *American Psychologist* 58(2), 93–115.

Currie, J., and J. Eveline. 2010. E-technology and work/life balance for academics with young children. *Higher Education* 62, 533–550.

Currie, J., and S. McConnell. 1992. Firm-specific determinants of the real wage. *Review of Economics and Statistics* 74, 297–304.

Dasgupta, N., and A. G. Greenwald. 2001. On the malleability of automatic attitudes: Combating automatic prejudice with images of admired and disliked individuals. *Journal of Personality and Social Psychology* 81, 800–814.

Dean, D. J., and C. L. Simpson. 2010. Workshop for Women Faculty. Association for Women in Science West Virginia Chapter Workshop presented at West Virginia University, Morgantown, November.

De Ruijter, J. M. P., J. J. Schippers, and A. Van Doorne-Huiskes. 2004. Comparable worth: Policy and measures. *Netherlands' Journal of Social Science* 40(1), 41–67.

DiPrete, T. A., G. M. Eirich, and M. Pittinsky. 2010. Compensation benchmarking, leapfrogs, and the surge in executive pay. *American Journal of Sociology* 115(6), 1671–1712.

Donovan, R. A., A. L. Pieper, and A. N. Ponce. 2007. Walking the maternal tightrope. *New England Journal of Public Policy* 22(1/2), 195–206.

DuMond, J. Michael, Barry T. Hirsch, and David A. Macpherson. 1999. Wage differentials across labor markets and workers: Does cost of living matter? *Economic Inquiry* 37(4), 577–598.

Eagly, A. H., and S. J. Karau. 2002. Role congruity theory of prejudice toward female leaders. *Psychological Review* 109(3), 573–598.

Eby, L. T., T. D. Allen, S. C. Evans, T. Ng, and D. L. DuBois. 2008. Does mentoring matter? A multidisciplinary meta-analysis comparing mentored and non-mentored individuals. *Journal of Vocational Behavior* 72, 254–267.

Edley, P. P. 2001. Technology, employed mothers, and corporate colonization of the lifeworld: A gendered paradox of work and family balance. *Women and Language* 24(2), 28–35.

———. 2004. Entrepreneurial mothers' balance of work and family: Discursive constructions of time, mothering and identity. In *Gender in Applied Communication Contexts,* ed. P. M. Buzzanell, H. Sterk, and L. H. Turner, 255–273. Thousand Oaks, CA: Sage.

Eliot, L. 2009. *Pink Brain, Blue Brain.* New York: Houghton Mifflin Harcourt.

Ellis, E. 2005. *EU Anti-Discrimination Law.* New York: Oxford University Press. http://fds.oup.com/www.oup.co.uk/pdf/0-19-926683-2.pdf.

Elvira, M. M., and M. E. Graham. 2002. Not just a formality: Pay system formalization and sex-related earnings effects. *Organization Science* 13(6), 601–617.

England, P., and N. Folbre. 1999. Who should pay for the kids? *Annals of the American Academy of Political and Social Science* 563, 194–207.

Engstrom, C. M., J. G. McIntosh, F. M. Ridzi, and K. Kruger. 2006. Salary determinants for senior student affairs officers: Revisiting gender and ethnicity in light of institutional characteristics. *NASPA Journal* 43, 243–263.

Ericksen, K. S., J. C. Jurgens, M. T. Garrett, and R. B. Swedburg. 2008. Should I stay at home or should I go back to work? Workforce reentry influences on a mother's decision-making process. *Journal of Employment Counseling* 45(4), 156–168.

Escriche, L. 2007. Persistence of occupational segregation: the role of the intergenerational transmission of preferences. *Economic Journal* 117, 837–857. doi: 10.1111/j.1468–0297.2007.02052.x.

Eurofound. 2011a. Discrimination. http://www.eurofound.europa.EU/areas/indus-trialrelations/dictionary/definitions/discrimination.htm.

———. 2011b. Equality between women and men. http://www.eurofound.europa.EU/areas/industrialrelations/dictionary/definitions/equalitybetweenwomenand-men.htm.

Faragher v. City of Boca Raton, 524 U.S. 775 (1998). http://supreme.justia.com/us/524/775/case.html.

Feldman, R., A. L. Sussman, and E. Zigler. 2004. Parental leave and work adaptation at the transition to parenthood: Individual, marital, and social correlates. *Applied Developmental Psychology* 25, 459–479.

Ferguson, K. E. 1985. *The Feminist Case Against Bureaucracy*. Philadelphia: Temple University Press.

Fitzgerald, K. 1998. Top pay levels keep going up. *Purchasing* 125(12), 42–52.

Fitzgerald, L. F. 1993. Sexual harassment. Violence against women in the workplace. *American Psychologist* 48(10), 1070–1076.

Frazier, P., N. Arikian, S. Benson, A. Losoff, and S. Maurer. 1996. Desire for marriage and life satisfaction among unmarried heterosexual adults. *Journal of Social and Personal Relationships* 13(2), 225–239.

Friedan, B. 1963/2001. *The Feminine Mystique*. New York: Norton.

Gartner, L. M., J., Morton, R. A. Lawrence, et al. 2005. American Academy of Pediatrics section on breastfeeding and the use of human milk. *Pediatrics* 115(2), 496–506.

Gerard, V. 2009. The White House Council on Women and Girls. Video file, March 11. http://www.whitehouse.gov/administration/eop/cwg (accessed September 6, 2012).

Gerson, K. 2009. Changing lives, resistant institutions: A new generation negotiates gender, work, and family change. *Sociological Forum* 24(4), 735–753.

Gettman, H. J., and M. J. Gelfand. 2007. When the customer shouldn't be king: Antecedents and consequences of sexual harassment by clients and customers. *Journal of Applied Psychology* 92, 757–770.

Gill, R., and S. Ganesh. 2007. Empowerment, constraint, and the entrepreneurial self: A study of white women entrepreneurs. *Journal of Applied Communication Research* 35(3), 268–293.

Gillespie, B. B., and H. S. Temple. 2011. *Good Enough Is the New Perfect: Finding Happiness and Success in Modern Motherhood*. New York: Harlequin.

Giscombe, K. 2007. Advancing women through the glass ceiling with formal mentoring. In *The Handbook of Mentoring at Work: Theory, Research, and Practice*, ed. B. R. Ragins and K. E. Kram, 549–572. Los Angeles: Sage.

Glass, J. 2004. Blessing or curse? Work-family policies and mother's wage growth over time. *Work and Occupations* 31(3), 367–394.

Government of Canada. 1994. *Case Studies on Effective Practices in the Employment of Persons with Disabilities: A Report*. Ottawa: The Group.

Grall, T.S.. 2011. *Custodial Mothers and Fathers and Their Child Support: 2009*. Washington, DC: U.S. Census Bureau.

Grant, J., T. Hatcher, and N. Patel. 2005. *Expecting Better: A State-by-State Analysis of Parental Leave Programs*, 2d ed. May. Washington, DC: National Partnership for Women and Families. http://www.nationalpartnership.org/site/DocServer/ParentalLeaveReportMay05.pdf?docID=1052/.

Greenstein, T. N. 2000. Economic dependence, gender and the division of labor at home: A replication and extension. *Journal of Marriage and Family* 62(2), 322–335.

Gunderson, M., and C. W. Riddell. 1992. Comparable worth: Canada's experience. *Contemporary Economic Policy* 10(3), 85–94.

Guy, M. E. 1993. Three steps forward, two steps backward: The status of women's integration into public management. *Public Administration Review* 53(4): 285–292.

———. 2003. The difference that gender makes. In *Public Personnel Administration: Problems and Prospects*, ed. S. W. Hays and R. C. Kearney, 265–269. Upper Saddle River, NJ: Prentice Hall.

Guy, M., M. Newman, and S. Mastracci. 2008. *Emotional Labor: Putting the Service in Public Service*. Armonk, NY: M.E. Sharpe.

Hayes, Jeff. 2011. *Women's Median Earnings as a Percent of Men's Median Earnings, 1960–2009 (Full-Time, Year-Round Workers) with Projection for Pay Equity in 2056*. Report, March. Washington, DC: Institute for Women's Policy Research. http://www.iwpr.org/publications/pubs/women2019s-median-earnings-as-a-percent-of-men2019s-median-earnings-1969-2009-full-time-year-round-workers-with-projection-for-pay-equity-in-2056.

Hays, S. 1996. *The Cultural Contradictions of Motherhood*. New Haven, CT: Yale University.

Hegewisch, Ariane, Claudia Williams, and Anlan Zhang. 2011. *The Gender Wage Gap: 2011*. Report, March 2012. Washington, DC: Institute for Women's Policy Research.

Heilman, M. E., A. S. Wallen, D. Fuchs, and M. M. Tamkins. 2004. Penalties for success: Reactions to women who succeed at male gender-typed tasks. *Journal of Applied Psychology* 3, 416–417. doi: 10.1037/0021–9010.89.3.416.

Hewlett, S. A., and C. B. Luce. 2005. Off-ramps and on-ramps. Keeping talented women on the road to success. *Harvard Business Review* (March), 1–10.

Heymann, J., A. Earle, and J. Hayes. 2007. *The Work, Family, and Equity Index: How Does the United States Measure Up?* Montreal: Project on Global Working Families. http://www.mcgill.ca/files/ihsp/WFEI2007FINAL.pdf.

Heymann, S. J., K. Penrose, and A. Earle. 2006. Meeting children's needs: How does the United States measure up? *Merrill-Palmer Quarterly* 52(2), 189–215.

Hindera, J. J., and C. D. Young. 1998. Representative bureaucracy: The theoretical implications of statistical interaction. *Political Research Quarterly* 51, 655–671.

Hochschild, A. R. 1989. *The Second Shift*. New York: Avon.

———. 1997. *Time Bind: When Work Becomes Home and Home Becomes Work*. New York: Metropolitan Books.

Hoffnung, M. 2004. Wanting it all: Career, marriage, and motherhood during college-educated women's 20s. *Sex Roles* 50(9/10), 711–723.

Holzer, H.J. 1990. The determinants of employee productivity and earnings. *Industrial Relations* 29(3), 403–422.

Holzer, H.J., and D. Neumark. 2000. Assessing affirmative action. *Journal of Economic Literature* 38(3), 483–568.

Hong, L., and S. E. Page. 2004. Groups of diverse problem solvers can outperform groups of high-ability problem solvers. *Proceedings of the National Academy of Sciences* 101(46), 16385–16389.

————. 2001. Problem solving by heterogeneous agents. *Journal of Economic Theory* 97: 123–163.

Hopcroft, R. L. 1996. The authority attainment of women: competitive sector effects. *American Journal of Economics and Sociology* 55(2), 163–184.

Hotchkiss, J. L., M. M. Pitts, and M. B. Walker. 2008. *Working with Children? The Probability of Mothers Exiting the Workforce at Time of Birth.* Working Paper 2008–08, February. Atlanta: Federal Reserve Bank of Atlanta.

Hsieh, C., and E. Winslow. 2006. Gender representation in the federal workforce. *Review of Public Personnel Administration* 26, 276–294. doi: 10.1177/0734371X05281785.

Huffman, M. L. 1995. Organizations, internal labor market policies, and gender inequality in workplace supervisory authority. *Sociological Perspectives* 38(3), 381–397.

Huffman, M. L., and P. N. Cohen. 2004. Occupational segregation and the gender gap in workplace authority: National versus local labor markets. *Sociological Forum* 19(1), 121–147.

Internal Revenue Service (IRS). 2011a. Ten facts about the child tax credit. IRS Tax TIP 2011–29, February 10. http://www.irs.gov/newsroom/article/0,,id=106182,00.html.

————. 2011b. Ten things to know about the child and dependent care practice. IRS Tax Tip 2011–46, March 7. http://www.irs.gov/newsroom/article/0,,id=106189,00.html.

Ip, S., M. Chung, G. Raman, P. Chew, N. Magula, D. DeVine, T. Trikalinos, and J. Lau. 2007. Breastfeeding and maternal and infant health outcomes in developed countries. *Evidence Report/Technology Assessment* April (153), 1–186.

Jacobs, J. A. 1992. Women's entry into management: Trends in earnings, authority, and values among salaried managers. *Administrative Science Quarterly* 37(2), 282–301.

Jain, H. C., and R. D. Hackett. 1989. Measuring effectiveness of employment equity programs in Canada: Public policy and a survey. *Canadian Public Policy/Analyse de Politiques* 15(2), 189–204.

Job Accommodation Network (JAN). 2011. *The ADA Amendments Act of 2008* (Accommodation and Compliance Series). Document, May 24. Washington, DC: U.S. Department of Labor, Office of Disability Employment Policy. http://askjan.org/bulletins/ADAAAwithRegs.pdf.

Johnson v. Transportation Agency, Santa Clara County, Cal., 480 U.S. 616 (1987). http://www.eeoc.gov/eeoc/foia/letters/2006/vii_affirmative_action.html.

Johnson, C. M., and G. Duerst-Lahti. 1992. Public work, private lives. In *Women and Men of the States: Public Administrators at the State Level,* ed. M. E. Guy, 61–88. Armonk, NY: M.E. Sharpe.

Johnson, T. D. 2008. *Maternity Leave and Employment Patterns of First-Time Mothers: 1961–2003.* Report P70–1133. Washington, DC: U.S. Census Bureau.

Karpinski, A., and J. L. Hilton. 2001. Attitudes and the implicit association test. *Journal of Personality and Social Psychology* 81(5), 774–788.

Kearney, R. C. 2003. The determinants of state employee compensation. *Review of Public Personnel Administration* 23, 305–322. doi: 10.1177/0734371 X03259279.

Keashly, L., and J. H. Neuman. 2009. Building a constructive communication climate: The workplace stress and aggression project. In *Destructive Organizational*

Communication, ed. P. Lutgen-Sandvik and B. Davenport Sypher, 339–363. New York: Routledge.

Kelly, R. M., M. E. Guy, J. Bayes, G. Duerst-Lahti, L. L. Duke, M. M. Hale, C. Johnson, A. Kawar, and J. R. Stanley. 1991. Public managers in states: A comparison of career advancement by sex. *Public Administration Review* 51(5), 402–412. doi: 10.2307/976409.

Kernaghan, K., and D. Siegel. 1991. *Public Administration in Canada*, 2d ed. Scarborough, Canada: Nelson.

Kim, C. 2004. Women and minorities in state government agencies. *Public Personnel Management* 33, 165–180.

Kim, J., and M. E. Wiggins. 2011. Family-friendly human resource policy: Is it still working in the public sector? *Public Administration Review* 71(5), 728–739.

Kirchmeyer, C. 2006. The different effects of family on objective career success across gender: A test of alternative explanations. *Journal of Vocational Behavior* 68, 323–346.

Kmec, J. A. 2005. Setting occupational sex segregation in motion. *Work and Occupations* 32, 322–354. doi: 10.1177/0730888405277703.

Kmec, J. A., and E. H. Gorman. 2010. Gender and discretionary work effort: Evidence from the United States and Britain. *Work and Occupations* 37(1), 3–36. doi: 10.177/0730888409352064.

Kraus, V., and Y.P. Yonay. 2000. The effect of occupational sex composition on the gender gap in workplace authority. *Social Science Research* 29, 583–605.

Krstic, I. 2003. Affirmative action in the United States and the European Union: Comparison and analysis. *Fata Universitatis. Series: Law and Politics* 1(7), 825–843. http://facta.junis.ni.ac.rs/lap/lap2003/lap2003-06.pdf.

Langer, S. 2000. Factors affecting CFO compensation. *Strategic Finance Magazine* 81(9), 38–44.

Leenders, M. R., and H. F. Fearon. 1997. *Purchasing and Supply Management*, 11th ed. Boston: McGraw-Hill.

Lewis, G. B., and D. Nice. 1994. Race, sex, and occupational segregation in state and local governments. *American Review of Public Administration* 24(4), 393–410.

Lipsky, M. 1980. *Street-Level Bureaucracy: Dilemmas of the Individual in Public Services*. New York: Russell Sage Foundation.

Lowery, B. S., C. D. Hardin, and S. Sinclair. 2001. Social influence effects on automatic racial prejudice. *Journal of Personality and Social Psychology* 81(5), 842–855.

Lowi, T. J. 1985. The state in politics: The relation between policy and administration. In *Regulatory Policy and the Social Sciences,* ed. R. G. Noll, 67–105. Berkeley: University of California Press.

Lutgen-Sandvik, P., and S. J. Tracy. 2012. Answering five key questions about workplace bullying: How communication scholarship provides thought leadership for transforming abuse at work. *Management Communication Quarterly* 26, 3–47.

Lyness, K. S., and M. E. Heilman. 2006. When fit is fundamental: Performance evaluations and promotions of upper-level female and male managers. *Journal of Applied Psychology* 91(4), 777–785.

Major, D., R. Cardenas, and C. Allard. 2004. Child health: A legitimate business concern. *Journal of Occupational Health Psychology* 9(4), 306–321.

Marini, F. 1971. *Toward a New Public Administration*. Scranton, PA: Chandler.

Marshall, A. M. 2005. Idle rights: Employees' rights consciousness and the construction of sexual harassment policies. *Law and Society Review* 39(1), 83–124.

Maume, D. J. Jr. 1999. Glass ceilings and glass escalators. *Work and Occupations* 26(4), 483–510.

McGuire, G. M., and B. F. Reskin. 1993. Authority hierarchies at work: The impacts of race and sex. *Gender and Society* 7(4), 487–506.

Meier, K. J. 1993. Representative bureaucracy: A theoretical and empirical exposition. In *Research in Public Administration*, ed. J. Perry, 1–35. Greenwich, CT: JAI.

Meier, K. J., and V. M. Wilkins. 2002. Gender differences in agency head salaries: The case of public education. *Public Administration Review* 62, 405–411.

Mesmer-Magnus, J. R., and C. Viswesvaran. 2006. How family-friendly work environments affect work/family conflict: A meta-analytic examination. *Journal of Labor Research* 27(4), 565–574.

Meyers, M., and J. Gornick. 2005. Policies for reconciling parenthood and employment: Drawing lessons from Europe. *Challenge* 48(5), 39–61.

Miller, W., B. Kerr, and M. Reid. 1999. A national study of gender-based occupational segregation in municipal bureaucracies: Persistence of glass walls? *Public Administration Review* 59(3), 218–230. doi: 10.2307/3109950.

Miree, C. E., and I. H. Frieze. 1999. Children and careers: A longitudinal study of the impact of young children on critical career outcomes of MBAs. *Sex Roles* 41(11/12), 787–808.

Mitra, A. 2003. Access to supervisory jobs and the gender wage gap among professionals. *Journal of Economics* 37(4), 1023–1044.

Moore, D. P. 2005. Career paths of women business owners. In *International Handbook of Women and Small Business Entrepreneurship*, ed. S. L. Fielden and M. J. Davidson, 42–51. Cheltenham, UK: Edward Elgar.

Moore, W. J., and J. Raisian. 1987. Union-nonunion wage differentials in the public administration, educational, and private sectors: 1970–1983. *Review of Economics and Statistics* 69(4), 608–616.

Morgan, J. 1997. 1997 salary survey: From checkers to chess. *Purchasing* 123(9), 1.

Naff, K. C. 1994. Through the glass ceiling: Prospects for the advancement of women in the federal civil service. *Public Administration Review* 54(3), 507–514.

Namie, G., and P. Lutgen-Sandvik. 2010. Active and passive accomplices: The communal character of workplace bullying. *International Journal of Communication* 4, 343–373.

National Institute for Occupational Safety and Health (NIOSH). 1996. *Violence in the Workplace*. DHHS (NIOSH) Publication Number 96–100, July. http://www.cdc.gov/niosh/docs/96-100/.

———. 2006. *Workplace Violence Prevention Strategies and Research Needs*. Report from the conference Partnering in Workplace Violence Prevention: Translating Research to Practice. November 17–19, 2004, Baltimore. http://www.cdc.gov/niosh/docs/2006-144/pdfs/2006-144.pdf.

National Partnership for Women and Families. 2009. *State Family and Medical Leave Laws that Are More Expansive than the Federal FMLA*. Washington, DC. http://www.nationalpartnership.org/site/DocServer/StatesandunpaidFMLLaws.pdf?docID=968/.

National Science Foundation (NSF). 2011. About the National Science Foundation. http://www.nsf.gov/about/.

National Women's Law Center. 2005. *The Paycheck Fairness Act: Helping to Close the Wage Gap for Women.* April. Washington, DC. http://www.pay-equity.org/PDFs/PaycheckFairnessAct_April2005.pdf.

———. 2009. Falling $hort in Every State: The Wage Gap and Harsh Economic Realities for Women Persist. Report, April. Washington, DC. http://www.nwlc.org/sites/default/files/pdfs/FallingShort2009web.pdf.

New Jersey Office of the Attorney General. 2011. The New Jersey Family Leave Act. Civil Rights Fact Sheet, rev. July 25. http://www.state.nj.us/lps/dcr/downloads/flafactsheet.pdf.

Newman, M. A. 1994. Gender and Lowi's thesis: Implications for career advancement. *Public Administration Review* 54(3), 277–284.

Newman, M., and K. Mathews. 1999. Federal family-friendly workplace policies: Barriers to effective implementation. *Review of Public Personnel Administration* 19(3), 34–48.

Ng, T. W. H., L. T. Eby, K. L. Sorensen, and D. C. Feldman. 2005. Predictors of objective and subjective career success: A meta-analysis. *Personnel Psychology* 58(2), 367–408. doi: 10.1111/j.1744-6570.2005.00515.x.

Ogden, J. A., G. A. Zsidisin, and T. E. Hendrick. 2002. Factors that influence chief purchasing officer compensation. *Journal of Supply Chain Management* 38(3), 30–38. doi: 10.1111/j.1745-493X.2002.tb00133.x.

O'Leary, A. 2007. How family leave laws left out low-income workers. *Berkeley Journal of Employment and Labor Law* 28(1), 1–62.

O'Leary-Kelly, A. M., L. Bowes-Sperry, C. A. Bates, and E. R. Lean. 2009. Sexual harassment at work: A decade (plus) of progress. *Journal of Management* 35, 503–529.

Olshfski, D., and R. Caprio. 1996. Comparing personal and professional characteristics of men and women state executives: 1990 and 1993 results. *Review of Public Personnel Administration* 16(1), 31–40.

O'Neill, J. E. 2011. Comparable worth. In *The Concise Encyclopedia of Economics*, ed. David R. Henderson. Indianapolis, IN: The Library of Economics and Liberty. http://www.econlib.org/library/Enc1/ComparableWorth.html.

O'Neill, O. A., and C. A. O'Reilly, III. 2010. Careers as tournaments: The impact of sex and gendered organizational culture preferences on MBAs' income attainment. *Journal of Organizational Behavior* 31(6), 856–876.

———. 2011. Reducing the backlash effect: Self-monitoring and women's promotions. *Journal of Occupational and Organizational Psychology* 84(4), 825–832.

Orazem, P. F., and J. P. Mattila. 1998. Male-female supply to state government jobs and comparable worth. *Journal of Labor Economics* 16(1), 95–121. doi: 10.1086/209883.

Organization for Economic Cooperation and Development (OECD). 2011a. About the OECD. http://www.oecd.org/about/.

———.2011b. *OECD 50th Anniversary Vision Statement.* Report C/MIN(2011)6. Meeting of the OECD Council at Ministerial Level, Paris, May 25–26. http://www.oecd.org/dataoecd/36/44/48064973.pdf.

Ortiz, J., K., McGilligan, and P. Kelly. 2004. Duration of beast milk expression among working mothers enrolled in an employer-sponsored lactation program. *Pediatric Nursing* 30(2), 111–119.

Padavic, B. F., and I. Reskin. 1994. *Women and Men at Work*. Thousand Oaks, CA: Pine Forge Press.

Page, S. E. 2007. *The Difference: How the Power of Diversity Creates Better Groups, Firms, Schools, and Societies*. Princeton, NJ: Princeton University Press.

Perrone, K. M., L. K. Webb, and R. H. Blalock. 2005. The effects of role congruence and role conflict on work, marital, and life satisfaction. *Journal of Career Development* 31(4), 225–238.

Pradel, D. W., H. R. Bowles, and K. L. McGinn, 2005. When does gender matter in negotiation? *Negotiation* 8(11), 9–10.

Prime, J., C. A. Moss-Racusin, and H. Foust-Cummings. 2009. *Engaging Men in Gender Initiatives: Stacking the Deck for Success*. New York: Catalyst.

Pullman, D., and T. Lemmens. 2010. Keeping the GINA in the bottle: Assessing the current need for genetic non-discrimination legislation in Canada. *Open Medicine* 4(2). http://www.openmedicine.ca/article/view/339/322.

Pyle, J. L., and M. S. Pelletier. 2003. Family and Medical Leave Act: Unresolved issues. *New Solutions* 13(4), 353–384.

Ramey, G., and V. A. Ramey. 2009. *The Rug Rat Race*. NBER Working Paper No. 15284, August. Cambridge, MA: National Bureau of Economic Research.

Ramoni-Perazzi, J., and D. Bellante. 2007. Do truly comparable public and private sector workers show any compensation differential? *Journal of Labor Research* 28(1), 118–133.

Ranson, G. 2005. No longer "one of the boys": Negotiations with motherhood, as prospect or reality, among women in engineering. *Canadian Review of Sociology and Anthropology* 42(2), 145–166.

Raver, J. L., and M. J. Gelfand. 2005. Beyond the individual victim: Linking sexual harassment, team processes, and team performance. *Academy of Management Journal* 48(3), 387–400.

Ray, R., J. C. Gornick, and J. Schmitt. 2010. Who cares? Assessing generosity and gender equality in parental leave policy designs in 21 countries. *Journal of European Social Policy* 20(3), 196–216.

Rayner, C., and H. Hoel. 1997. A summary review of literature relating to workplace bullying. *Journal of Community and Applied Social Psychology* 7, 181–191.

Rees, A. 1993. The role of fairness in wage determination. *Journal of Labor Economics* 11(1), 243–252.

Riccucci, N. M. 2009. The pursuit of social equity in the federal government: A road less traveled? *Public Administration Review* 69(3), 373–382. doi: 10.1111/j.1540-6210.2009.01984.x.

Riggs, F. 1970. *Administrative Reform and Political Responsiveness: A Theory of Dynamic Balancing*. Thousand Oaks, CA: Sage.

Rindfuss, R. R., K. B. Guzzo, and S. P. Morgan. 2003. The changing institutional context of low fertility. *Population Research and Policy Review* 22(5/6), 411–438.

Roberts, G. E., J. A. Gianakis, C. McCue, and X. H. Wang. 2004. Traditional and family-friendly benefits practices in local governments: Results from a national survey. *Public Personnel Management* 33(3), 307–330.

Rousseau, D. M. 2005. *I-Deals: Idiosyncratic Deals Employees Bargain for Themselves*. Armonk, NY: M.E. Sharpe.

Saltzstein, A. L., Y. Ting, and G. H. Saltzstein. 2001. Work-family balance and job satisfaction: The impact of family-friendly policies on attitudes of federal government employees. *Public Administration Review* 61(4), 452–467.

Santere, R. E., and J. M. Thomas. 1993. The determinants of hospital CEO compensation. *Health Care Management Review* 18(3), 31–40.

Sarfaty, S., D. Kolb, R. Barnett, L. Szalacha, C. Caswell, T. Inui, and P. L. Carr. 2007. Negotiation in academic medicine: A necessary career skill. *Journal of Women's Health* 16(2), 235–244.

Schat, A. C. H., M. R. Frone, and E.K. Kelloway. 2006. Prevalence of workplace aggression in the U.S. workforce: Findings from a national study. In *Handbook of Workplace Violence,* ed. E.K. Kelloway, J. Barling, and J.J. Hurrell Jr., 47–89. Thousand Oaks, CA: Sage.

Schulman, K. and H. Blank. 2011. *State Childcare Assistance Polices: Reduced Support for Families in Challenging Times.* Washington, DC: National Women's Law Center. http://www.nwlc.org/sites/default/files/pdfs/state_child_care_assistance_policies_report2011_final.pdf.

Shapiro, M., C. Ingols, and S. Blake-Beard. 2008. Confronting career double binds. Implications for women, organizations, and career practitioners. *Journal of Career Development* 34(3), 309–333.

Sharp, E., and L. Ganong. 2007. Living in the gray: Women's experiences of missing the marital transition. *Journal of Marriage and Family* 69(3), 831–844. doi:10.1111/j.1741-3737.2007.00408.x.

Shields, S. A., M. J. Zawadzki, and N. R. Johnson. 2011. The impact of the workshop activity for gender equity simulation in the academy (WAGES-Academic) in demonstrating cumulative effects of gender bias. *Journal of Diversity in Higher Education* 4(2), 120–129.

Singh, R., B. R. Ragins, and P. Tharenou. 2009. What matters most? The relative role of mentoring and career capital in career success. *Journal of Vocational Behavior* 75, 56–67.

Slaughter, A.-M. 2012. Why women still can't have it all. *Atlantic* (July/August).

Smith, J. P., and F. Welch. 1984. Affirmative action and labor markets. *Journal of Labor Economics* 2(2), 269–302.

Smith, R. 2002. Race, gender, and authority in the workplace: Theory and research. *Annual Review of Sociology* 28, 509–542.

Society for Human Resource Management (SHRM). 2010. *2010 Employment Benefits: Examining Employee Benefits in the Midst of a Recovering Economy.* Research Report, June. http://www.shrm.org/Research/SurveyFindings/Articles/Documents/10-0280%20Employee%20Benefits%20Survey%20Report-FNL.pdf.

Solnick, S. J. 2001. Gender differences in the ultimatum game. *Economic Inquiry* 30(2), 189–200.

South, S. J., and G. Spitze. 1994. Housework in marital and nonmarital households. *American Sociological Review* 59(3), 327–347.

Spangler, A. 2000. Breastfeeding and the working mother: Planning and preparing to combine working and breastfeeding. In *Amy Spangler's Breastfeeding: A Parent's Guide,* 7th ed., 109–120. Atlanta, GA: Abby Drue, Inc.

Spivak, G. C., and S. Gunew. 1993. Questions of multiculturalism. In *The Cultural Studies Reader,* ed. S. During, 193–202. London: Routledge.

Stewart, K. D., M. M. Dalton, G. A. Dino, and S. P. Wilkinson. 1996. The development of salary goal modeling. *Journal of Higher Education* 67(5), 555–576.

Stivers, C. 1993. *Gender Images in Public Administration: Legitimacy and the Administrative State.* Newbury Park, CA: Sage.

————. 2000. *Bureau Men, Settlement Women: Constructing Public Administration in the Progressive Era*. Lawrence: University Press of Kansas.

Stone, P., and A. Kuperberg. 2005. Anti-discrimination vs. anti-poverty? A comparison of pay equity and living wage reforms. *Marriage, Work, Poverty and Children* 27(3/4), 23–37.

Stuhlmacher, A. F., and A. E. Walters. 1999. Gender differences in negotiation outcome: A meta-analysis. *Personnel Psychology* 52, 653–677.

Sweeney, M. M. 2002. Two decades of family change: The shifting economic foundations of marriage." *American Sociological Review* 67(1), 132–147.

Taniguchi, H. 1999. The timing of childbearing and women's wages. *Journal of Marriage and the Family* 61(4), 1008–1019.

Taylor, C. 2010. Occupational sex composition and the gendered availability of workplace support. *Gender and Society* 24(2), 189–212. doi: 10.1177/0891243209359912.

Taylor-Mill, H. 1851. Enfranchisement of women. *Westminister Review* (July), 295–296.

Teamsters v. United States, 431 U.S. 324 (1977). http://supreme.justia.com/cases/federal/us/431/324/case.html.

Tharenou, P. 2005. Does mentor support increase women's career advancement more than men's? The differential effects of career and psychosocial support. *Australian Journal of Management* 30, 77–109.

Thomas, S. 2002. The personal is political: Antecedents of gendered choices of elected representatives. *Sex Roles* 47(7/8), 343–353.

Thompson, V. A. 1975. *Without Sympathy or Enthusiasm: The Problem of Administrative Compassion*. Tuscaloosa: University of Alabama Press.

Tong, R. 2008. *Feminist Thought: A More Comprehensive Introduction*, 3d ed. Boulder, CO: Westview Press.

Toossi, M. 2002. A Century of Change: the U.S. labor force, 1950-2050. *Monthly Labor Review* (May), 15–28. http://www.bls.gov/opub/mlr/2002/05/art2full.pdf.

Tower, L. E., and M. G. Alkadry. 2008. The social costs of career success for women. *Review of Public Personnel Administration* 28, 144–165.

Trix, F., and C. Psenka. 2003. Exploring the color of glass: Letters of recommendation for female and male medical faculty. *Discourse and Society* 14(2), 191–220.

Trommer, D. 1995. Buyers who expect more, make more. *Electronic Buyers' News* 978, 1–3.

U.S. Bureau of Labor Statistics. 2003. Women at work: A visual essay. *Monthly Labor Review* 126(10), 45–50. http://www.bls.gov/opub/mlr/2003/10/ressum3.pdf.

————. 2011. *Current Population Survey of Households and Individuals*. Washington, DC.

U.S. Census Bureau. 2001. Current Population Survey. March. Washington, DC: Government Printing Office. http://www.census.gov.

U.S. Department of Commerce Economics and Statistics Administration and the Executive Office of the President Office of Management and Budget. 2011. *Women in America: Indicators of Social and Economic Well-Being*. Report, March. http://www.whitehouse.gov/sites/default/files/rss_viewer/Women_in_America.pdf.

U.S. Department of Labor (DOL). n.d.a. About the Office of Federal Contract Compliance Programs (OFCCP). http://www.dol.gov/ofccp/aboutof.html.

———. n.d.b. Civil Rights Center (CRC). http://www.dol.gov/oasam/programs/crc/about-crc.htm (accessed September 6, 2012).

———. n.d.c. Equal Employment Opportunity. http://www.dol.gov/dol/topic/discrimination/index.htm.

———. 2002. Facts on Executive Order 11246—Affirmative Action. Office of Federal Contract Compliance Programs (OFCCP), rev. January 4. http://www.dol.gov/ofccp/regs/compliance/aa.htm.

———. 2008. DOL's final rule on family and medical leave. Fact sheet, November 17. http://www.dol.gov/whd/fmla/finalrule/factsheet.pdf.

———. 2012. *Need Time? The Employee's Guide to the Family and Medical Leave Act.* Wage & Hour Division Guide, WH-1506, August. http://www.dol.gov/whd/fmla/employeeguide.pdf.

USDA. n.d. Office of Human Resource Management. Frequently Asked Questions. http://www.dm.usda.gov/employ/worklife/worklife/faq.htm.

U.S. Equal Employment Opportunity Commission (EEOC).

———. n.d.b. Filing a Charge of Discrimination. http://www.eeoc.gov/employees/charge.cfm.

———. n.d.c. Laws Enforced by the EEOC. http://www.eeoc.gov/laws/statutes/index.cfm.

———. 1963. The Equal Pay Act of 1963. http://www.eeoc.gov/laws/statutes/epa.cfm.

———. 1964. Title VII of the Civil Rights Act of 1964. http://www.eeoc.gov/laws/statutes/titlevii.cfm.

———. 1978. The Pregnancy Discrimination Act of 1978. http://www.eeoc.gov/laws/statutes/pregnancy.cfm.

———. 1990. *Policy Guidance on Current Issues of Sexual Harassment.* Number N-915-050, March 19. http://www.eeoc.gov/eeoc/publications/upload/current-issues.pdf.

———. 2009. *Data Warehouse.* Washington, DC.

———. 2010. Employment Tests and Selection Procedures. September 23. http://www.eeoc.gov/policy/docs/factemployment_procedures.html.

U.S. Government Accountability Office (GAO). 1995. *Federal Affirmative Employment: Progress of Women and Minority Criminal Investigators at Selected Agencies.* Report to the Honorable William L. Clay, House of Representatives, April. http://www.gao.gov/assets/230/221220.pdf.

U.S. Office of Personnel Management (OPM). 2009. *Federal Equal Opportunity Recruitment Program Report to Congress 2009.* Washington, DC.

Valian, V. 1998. *Why So Slow? The Advancement of Women.* Cambridge, MA: MIT Press.

Vandell, D. L., and B. Wolfe. 2000. *Childcare Quality: Does It Matter and Does It Need to Be Improved?* Special Report no. 78, November. Madison: Institute for Research on Poverty, University of Wisconsin–Madison.

Visible Minority Consultation Group, Canada. 1993. *Distortions in the Mirror: Reflections of Visible Minorities in the Public Service of Canada.* Report of the Visible Minority Consultation Group to the Secretary of the Treasury Board and the Employment Equity Council of Deputy Ministers.

Von Bergen, C. W. 2008. "The times they are a-changin'": Family responsibilities discrimination and the EEOC. *Employee Responsibilities and Rights Journal* 20(3), 177–194.

Waldfogel, J. 2001. International policies toward parental leave and childcare. *Future of Children* 11(1), 99–111. http://futureofchildren.org/futureofchildren/publications/docs/11_01_06.pdf.

Webber, G., and C. Williams. 2008. Mothers in "good" and "bad" part-time jobs. Different problems, same results. *Gender and Society* 22(6), 752–777.

Weber, M. 1967. *Max Weber on Law in Economy and Society,* ed. Max Rheinstein. New York: Touchstone.

Weiler, S., and A. Bernasek. 2001. Dodging the glass ceiling? Networks and the new wave of women entrepreneurs. *Social Science Journal* 38, 85–103.

Wheary, J., T. M., Shapiro, and T. Draut. 2007. *By a Thread: The New Experience of America's Middle Class*. New York: Dēmos. http://www.demos.org/sites/default/files/publications/ByAThread_MiddleClass_Demos.pdf.

White House. n.d.a. About the Middle Class Task Force. http://www.whitehouse.gov/strongmiddleclass/about.

———. n.d.b. National Equal Pay Enforcement Task Force. http://www.whitehouse.gov/sites/default/files/rss_viewer/equal_pay_task_force.pdf.

White House. 2010. Vice President Biden Holds Middle Class Task Force Event on Work and Family. Press release, July 20. http://www.whitehouse.gov/the-press-office/vice-president-biden-holds-middle-class-task-force-event-work-and-family.

White House Council on Women and Girls. 2011. http://www.whitehouse.gov/administration/eop/cwg.

Whyte, W. H., Jr., 1956. *The Organization Man*. New York: Doubleday.

Wieclaw, J., E. Agerbo, P. B. Mortensen, H. Burr, F. Tuchsen, and P. J. Bonde. 2006. Work related violence and threats and the risk of depression and stress disorders. *Journal of Epidemiology and Community Health* 60, 771–775.

Wilson, W. 1887. The Study of Administration. *Political Science Quarterly* 2, 191–222.

Williams, J. C. 2010. *Reshaping the Work-Family Debate: Why Men and Class Matter.* Cambridge, MA: Harvard University Press.

Williams, J. C., and H. Boushey. 2010. *The Three Faces of Work-Family Conflict.* San Francisco: Center for WorkLife Law.

Williams, J. C., and H. C. Cooper. 2004. The public policy of motherhood. *Journal of Social Issues* 60, 849–865.

Willness, C. R., P. Steel, and K. Lee. 2007. A meta-analysis of the antecedents and consequences of workplace sexual harassment. *Personnel Psychology* 60, 127–162.

Wolfinger, N. H., M. A. Mason, and M. Goulden. 2010. Alone in the ivory tower. *Journal of Family Issues* 31, 1652–1670.

Wollstonecraft, M. 1787. *Thoughts on Education of Daughters: With Reflections on Female Conduct in the More Important Duties of Life.* London: Joseph Johnson.

WomensHealth.gov. 2012a. Business case for breastfeeding. U.S. Dept. of Health and Human Services. http://www.womenshealth.gov/breastfeeding/government-in-action/business-case-for-breastfeeding/.

————. 2012b. Why breastfeeding is important. U.S. Dept. of Health and Human Services. http://www.womenshealth.gov/breastfeeding/why-breastfeeding-is-important/.

Woodring, B. K. 2010. Employment status of married-couple families by presence of own children under 18 years: 2008 and 2009. American Community Service Brief ACSBR/09–10, October. Washington, DC: U.S. Census Bureau. https://www.census.gov/prod/2010pubs/acsbr09-10.pdf.

Wright, E. O., J. Baxter, and G. E. Birkelund. 1995. The gender gap in workplace authority: a cross-national study. *American Sociological Review* 60(3), 407–435.

Yeh, C-N., S. Suwanakul, and Y-M. Lim. 1998. The determinants of faculty salaries at a public university. *Journal of Collective Negotiations in the Public Sector* 27(1), 37–43.

Yost, C. W. 2004. *Work + Life: Finding the Fit That's Right for You.* New York: Riverhead Books.

Young, I. M. T. 1990a. *Justice and the Politics of Difference.* Princeton, NJ: Princeton University Press.

————. 1990b. Throwing like a girl: A phenomenology of feminine body comportment, motility, and spatiality. In *Throwing Like a Girl And Other Essays in Feminist Philosophy and Social Theory*, 27–45. Bloomington: Indiana University Press.

Young, M. C. 2010. Gender differences in precarious work settings. *Relation Industrielles* 65(1), 74–97.

Index

Page numbers in *italics* indicate figures and tables.

Childbearing *(continued)*
  and Mommy Track, 142–144
  stay-at-home mothers, 143
Child care
  benefits for, 91–92, *93*, 94
  federal subsidy of, 47–48
  international, 48, *49*
  onsite, *91*
  and poverty reduction, 52
  quality of, 48–49
  and societal attitudes toward children,
    46–47, 54
  state subsidy of, 48, 49–50
Child Care and Development Block
    Grant (CCDBG), 48
Childrearing style, 75–76
Chopin, I., 30
Chow, S.Y., 163
Civil Rights Act of 1964, 28, 29–30. *See
    also* Title VII
Civil Rights Act of 1991, 31, 65
Civil Rights Center, 64, 67, 175
Civil Rights Movement, 8, 29
Class action lawsuits, 31, 34, 56, 65
  Dukes v. Wal-Mart, 63–64
Clerical positions, segregation into, 118
Clinton, Hillary, 168
Cognitive work, 135
Cohen, C.F., 79, 80
Cohen, P.N., 119, 144, 147
Collective bargaining, and pay level,
    146–147
Commerce, Department of, 102
Comparable worth, 35–38, 173
Compressed workweek, *82*, 85, *89*
Condo, E., 102, 107, 108
Congress, U.S. representation of women
    in, 97
Consumerist-based argument for
    diversity, 4, 11–12
Contractors, federal, 58, 59
Cooper, H.C., 46, 52, 85
Cornwell, C., 107
Cost of living, and pay level, 148
Council on Women and Girls, 56, 59, 60,
    67, 175

Courts. *See also* Supreme Court (U.S.)
  affirmative action backlash in, 58
  EEOC lawsuits in, 65
  and family responsibility
    discrimination, 51
  and pay equity, 36
Criminal investigation jobs, 119, *124*
Crittenden, A., 50, 79
Crosby, F.J., 59
Currie, J., 75, 146
Czech Republic, 38

D

Dasgupta, N., 24
Dean, D.J., 77, 81
Defense, Department of, 124
Demographic change, 13–15, *72*
Dependent care accounts, 92
De Ruiter, J.M.P., 37
Diaper-changing stations, and gender
    images, xiii–xiv
Direct sexual behavior, 161
Disability legislation, 38–39
Discrimination
  employment. *See* Legislation,
    workplace; Pay equity
  family responsibility, 51–53, *53*
  implicit bias, 19, 20, 22–24, *24*, 53, 58,
    112, 173–174
  institutional, 24–25, 174
  and structural constraints, 86
Disparate impact, 31
Disparate treatment, 30
Distributive agencies, 102, *103*, 103,
    104–105, 107, 119, *120*, 124
Diverse workplace
  active *v.* passive representation in,
    15–17
  and administrative reform, 10–11
  challenge of group norms in, 15
  consumerist-based argument for, 4,
    11–12
  defined, 4
  and demographic change, 13–15
  equity-based arguments for, 4–11
  and implicit bias, 23

About the Authors

Dr. Mohamad G. Alkadry is an associate professor and director of the Florida International University (FIU) Master of Public Administration Program. He also serves as an affiliate faculty member of the FIU Women's Center. He received his PhD from Florida Atlantic University (2000) and his Masters of Public Policy and Public Administration from Concordia University in Quebec (1996). His undergraduate work was done at Carlton University in Canada (2002, 2004) and the American University of Beirut in Lebanon. Dr. Alkadry is the author of more than thirty peer-reviewed articles and is coeditor (with Hugh Miller) of *These Things Happen: Stories from the Public Sector*.

Dr. Leslie E. Tower is an associate professor at West Virginia University, holding a dual appointment in the School of Social Work and Department of Public Administration. She has published research on women and work, adult learners, and violence against women. As a co-principal investigator on the National Science Foundation (NSF) WVU ADVANCE Institutional Transformation (IT) Grant, she leads its work–life policy development component. She is co-chair of the Council on the Role and Status of Women in Social Work Education (Women's Council) for the Council on Social Work Education (CSWE). CSWE is the sole accrediting body of social work education. The Women's Council has several responsibilities, including "work[ing] to eliminate all procedures within academia that hinder the full participation of women." Dr. Tower is a passionate advocate for policies that support women's full participation in society.